D1496465

ADVANCE PRAISE FOR

FREEDOM THROUGH CORRECT KNOWING

"This wonderful book introduces the English-speaking public to the very rich Tibetan monastic philosophical tradition. The introduction by Geshe Namdak and the translation with commentary are not by a Western academic scholar but by the Sera Jey monks themselves. There, the reader will find a good reflection of the depth of their tradition. A great work for anybody interested in a deeper immersion in Buddhist philosophy."
—Georges Dreyfus, Jackson Professor of Religion, Williams College

"In the present so-called post-truth era, where misinformation abounds, it is crucial to be able to differentiate between fact and fiction and between valid and invalid ways of knowing something. *Freedom through Correct Knowing* provides the Buddhist analytical tools needed for this task, as interpreted by two of the greatest Tibetan Gelugpa scholars, Khedrup Jé and his commentator Purbu Chok. To open up the meaning of the technical language of the text, the editors have interspersed clear explanations and have added generous appendices with background material. The translators and editors are to be congratulated on this beautifully written, welcome contribution to our understanding of how the mind works."
—Dr. Alexander Berzin, founder, studybuddhism.com, a project of the Berzin Archives

"The skill with which Mahāyāna practitioners exercise vigilance over their superimposing false knowledge upon the world derives from their study of *pramāṇa* theory. Here we have a penetrating digest of the central aspects of these classical investigations into knowing. *Correct Knowing* is eloquent both by the standards of traditional Tibetan inquiry and by maintaining a flowing, clear, contemporary English prose that renders this journey through Buddhist epistemology accessible to the reader."
—Kenneth Liberman, professor emeritus, University of Oregon

FREEDOM THROUGH CORRECT KNOWING

On Khedrup Jé's Interpretation of Dharmakīrti's
Seven Treatises on Valid Cognition

Translated with commentary
by the Sera Jey English Translation Department,
under the review of
Geshe Tenzin Namdak and Ven. Tenzin Legtsok

Wisdom Publications
199 Elm Street
Somerville, MA 02144 USA
wisdomexperience.org

Copyright © 2022 Sera Jey Monastic University

All rights reserved.

No part of this book may be reproduced in any form or by any means,
electronic or mechanical, including photography, recording, or by any
information storage and retrieval system or technologies now known
or later developed, without permission in writing from the publisher.

Library of Congress Cataloging-in-Publication Data
Names: Namdak, Tenzin, 1926– translator. | Legtsok, Tenzin, translator.
Title: Freedom through correct knowing: on Khedrup jé's Interpretation of
    Dharmakīrti's seven treatises on valid cognition / by the Sera Jey English Translation
    Department, under the review of Geshe Tenzin Namdak and Ven. Tenzin Legtsok
Description: First. | Somerville, MA, USA: Wisdom Publications, [2022] |
    Includes bibliographical references and index.
Identifiers: LCCN 2021054568 (print) | LCCN 2021054569 (ebook) |
    ISBN 9781614296997 | ISBN 9781614297291 (ebook)
Subjects: LCSH: Dge-legs-dpal-bzang-po, Mkhas-grub-rje, 1385–1438.
    Tshad ma sde bdun gyi rgyan yid kyi mun sel. | Dharmakīrti, active 7th century. |
    Buddhist logic—Early works to 1800. | Nyaya.
Classification: LCC B133.D654 M5534 2022 (print) | LCC B133.D654 (ebook) |
    DDC 181/.043—dc23/eng/20211209
LC record available at https://lccn.loc.gov/2021054568
LC ebook record available at https://lccn.loc.gov/2021054569

ISBN 978-1-61429-699-7   ebook ISBN 978-1-61429-729-1

26 25 24 23 22
5 4 3 2 1

Cover design by Jess Morphew. Interior design by Gopa & Ted2, Inc.

Printed on acid-free paper that meets the guidelines for permanence and durability
of the Production Guidelines for Book Longevity of the Council on Library Resources.

Printed in Canada.

Contents

The Dalai Lama

Foreword

While one may engage in the teachings of Buddha Shakyamuni by means of faith, the ideal way to truly appreciate and embrace the doctrine of the Buddha is through inquiry and critical reasoning. The Buddha himself has said:

> Oh, monks and scholars, just as you test gold
> by burning, cutting, and rubbing,
> so too examine my speech well;
> do not accept it merely out of respect.

Taking this to heart, many ancient Indian masters subjected the Buddha's teaching to critical examination. Debate among Buddhists and non-Buddhist philosophers was an important feature of philosophical inquiry in ancient India. Such debate played a crucial role in the development of a system of thought called *pramāṇa*, the discipline of logic and epistemology. Dignāga (6th century) and Dharmakīrti (6–7th centuries) are recognized as the pioneers of Buddhist logic and epistemology.

Dignāga's *Pramāṇasamuccaya*, followed by Dharmakīrti's *Seven Texts on Valid Cognition*, came to be considered the authoritative works on logical reasoning. Ever since these texts were translated into Tibetan, logic and epistemology became firmly integrated into the monastic curriculum in Tibet. Hundreds of commentarial treatises, particularly on Dharmakīrti's *Pramāṇavārttika*, were written in Tibetan.

Khedrup Gelek Palsang, one of the main disciples of Jé Tsongkhapa, was a great philosopher and practitioner credited with thirteen volumes of scholarly works. *Clearing Mental Darkness: An Ornament to the Seven Texts on Valid Cognition*, was his first among several classical texts on logic and epistemology. It remains popular today among Tibetan scholars, particularly in Geluk monasteries.

Freedom through Correct Knowing presents important sections of Khedrup Gelek Palsang's *Clearing Mental Darkness*, with clarification from Purbu Chok Jampa Gyatso's *The Magic Key to the Path of Reasoning*. I commend the team of translators of Sera Je Monastery and all those involved in this important initiative. I hope this book will help many apply reasoning in their study and practice.

11 January 2022

PREFACE

FREEDOM through CORRECT KNOWING is a translation with commentary of the main sections explaining minds and objects of consciousness, the four noble truths, and the path to liberation from *Clearing Mental Darkness: An Ornament of Dharmakīrti's Seven Treatises on Valid Cognition* (*Tshad ma sde bdun gyi rgyan yid kyi mun sel*), by Khedrup Gelek Palsang (1385–1438), one of the foremost students of Lama Tsongkhapa. Lama Tsongkhapa (1357–1419) was a great Tibetan scholar and accomplished practitioner who founded the Geluk tradition, the tradition that is followed by Sera Jey Monastic University. Monastic universities founded in Tibet, like Sera Jey, were modeled on the great ancient Indian monastic universities of Nālandā, Vikramaśhīla, and Odantapuri. To this day their main bases of study are treatises by the great Buddhist pandits of Nālandā monastery. Thanks to the kindness of the Indian government, after the Chinese occupation of Tibet in 1959 many Tibetan monks were able to reestablish some of their monasteries in India under the spiritual guidance of His Holiness the Fourteenth Dalai Lama. Among these, Sera Jey Monastic University is one of the largest and most renowned institutions in the world for studying and practicing Buddhist philosophy.

Currently at Sera Jey Monastic University, about three thousand monks are preserving the precious Buddhist teachings of lovingkindness, compassion, wisdom, and the view of ultimate reality by engaging in an intensive program of study consisting of debate, memorization, oral commentary and explanation, prayers, abiding in monastic discipline, and meditation. To complete the program takes from nineteen to twenty-five years, depending on the level of geshe degree one wishes to obtain. During this intensive study, the monks learn five major philosophical subjects, each based on classic Indian Buddhist texts: Pramāṇa (Valid Cognition), Pāramitās (Perfections), Madhyamaka (Middle Way), Vinaya (Monastic Discipline), and Abhidharma (Phenomenology). The main topic of this book is valid cognition.

Freedom through Correct Knowing is a project of the English Translation Department of Sera Jey Monastic University. This department runs a translators' training program that was started because of the increased need for English-speaking teachers and translators who are well versed in the full breadth and depth of Buddhist philosophy as transmitted through the oral traditions of the monastic universities. Students of the program simultaneously follow the traditional geshe study curriculum of the monastery.

When His Holiness the Dalai Lama heard about the Translation Department, he suggested translating the main parts of Khedrup Jé's *Clearing Mental Darkness* concerning awareness and knowers. This text is frequently referred to during the entire duration of the geshe study program, especially while studying subjects related to consciousness, logic, the two truths, and the four noble truths.

Certain sections of the text are quite challenging, especially in the beginning when the various objects and how they appear to different states of consciousness are explained. This is the groundwork for understanding how things appear and what actual reality is. It helps us to understand wrong views and distorted perceptions and how to eliminate these disturbing states of mind by applying their antidotes. The impressive sections on the two types of reality, conventional and ultimate, and the four noble truths, leads us gradually to generate renunciation, bodhichitta, and the view of emptiness. Sustained contemplations on emptiness will eventually result in developing the powerful consciousness called "yogic direct perception," a direct realization of emptiness, the actual antidote to the root of all suffering. This realization, as Khedrup Jé clearly explains, brings samsara to an end. He mentions these points also as the reason for composing *Ocean of Reasonings: An Extensive Explanation of [Dharmakīrti's] Commentary on Valid Cognition*:

What path and which stages did the Bhagavan depend upon to achieve the state of full enlightenment of omniscience? After enlightenment, how did [the Buddha] perfectly lead disciples on the two common paths of liberation? Those who wish to attain these liberating [paths], need to understand their objects of knowledge and meditation. To eliminate wrong views and generate the unmistaken realizations regarding the paths and results of liberation and omniscience, I composed this commentary.[1]

Clearing Mental Darkness is not an easy text, and the meaning of many passages can have different interpretations. Since a mere direct translation of the text by itself would only be useful for a small group of specialists, in discussion with the then-current abbot of Sera Jey, Khensur Rinpoche Geshe Lobsang Delek, we deemed that the translation should be made accessible to a more general audience and therefore decided to add explanations interspersed with the translation. Thereby the translation of Khedrup Jé's text is clearly differentiated from the commentarial text, which begins and ends with a small ornament: ☙ . . . ☙. Our explanations are mainly based on Purbu Chok Jampa Gyatso's textbooks on collected topics, *The Magic Key to the Path of Reasoning: A Presentation of Collected Topics Revealing the Meaning of the Texts on Valid Cognition (Tshad ma'i gzhung don 'byed pa'i bsdus grva'i rnam bzag rigs lam 'phrul gyi lde mig)*, and *Explanation of the Presentation of Objects and Object-Possessors as Well as Awarenesses and Knowers (Yul yul chan dang blo rigs gi rnam par bshad pa)*. These are the most basic textbooks that Sera Jey Monastery uses with regard to these topics.

A glossary is given at the end of this book containing key technical terms in English along with their Tibetan and Sanskrit glosses. The classical Tibetan definition of every term is given first, usually followed by a more idiomatic English explanation. Many of the classical definitions from Tibetan textbooks are not definitions as Western readers would expect them; rather they are stock definitions structured for stylized Tibetan debate, rendered in opaque literal English. These have been widely adopted in Western Buddhist curricula for the study of logic and debate. They are important because understanding the Tibetan exegetical tradition of this topic hinges on being conversant with them. Anyone studying this subject in a Geluk center or with a geshe will have to contend with them. The English explanations use more standard philosophical terms.

The texts cited by Khedrup Jé and those referenced in our commentary are mainly works composed in either Sanskrit or Tibetan. The endnotes to these give the author's name and either the Sanskrit titles for Sanskrit works or an English translation of works penned in Tibetan. In the bibliography the Tibetan titles for all these works are given in the Turrell Wylie system.

The Tibetan print we have used as a basis for this translation is by the Institute of Tibetan Classics, vol. 21, *Dpal dge ldan pa'i tshad ma rig pa' gzhung gces btus* (*Geluk Epistemology*). An English translation by Jonathan Samuels of this volume is soon to be published by Wisdom Publications and will contain a complete translation of Khedrup Jé's *Clearing Mental Darkness*. Throughout the translation, correlate Tibetan page numbers are given in brackets.

ACKNOWLEDGMENTS

First and foremost, I would like express my deepest gratitude to His Holiness the Fourteenth Dalai Lama for giving us the opportunity to work on this translation project. It started with His Holiness's advice to translate sections of Khedrup Jé's *Clearing Mental Darkness* dealing with awareness and knowers, the explanation of consciousness, the four noble truths, and the path to liberation.

Second, I would like to sincerely thank Khensur Rinpoche Geshe Lobsang Delek, the former abbot of Sera Jey Monastery, for his practical advice regarding this project and his kindhearted way of taking care of the monastery.

I also would like to thank the administration of Sera Jey Monastic University and the Sera Jey Secondary School for giving their support toward the English Translation Department.

I have to express enormous thanks and appreciation to the students of the English Translation Department who worked on this translation: Venerables Tenzin Thinley, Thupten Gyaltsen, Lobsang Kalden, Karma Samten, Jampa Mönlam, Lobsang Tsundru, Rinchen Ngodup, Konchok Dhondup, Thinley Amgyal, Lobsang Phuntsok, Lobsang Thuptop, Lobsang Thupten, Jigme Wangyal, Yeshe Tsering, Kalsang Namgyal, Jampa Khenrab, Jampa Topdhen, and Tsepak Gonpo. I also give immense thanks to the Western monks who extensively edited and proofread the translation: Venerables Tenzin Legtsok, Tenzin Gache, and Daniel Frey. Finally, I'd like to thank our editor, Mary Petrusewicz, and the entire team at Wisdom Publications who have helped bring this book to fruition and make it available to a wide audience.

Khedrup Jé's *Clearing Mental Darkness* is not an easy text, and the meaning of many passages can have different interpretations. Because of being low in acquired knowledge and learning, and saturated with wrong views and defilements, taking the lamas and deities as my witness, I confess my mistakes to the wise.

Tenzin Namdak
Sera Jey Monastic University

INTRODUCTION

*F*REEDOM *through* CORRECT KNOWING is a translation with commentary of several important sections of Khedrup Gelek Palsang's
(1385–1438) *Clearing Mental Darkness: An Ornament of the Seven Treatises on Valid Cognition* (*Tshad ma'i bstan bcos sde bdun gyi rgyan yid kyi
mun sel*). The parts we have chosen to translate concern awareness and
knowers (*blo rig*), the four noble truths, and the path to liberation. "Awareness and knowers" is a term used to describe a general topic and correlate
genre of texts concerning the enumeration and descriptions of various
types of consciousness. Knowing about the mind is essential for eliminating suffering and achieving both temporary and ultimate happiness,
the central goals of Buddhist practice. Texts on awareness and knowers
are based on the sūtra teachings of the Buddha elucidated by the scholars of the ancient Indian universities like Nālandā. The primary source
for this subject is Dignāga's (480–540) *Compendium of Valid Cognition* (*Pramāṇasamuchachaya, Tshad ma kunlasbtus pa*). Another Indian
master, Dharmakīrti (600–660), wrote seven commentaries on valid
cognition, the most famous being *Commentary on (Dignāga's) Compendium of Valid Cognition* (*Pramānavarttikakārikā, Tshad ma rnam
'grelgyitshigle'urbyas pa*). In the Tibetan Buddhist tradition these are
deemed the most authoritative Indian texts on logic and basic functions
of the mind.

Many Indian texts were translated into Tibetan before the decline of
Buddhism in India, after which Tibetan scholars continued the tradition
of composing commentaries to clarify and make relevant to current audiences the meaning of preceding sūtras and commentaries. In the twelfth
century the first Tibetan text on the subject of valid cognition, called *Valid*

Cognition Eliminating the Darkness of the Mind (*Tshad ma sde bdun yid kyi mun sel*), was composed by the scholar Chapa Chökyi Sengé (Phywa pa Chos kyi seng ge, 1109–69). Shortly after this text was composed Sakya Paṇḍita Kunga Gyaltsen (Sa pan Kun dga' Rgyal mtshan, 1182–1251) composed *The Treasury of Reasoning* (*Tsad ma rigs gter*). Sakya Paṇḍita was a great master of the Sakya tradition of Buddhism in Tibet, the other traditions being Nyingma, Kagyü, and Geluk. Lama Tsongkhapa, the founder of the Geluk tradition, although he taught extensively on this topic, did not author a detailed text exclusively on awareness and knowers. Khedrup Jé, one of Lama Tsongkhapa's two main disciples, composed *Clearing Mental Darkness*, the first extensive exposition on this topic by a Geluk scholar. From among the four systems of Buddhist philosophy, Vaibhāṣhika (Great Exposition), Sautrāntika (Sūtra), Chittamātra (Mind-Only), and Madhyamaka (Middle Way), and the Madhyamaka variants Prāsaṅgika (Consequence) and Svātantrika (Autonomy), the subject here, awarenesses and knowers, is mainly explained according to the Sautrāntika and Chittamātra. The same basic classifications and ways of defining various functions of consciousness are used in other schools with slight modifications. Khedrup Jé's text, *Clearing Mental Darkness*, presents not only awareness and knowers, the explanation of consciousness, the four noble truths, and the path to liberation, but also gives an elaborate explanation of signs and reasoning (*rtags rigs*). Signs and reasoning is a topic of study and an associated genre of Buddhist texts that explain logic and valid reasoning. This book presents only the awareness and knowers, four noble truths, and path to liberation sections of Khedrup Jé's *Clearing Mental Darkness* without delving into the signs and reasoning section of his text.

In many Tibetan philosophical texts like *Clearing Mental Darkness,* it is common to divide the presentation of each subject into three parts—namely, refuting others' assertions, positing the author's own assertions, and dispelling objections to the author's position. While the middle part, positing the author's own assertions, is explained in a quite straightforward way, most of the subject matter in the first and last sections is presented in the form of debates between holders of various positions. If one is not

familiar with the structure of debate in classical Indian and Tibetan philosophy, then such presentations are almost impossible to follow without
oral commentary. Therefore this translation focuses mainly on the sections
positing the author's own assertions with some additional debates from
the sections in which others' positions are refuted and objections to the
author's own position are dispelled. We have not translated Khedrup Jé's
text in its entirety. Since page numbers of the Tibetan text we've used as a
basis for this translation are given in brackets, one can get a sense of how
much text has been omitted from this translation.

A text like Khedrup Jé's is not composed for those totally new to Buddhist philosophy. It assumes some background knowledge of basic Buddhist terminology, logic, epistemology, and worldview. Also, a work like
Clearing Mental Darkness is not intended to be read in isolation but is
best understood through discussion with others engaged in studying and
contemplating these topics, as well as with reference to other related texts.
One has to remember that when Khedrup Jé composed this work the audience he most likely had in mind was other monastics like himself who were
steeped in traditional Buddhist studies and practice at various monasteries
and hermitages throughout Tibet. Even most literate lay Tibetans would
not be able to understand much of this text. For English readers, a straight
translation of the Tibetan alone would be largely incomprehensible. For
that reason we have tried to provided explanations interspersed with the
translation to bridge this gap between you the reader and the intended
Tibetan audience. A few topics that are invaluable for understanding this
text, however, such as the structure of a syllogism and the divisions of mental factors, cannot be succinctly explained without greatly impinging on
the flow of Khedrup Jé's work. Therefore in several appendixes we have
given brief explanations of such topics together with charts and tables.

In the seven chapters constituting Khedrup Jé's presentation of mind and
awareness, he primarily explains the full range of *objects*, including all phenomena that can be known, and *object possessors*, things that engage objects,
such as consciousness and persons. In the first chapter, Khedrup Jé starts
by explaining objects of knowledge. This presentation is filled out with an

extensive discussion of three different twofold divisions of phenomena, first into manifest and hidden phenomena, then specifically characterized and generally characterized phenomena, and finally into the two truths— ultimate and conventional truths. He not only explains how objects exist in various ways but also the ways they can be realized, either in a direct non-conceptual manner, as with manifest phenomena like colors, or in a conceptual manner by depending on inference, as in the case of hidden phenomena like the fact that all humans are mortal. Another way of distinguishing how a mind realizes its object is either explicitly or implicitly. This presentation leads to the following questions: Which types of consciousness realize their objects and which do not realize an object? When is a consciousness considered to be valid, in the sense of realizing its object, and when not?

The answers to these questions are given in chapters 2 and 3. Chapter 2 gives an explanation of various non-valid awarenesses. These include both consciousnesses that don't realize their object and those that, although they realize their object, are not valid because they do not realize their objects newly by their own power but are induced by a valid cognizer that precedes them. The latter are known as subsequent cognizers. Khedrup Jé makes this presentation of non-valid awareness within the twofold division of conceptual and non-conceptual consciousness.

Chapter 3 explains what it means to be a valid cognizer and divides valid cognizers into various categories. In chapter 4, the first division, valid direct perceivers, is discussed. This chapter elaborately explains how these types of consciousness come into being and how they are produced in dependence on various causes and conditions. The Sautrāntika and Chittamātra have different interpretations regarding these points. Khedrup Jé clearly explains these differences and their supporting reasons in the form of interesting logical debates between these two schools. Valid direct perceivers are essentially direct perceivers that are characterized as being valid cognizers. Chapter 4 further defines the four main categories of direct perceivers: sense direct perceivers, mental direct perceivers, self-knowing direct perceivers, and yogic direct perceivers.

Having studied yogic direct perceivers, one comes to see the need to understand the four noble truths. In chapter 5, Khedrup Jé gives a brilliant elucidation of these essential teachings of the Buddha. He clearly indicates that the understanding of the four noble truths depends on developing different types of valid cognizers in one's own mental continuum and offers a very lucid presentation of how to progress on the spiritual paths of liberation and enlightenment. He also eloquently explains how to develop an unmistaken realization of the fundamental reality of selflessness of persons and phenomena, and the need to meditate on these aspects of the path over a prolonged period of time in order to eliminate ignorance, the root cause of all mental afflictions and samsaric suffering.

The realizations of the path, explained in chapter 6, are results of valid cognizers. These results are of two types: interrupted and uninterrupted. Interrupted results include the various realizations and goals a Buddhist practitioner strives for, such as desirable rebirth, liberation, and enlightenment. Uninterrupted results of valid cognizers are results immediately arising from a valid cognizer, such as a concept thinking, this is a table, arising immediately subsequent to an eye consciousness observing the visible form of a table. In chapter 6 the different categories of these results are discussed together with debates between the Sautrāntika and Chittamātra regarding their interpretations of the results of valid cognizers.

As explained in previous chapters, one needs to develop the yogic perception directly realizing selflessness in order to eliminate ignorance and thereby progress on the paths to liberation and enlightenment. Direct realization of selflessness can only come about by having realized it in a conceptual manner—that is, by generating a valid inference realizing selflessness—first. How to generate this kind of inference is precisely explained in chapter 7.

In order to give readers some sense of the two main authors involved here, Khedrup Jé Gelek Palsang and Purbu Chok Jampa Gyatso, whom we mainly rely on for additional explanations, brief biographies of these two eminent Buddhist scholars are given at the close of this introduction.

Khedrup Jé refers often to the generation of a correct sign or reason throughout the text when discussing how to use logical reasoning to establish the existence or non-existence of various phenomena. Logical proofs are very important to generate a correct understanding of reality but are not easy to understand. Appendix 1 gives a summary of the main aspects of logic and reasoning for the reader's reference.

On several occasions in the text there are references to main minds and mental factors. Because the actual text of Khedrup Jé's *Clearing Mental Darkness* doesn't list or explain mental factors, appendix 2 gives an overview of the relation between main minds and mental factors and lists the mental factors according to Vasubandhu's *Treasury of Knowledge* (*Abhidharma-kosha*) and Asaṅga's *Compendium of Knowledge* (*Abidharmasamucchaya*).

In the explanation of the four noble truths, karma and afflictions are explained as the origin of suffering. As Khedrup Jé doesn't explicitly explain these two objects of abandonment, appendix 3 gives a brief explanation of how karma is created and how some of the main afflictions are defined.

The view of selflessness is mentioned in many parts of the text and is at the heart of Buddhist practice and worldview. In order to give an overview of this as explained by the different schools of Buddhist philosophy, appendix 4 summarizes the main Buddhist views on selflessness.

In chapters 5 and 6, the relations between consciousness and the spiritual paths of liberation and enlightenment are explained in great detail from the point of view of the different valid cognizers needed to produce these paths. Appendix 5 gives an overview of the different spiritual paths Khedrup Jé is referring to in this context.

The section "Negating the Selves of Persons and Phenomena" in chapter 5 gives an explanation of how to realize selflessness according to the Sautrāntika and Chittamātra schools. In order to know how this presentation relates to the more commonly known explanation of the Prāsaṅgika Madhyamaka, appendix 6 explains a simplified form of realizing selflessness according to that school.

Throughout this text corresponding page numbers of the Tibetan-language version of Khedrup Jé's *Clearing Mental Darkness* are given in brackets—for example, [15]. Among the many prints of this text available in Tibetan, we have used as a basis of our translation the version published by the Institute of Tibetan Classics (ITC) in 2006. In endnotes we have also given references to citations for the various works quoted by Khedrup Jé as given in notes to the ITC print.

BIOGRAPHIES OF KHEDRUP JÉ GELEK PALSANG AND PURBU CHOK JAMPA GYATSO[2]

Khedrup Jé Gelek Palsang, the third holder of the Ganden Throne, was born in Tsang in 1385. He was renowned as the reincarnation of the great Indian scholar Devendrabuddhi, a master of Buddhist logic whom he cites frequently in his composition translated below. From a young age, spurred on by a fierce faith and perseverance for studying and contemplating all academic subjects, he traveled to Ngamring and Sakya to study at the feet of many great masters. Everyone he encountered was amazed at the power of his intellect.

He received ordination as a novice monk from Khedrup Sengye Gyaltsen, who gave him the name Khedrup Gelek Palsang. He studied sūtra and tantra with Lamdré Yeshe Pal, Kunga Gyaltsen, and Jé Rendawa. In 1405 he received full monastic ordination, with Jé Rendawa acting as his abbot. In 1407, at age twenty-three, he traveled to Ü (i.e., central Tibet), where he met the unequaled Tsongkhapa, who was staying at the Sera hermitage. Tsongkhapa was highly pleased by the young man's penetrating questions and subtle points of doubt regarding the texts, and subsequently gave him extensive teachings and empowerments. Thereafter, Khedrup Jé became a treasure of qualities of teaching, debate, and composition, and also an accomplished practitioner. Tsongkhapa indicated that he considered Khedrup Jé his heart disciple. Khedrup Jé also received extensive profound teachings from Rendawa Shönu Lodrö, Namkha Paljor, Lamdré Yeshe Pal, Kunga Gyaltsen, and Gyaltsab Darma Rinchen. After that, he traveled to Tsang (in central Tibet), where he founded the monastic seat of Nyangtö Changra. On account of his extensive activities there, he was sometimes referred to as "Khedrup Changrawa." He founded the monasteries of Riwo Dacheng and Gyaltse Palkhor Dechen Chöde. He later stayed in meditation retreat at Riwo Dacheng but also continued to give teachings on sūtra and tantra to many disciples.

At age forty-five, together with Gyaltsab Darma Rinchen, he traveled to Ü, where Gyaltsab Jé served as the second holder of the Ganden Throne after Tsongkhapa. Khedrup Jé took this position himself in 1431 and held it for eight years, during which he passed the time teaching, debating, and writing. At age fifty he composed a major commentary on the *Kālachakra Tantra* entitled *Stainless Light* (*Dri med 'od rgya cher bshad pa de kho na nyid snang ba*). At Ganden, he founded the school of dialectics and initi- ated the tradition of commemorating Lama Tsongkhapa's passing on the twenty-fifth of the tenth Tibetan month. He passed away in 1438 at age fifty-three. He composed many important texts, such as *Illumination of the Difficult Points, An Explanation of [Haribhadra's] Commentary on the Clear Meaning* (*Rtogs dka'i snang ba*), a commentary on Prajñāpāramitā; *Dose of Emptiness Called the "Eye Opener of Good Fortune"* (*Stong thun skal bzang mig byed*), an exposition on emptiness in the major Indian schools; a synthesized commentary on Dharmakīrti's philosophy of logic and epis- temology, parts of which are translated in *Clearing Mental Darkness: An Ornament of Dharmakīrti's Seven Treatises on Valid Cognition* (*Tshad ma sde bdun gyi rgyan yid kyi mun sel*), and *Ocean of Reasonings: An Extensive Explanation of [Dharmakīrti's] Commentary on Valid Cognition* (*Tshad ma rigs pa'i rgya mtsho*), commentaries on valid cognition; *Ford of Faith* (*Rnam thar dad pa'i 'jug ngogs*), a biography of Tsongkhapa; and others.

The master Purbu Chok Jampa Gyatso was born to a nomadic family in the Dzachu Ortok region of Kham (in eastern Tibet) in 1825. His father was named Jamchö, and his mother, Tsering Drolkar. At the age of five he was recognized as the incarnation of the great Sera Jey scholar the third Purbu Chok Rinpoche and was invited to the Ü region, where he stayed at the Purchok hermitage. The local lama there taught him writing, recitation, and other basic subjects.

At age ten he entered Sera Jey Monastery. That same year he offered a tuft of hair, signifying his going forth into life as a monk, to the tenth

Dalai Lama Tsultrim Gyatso, who gave him the name Jampa Tsultrim
Gyatso. Afterward, he received ordination as a getsul (novice) from the
Panchen Lama Tenpai Nyima. Relying on his tutor Geshe Drakpa Tsön-
drü, he studied the great Buddhist texts. At age fourteen, he participated
in the Rikchung debates, for having excelled in his Prajñāpāramitā studies. After that, he debated before the great assembly of Sera Jey and Mey
Monasteries. At age twenty, he received full monastic (gelong) ordination,
again from Panchen Tenpai Nyima. At age twenty-one, he sat for his Lha-
rampa Geshe exam during the Mönlam Chenmo in Lhasa, having become
a great scholar of sūtra and tantra. He gave many teachings, such as Drops
of the River Ganges, a guru yoga practice related to Ganden Lha Gyama
(the guru yoga practice of Lama Tsongkhapa); the guru yogas of Guhya-
samāja, Heruka, Yamantaka, Hayagriva, and White Mahakala; and composed texts such as *The Magic Key to the Path of Reasoning: A Presentation
of Collected Topics Revealing the Meaning of the Texts on Valid Cognition*
(*Tshad ma'i gzhung don 'byed pa'i bsdus grva'i rnam bzag rigs lam 'phrul
gyi lde mig*); *Explanation of the Presentation of Objects and Object-Possessors
as Well as Awarenesses and Knowers* (*Yul yulchen dang blo rigs gir nam par
bshad pa*); and a biography of Jetsun Ngawang Losang Tenpai Gyaltsen
Khyenrab Trinle Gyatso. At age thirty-seven he accepted the position of
tutor for the twelfth Dalai Lama, Trinle Gyatso, and at age fifty-five he
became the tutor of the thirteenth Dalai Lama Thupten Gyatso, to whom
he gave extensive teachings on sūtra and tantra. He passed away in 1894
at age sixty-nine.

Tenzin Namdak
Sera Jey Monastic University

CHAPTER ONE

OBJECTS OF KNOWLEDGE

I N ORDER TO UNDERSTAND consciousness, it is important to know about the objects that consciousness can apprehend, experience, and realize. This chapter explains those objects. There are various ways to divide objects, such as into permanent and impermanent phenomena, conventional and ultimate truths, and more. By looking at the whole collection of things that exist, we quickly come face to face with many questions that draw us into deeper ways of thinking about the world and ourselves that are essential for spiritual development. What does it mean for something to exist versus not exist? How do things exist? Is mind or awareness a necessary condition for existence or a coincidental outcome of the physical world? What are major differences in the types of things there are and differences in how they exist? Within the various types of things that exist, what are we? How do we come into existence? How do we go out of existence? Is the way we perceive ourselves and the world of existent phenomena accurate or deluded, true or false? Is there any purpose to our existence, does it have meaning, or is it ultimately devoid of these? All these profoundly important questions are swimming beneath the surface of this entire work. Because they are deep and complex issues, if we jump directly into a discussion of them, we will likely end up in a muddle of confusion. Rather, we begin by looking simply at what kinds of objects exist, how they are different, and how they are similar. Then we will look at how we perceive these objects in both clear and distorted ways. Gradually, the path to spiritual realization, which is necessarily realization of the most fundamental truths, comes to light.

The initial way to present objects of knowledge here is by dividing them into two different types: manifest and hidden phenomena. These two types of phenomena are commonly distinguished according to how an ordinary person first realizes them; however, here Khedrup Jé defines them in a slightly different way.

The more common way of distinguishing manifest and hidden phenomena is as follows. Manifest phenomena, like the color blue, are delineated as those that can be initially realized by a valid direct perceiver of an ordinary being, like a sense consciousness—for example, the eye consciousness apprehending the color blue. Blue is a manifest phenomenon. Conversely, hidden phenomena are delineated as those phenomena that an ordinary being needs to initially realize in dependence on conceptual consciousness using reasoning. For example, the fact that sound is impermanent, meaning that it continually changes through even the shortest units of time, is a hidden phenomenon. It is something that ordinary people cannot experience with their ear consciousness but can come to know through reason. An ordinary person first generates an inferential consciousness realizing that sound is impermanent in dependence on the reason that sound is a product. Hidden phenomena can be further divided into two: slightly hidden and very hidden phenomena. Sound being impermanent is an example of the first. An example of a very hidden phenomenon is the subtle workings of karma whereby, for instance, a particular individual's specific act of generosity results in a specific instance of gain or prosperity for that person. An ordinary being cannot initially know such a thing either through direct valid cognition or through typical reasoned inference based on the power of fact. Rather, they may generate a scriptural inference or inference through belief in dependence upon reasoning establishing that statements expressing such very hidden phenomena are unmistaken. Chapter 7 will explain the kinds of consciousnesses realizing slightly and very hidden phenomena in more detail. Here the focus is on the objects themselves.

Khedrup Jé distinguishes manifest and hidden phenomena simply on the basis of whether or not they are explicitly realized by a valid direct perceiver or an inferential valid cognizer, respectively. He does not consider how phenomena are initially realized by an ordinary person. His position will be fleshed out below.

Objects can also be divided according to whether they are realized explicitly or implicitly. In both cases the consciousness knows its object, but the manner of doing so varies. A valid cognizer that explicitly realizes its object does so through the force of the object appearing; the object must appear to that consciousness. For implicit realization the object need not appear to the consciousness realizing it. This is the second way of classifying objects discussed below.

Another important division of objects is into specifically characterized phenomena and generally characterized phenomena, referring to objects that are impermanent and permanent, respectively. This division is made according to how phenomena exist, whether they are merely imputed by conceptual consciousness or are established by their own characteristics. All phenomena, or objects of knowledge, can also be divided into the two truths: conventional and ultimate truths. Khedrup Jé presents these two ways of classifying phenomena as a third and fourth way to explain objects of knowledge. The last division Khedrup Jé explains is the division from the point of view of the mode of apprehension, where he discusses a classification of four objects made according to how they function with respect to different consciousnesses experiencing them: appearing objects, apprehended objects, determined objects, and objects of engagement.

In the following passage Khedrup Jé first explains the structure of his work. ⁙

An extensive presentation of the actual text
A detailed presentation of the meaning of this text's subject matter has three headings:

- A presentation of objects that are objects of knowledge.
- A presentation of awarenesses that are agents of knowing [which will be explained in chapters 2 and 3 on non-valid awareness and valid cognizers].
- A presentation of how consciousnesses engage their objects. [This

section explains signs and reasoning and is not a part of the translation in this book.] [15][3]

Objects of knowledge

Concerning the first [a presentation of objects that are objects of knowledge], there are three headings: enumerations, definition, and divisions.

- **Enumerations:** In our own system, object, object of knowledge, object of comprehension, existent, and established base are synonyms. [18]
- **Definition:** In our own system, the definition of an object is that which is known by an awareness. [20]
- **Divisions:** In our own system, there are four ways of dividing objects.

❧ To make the presentation more accessible the following outline is used for Khedrup Jé's discussion of various objects:
- manifest and hidden phenomena
- explicit and implicit realization
- specifically and generally characterized phenomena
- conventional and ultimate truths
- mode of apprehension ❧

[22] First, when divided in terms of (1) the mode of realization or (2) the mode of appearance of an object possessor that is a valid cognizer, there are the two, manifest phenomena and hidden phenomena, and the two, specifically characterized phenomena and generally characterized phenomena, respectively.

1.1 MANIFEST AND HIDDEN PHENOMENA

Therefore, first of all, manifest and hidden phenomena will be explained. This [explanation] has three parts: definitions, divisions, and an analysis of whether they are contradictory or non-contradictory.

- **Definitions:** In our own system, the definition of manifest phenomenon is that which is explicitly realized by a valid direct perceiver. The definition of hidden phenomenon is that which is explicitly realized by an inferential valid cognizer.

- **Divisions:** In our own system, when manifest phenomena are divided there are two: objects explicitly engaged by the action of a self-knowing direct perceiver and objects explicitly engaged by the action of an other-knowing direct perceiver.

❖ Whatever is explicitly realized by a valid direct perceiver is realized within appearing to that perceiver, and whatever appears to a direct perceiver is necessarily an impermanent phenomenon. Permanent phenomena cannot appear to a direct perceiver. Therefore, all manifest phenomena are impermanent. Whatever is explicitly realized by an inferential cognizer must also be realized within appearing to that cognizer; however, whatever appears to an inferential cognizer is not necessarily permanent or impermanent: both permanent and impermanent phenomena appear to and are explicitly realized by inferential cognizers. Therefore, all phenomena are hidden phenomenon.

To understand the division of manifest phenomena one has to understand the difference between self-knowing and other-knowing direct perceivers. Purbu Chok defines *a self-knowing valid direct perceiver* as: "a knower that is new and incontrovertible, free from conceptuality, only directed inward and is just an apprehender."[4] Self-knowing consciousness is directed only inward as it perceives a consciousness within the continuum of the person who has this knower. This consciousness does not engage in external objects, like forms. It enables one to remember a particular experience or object by perceiving the particular consciousness that realizes the object that is later remembered. For example, when we see a flower, in addition to an eye consciousness seeing the flower we have a self-knowing direct perceiver that perceives the eye consciousness seeing the flower. This self-knowing direct perceiver does not engage the flower, which is an external object, but only engages the eye consciousness, which is an internal object. It is because this self-knower perceives our eye consciousness seeing a flower that later we are able to recall having seen the flower. Conversely, *an other-knower* is a consciousness that is directed outward and engages external objects, such as an eye consciousness seeing a flower. Every instance of an other-knower has a self-knower that is concomitant with it. Therefore, all other-knowing consciousnesses are *objects explicitly engaged by the action of a self-knowing direct perceiver*, and all other manifest phenomena are *objects explicitly engaged by the action of an other-knowing direct perceiver.*

In the following section Khedrup Jé discusses the difference between manifest and hidden phenomena in general and the difference between them in relation to a particular awareness. Purbu Chok explains manifest phenomena as objects that are directly realized by a valid direct perceiver—for example, the eye consciousness perceiving the color blue.[5] He defines hidden phenomena as objects that are realized in a hidden way by the conceptual consciousness that apprehends them. For Purbu Chok all phenomena are hidden phenomena because all phenomena are objects realized in a hidden way by the conceptual consciousness that apprehends them.[6] Conversely, only functioning things are manifest phenomena because only they are objects realized directly by a valid direct perceiver. Likewise, Khedrup Jé explains that a phenomenon like the fire on a smoky mountain pass is a hidden phenomenon in relation to the inference that realizes it and is also a manifest phenomenon in relation to a valid direct perceiver. Therefore, according to Khedrup Jé, although in general manifest and hidden phenomena are not mutually exclusive, in relation to a particular awareness they must be mutually exclusive. For example, in relation to an inferential cognizer realizing that fire exists on a distant mountaintop from which smoke is rising, fire is a hidden phenomenon and not a manifest phenomenon. In relation to that inference the existence of fire on the distant mountaintop has to be realized in dependence on the reason of the existence of smoke. Such a fire is too far away to be seen by the eye consciousness of the person possessing this inferential cognizer. However, for a person actually on the mountaintop that perceives this fire at close range, fire is a manifest phenomenon and not a hidden phenomenon in relation to their eye consciousness perceiving the fire. Khedrup Jé starts his analysis with the following. ⚜

- **Analysis:** Third, an analysis of whether or not they [i.e., manifest and hidden phenomena] are contradictory or non-contradictory. There is no contradiction between being an object of comprehension that is a manifest phenomenon and being an object of comprehension that is a hidden phenomenon. [25] This is because there is no contradiction between being the explicit object of comprehension of a valid direct perceiver and being the explicit object of comprehension of an inferential valid cognizer. Since with respect to whichever awareness in relation to which something is a manifest phenomenon it is necessarily not a hidden phenomenon with respect to that awareness, therefore, it *is* contradictory for one phenomenon to be both now manifest and now hidden with respect to the same awareness.

[If someone objects], "In that case, it follows that direct and inferential valid cognizers are non-contradictory because manifest and hidden objects of comprehension are non-contradictory. If there is no pervasion, then it follows that the enumeration of objects of comprehension into manifest and hidden phenomena doesn't entail the enumeration of valid cognizers into direct and inferential valid cognizers."

[To this our system responds], "If so, it follows that non-established, contradictory, and non-ascertained signs are not mutually exclusive, because the [three] branches [i.e., the three modes of ascertainment] of the definition of correct signs—the property of the subject, the forward pervasion, and the counter pervasion—are not mutually exclusive. If you say there is no pervasion, then it follows that the thing which clarifies, [the branches of] the definition of correct signs, being definitely enumerated as three does not entail that the basis to be clarified, counterfeit signs such as non-established signs and so forth, are definitely enumerated as three. What do you say to that?"

꠳ The response of our own system refers to inference that depends upon a correct sign that proves the probandum. The probandum is something to be proven, a quality of a particular object—for example, it can be established that the object sound has the quality of being impermanent; "impermanent" is a property, characteristic, or quality of sound. Sound's impermanence is its property of changing from moment to moment. In this case, a correct sign or reason to prove the probandum that sound is impermanent could be the sign "a product." A product is something produced from or arising from its causes and conditions. All things that are produced by their specific causes and conditions also have the property of continually changing from moment to moment. This sign, a product, proves sound to be impermanent because (1) sound is a product, and (2) whatever is a product is necessarily impermanent.

The generation of a consciousness realizing a sign proving a probandum requires three modes of ascertainment that will first individually be realized, after which a simultaneous ascertainment arises. Based on this simultaneous realization, an inference can be generated. These three modes for the establishment of "sound being impermanent" by the sign "a product" are: (1) "property of the subject": product is established to be a property of the subject "sound" because sound is a product; (2) "the forward pervasion": whatever is a product is necessarily impermanent; and (3) "the counter pervasion": whatever is not impermanent is necessarily a nonproduct. For more about correct signs and the generation of inference, see appendix 1 and chapter 7. The three modes of ascertainment of this valid reasoning proving sound to be impermanent by the sign "a product" are not mutually exclusive; however, the three incorrect signs, mentioned here by Khedrup Jé in the last lines above, non-established, contradictory, and non-ascertained signs, are mutually exclusive. Here our own system throws at the opponent the absurd consequence that these three incorrect signs are not mutually exclusive by using a similar incorrect pervasion as the opponent used. The opponent argued that direct and inferential valid cognizers are non-contradictory because manifest and hidden objects of comprehension are non-contradictory.

The three types of incorrect signs, non-established, contradictory, and non-ascertained signs, are as follows. A non-established sign means that the sign is not established as a property of the subject. For example, in the proof statement, the horns of a rabbit are impermanent because of being a product. The horns of a rabbit are not established as a product because they are non-existent. A contradictory sign means that the sign is contradictory in relation to the probandum—for example, saying that sound *is not impermanent* because of being a product. Whatever is a product *is necessarily impermanent*, so one cannot prove that sound *is not impermanent* with the sign "a product." A non-ascertained sign means that although the sign is established as a property of the subject, it is indefinite in relation to the similar and discordant class in the proof. For example, if one states that sound is impermanent because it is an object of knowledge, it is true that being an object of knowledge is a property of sound. However, it is not definite that whatever is an object of knowledge is impermanent, nor is it definite that whatever is an object of knowledge is not impermanent. There are some instances of object of knowledge that are impermanent, like pot, and some that are not impermanent, like the absence of hair on the palm of your hand. Therefore, although the sign, object of knowledge, is a property of sound, from this sign it cannot be ascertained that sound either is or is not impermanent. In short, just as these three incorrect signs being mutually exclusive does not entail that the three modes of ascertainment are mutually exclusive, the fact that manifest and hidden phenomena are not mutually contradictory does not entail that direct and inferential cognizers are not contradictory.

However, one should note that many other Buddhist scholars give different definitions of manifest and hidden phenomena from Khedrup Jé's and do assert that the two are mutually exclusive.

Khedrup Jé continues the debate: ⚬

[25] If [the opponent] responds, "In that case, how do you explain the following verse [of Dharmakīrti's *Exposition of Valid Cognition*]?":

Other than manifest and hidden phenomena,
there aren't other objects of comprehension.
Therefore, because there are two objects of comprehension,
valid cognizers are asserted as two.[7]

Our [own system's] response is, "In that case, how do you explain the
following passage [from Dharmakīrti's *Exposition of Valid Cognition*]?":

As for the three modes of a syllogism,
they also express the establishment of
the antidote to that syllogism's
[non-established, contradictory, and non-ascertained signs].[8]

Therefore, that the two objects of comprehension, manifest and hidden
phenomena, are not contradictory does not entail that the two valid cognizers, direct and inferential valid cognizers, must be non-contradictory.
This is because within manifest and hidden objects of comprehension
being not contradictory in general, it isn't necessary that [a phenomenon]
being manifest and being hidden with regard to one [particular] valid cognizer are non-contradictory.

Devendrabuddhi said:

As for the definitions of manifest and hidden phenomena, they
are also dependent on the one realizing and the current circumstance. If that were not the case, when the particular circumstances of the one looking and what appears to them change,
the manifest and hidden phenomena would change into one
another. Therefore, the definitions [of manifest and hidden
phenomena] would become mixed up.[9]

The meaning of this passage is as follows; explanations of how to ascertain
the individual definitions of manifest and hidden phenomena are explanations of how to ascertain each in dependence on the one realizing and

the current circumstance. They are not explanations of how to ascertain manifest and hidden phenomena in just any way without reference to those. This is because in some circumstances a manifest phenomenon may become a hidden phenomenon, and a hidden phenomenon may become a manifest phenomenon. Thereby the definitions would become mixed up; therefore they are not mutually exclusive. This is the meaning of what was quoted above.

If explained like that [the meaning] matches well with the explanation of Śhākyabuddhi. Śhākyabuddhi says in his explanation of this [passage by Devendrabuddhi]:

> They appear mixed up because a manifest phenomenon will become a hidden phenomenon, and a hidden phenomenon will also become manifest phenomenon in other [circumstances].[10]

Therefore don't spread distorted terms or statements by holding the meaning of the commentary of Devendrabuddhi to be that manifest phenomena and hidden phenomena are established as contradictory because they are [contradictory] with regard to one individual realizing.

᚛ In short, a phenomenon that is explicitly realized by a valid direct perceiver is a manifest phenomenon, and one that is explicitly realized by an inferential valid cognizer is a hidden phenomenon. While these two are mutually exclusive with regard to a specific knower and set of circumstances, they are not mutually exclusive in general. Thus, according to Khedrup Jé's definitions, an elephant is both a manifest and hidden phenomenon in general because it is both an object explicitly realized by an eye consciousness seeing it and by an inferential conscious realizing it. For instance, a person might generate an inferential cognizer knowing that an elephant visited a particular place based on the sign of tracks and droppings of an elephant in that place at a later time. For a person who actually saw the elephant in that place earlier, and for their eye consciousness, the elephant was a manifest and not a hidden phenomenon. In the case of a person who later comes to that place and sees the tracks and droppings of the elephant, thereby generating an inferential cognizer knowing that an elephant visited that place, for this person and this inferential cognizer the elephant at that place is a hidden and not a manifest phenomenon. If this person lies there in wait and the elephant comes again, then the elephant in that place becomes a manifest phenomenon for that person.

Becoming familiar with the distinction between manifest and hidden phenomenon helps us generate clarity about what kinds of things we know and how we know them. Many of the objects that trigger our attachment and aversion on a daily basis are manifest phenomena. Most of the objects that need to be realized on the path to liberation from samsara and full enlightenment, such as impermanence and selflessness, the truth of suffering, the truth of cessation, and so forth, are hidden phenomena. In the definition of both these types of phenomena it was stated that they are "explicitly realized." Now we compare this type of realization with implicit realization.

1.2 Explicit and Implicit Realization

In the next section Khedrup Jé divides objects according to how they are realized in either an explicit or implicit manner. ⁙

[26] Someone might ask, well then, what is the meaning of explicit and implicit realization? [The response to] this has three parts:
- The general meaning of explicit realization and implicit realization
- The meaning of explicit realization and implicit realization for a valid direct perceiver
- The meaning of explicit realization and implicit realization for a valid inferential cognizer

First, [the general meaning of explicit realization and implicit realization]: [27]
- The meaning of *explicitly realizing an object*: certain knowing that is induced by the power of a valid cognizer turning its attention toward

an object and [that object] appearing to it, and that subsequently induces ascertainment without relying on other awarenesses.

• The meaning of *implicit realization*: although [a specific valid cognizer] does not presently turn its attention toward that [implicit] object, by the force of that valid cognizer explicitly comprehending its [explicit] object of comprehension, since it has already eliminated superimposition[11] regarding that [implicit] object in accordance with the occasion, in the future, ascertainment [of that object] will arise through merely turning awareness toward that object without having relied on other valid cognizers.

⚘ In order to understand the two meanings posited here, it is helpful to compare them. In both cases the aim is to know or ascertain an object; however, the manner of doing so varies. There are two distinguishing features that set explicit realization apart from implicit realization. The first is that a valid cognizer explicitly realizing an object turns its attention to that object that is explicitly realized. The second feature of explicit realization is that the object explicitly realized must appear to the consciousness that explicitly realizes it. This stands in contrast to the two main distinguishing features of implicit realization. First of all, when a consciousness implicitly realizes object A, it does not turn its attention to A but rather turns its attention to object B, which it explicitly realizes. Through the force of explicitly realizing object B, superimpositions are cleared away with respect to object A. An example of implicit realization is the clearing away of the superimposition that sound is not a non-product by a conceptual consciousness explicitly realizing that sound is a product. Through turning its attention toward the fact that sound is a product, this consciousness implicitly realizes that sound is not a non-product without having explicitly engaged this fact. Similarly, when we hear a voice and recognize it as that of our mother, we implicitly realize that it is not the voice of our father. Although not expressly stated above, a second feature of implicit realization is that the object implicitly realized does not appear to a consciousness that implicitly realizes it. If a consciousness implicitly realizes object A, then object A does not appear to that consciousness. ⚘

As for the second [the meaning of explicit and implicit realization for a valid direct perceiver]:
Eliminating superimposition in relation to its object of comprehension through that object's aspect explicitly appearing is the meaning of *a valid direct perceiver's explicit realization*. For example, the valid direct perceiver apprehending blue eliminates superimposition regarding blue through the aspect of blue explicitly appearing.

Eliminating superimposition in relation to an object that *does not* appear to it by the force of having eliminated superimposition with regard to its object of comprehension through the aspect of [the object of comprehension] having directly appeared is the meaning of *a valid direct perceiver's implicit realization*. An example of this is when by the force of inducing ascertainment through the aspect of a place devoid of vase explicitly appearing, although the aspect of the non-existence of vase at that place does not explicitly appear, the superimposition of the existence of vase is eliminated [through the appearance of "that place" that is devoid of vase that appears]. Through merely turning awareness toward it, ascertainment of the non-existence of vase will be induced.

Furthermore, that valid sense direct perceiver apprehending a place devoid of vase, which is able to induce ascertainment of the lack of vase in a place devoid of vase through its own power, is not a direct perceiver to the lack of vase in that place. This is because (1) it [i.e., a place devoid of vase] and the lack of vase are factually different, and (2) to that [direct perceiver], the aspect of the lack of vase does not explicitly appear. It is also not an inferential cognizer, because the meaning generality[12] of lack of vase does not appear to it. However, to that [object, lack of vase], it is a valid cognizer. If it is asked why, [we respond as follows]. It follows that the subject, that kind of direct perceiver, is a valid cognizer with regard to the lack of vase in a place devoid of vase, because (1) that lack of vase is its object, and (2) to that lack of vase it is a valid cognizer that induces certainty through its own power by eliminating the superimposition of the opposite [i.e., the presence of vase].

If it is said that the earlier part of the sign [i.e., part 1] is not established, [we respond as follows]. The subject, object of knowledge: it [absurdly] follows that if something is the object of an awareness, it is necessarily the explicit object of that awareness, because that lack of vase is not the object of that valid sense direct perceiver. If this is accepted, then it absurdly follows that if something is the object of expression of an expressive sound, it is necessarily the explicit object of expression of that sound.

⚡Language is often used to convey implied or indirect meanings. For example, when it is said that "money doesn't grow on trees," it is implied that money is only earned through effort. That money is only earned through effort is an object implicitly expressed by the phrase, or expressive sound, "money doesn't grow on trees." The mere reality that money doesn't in fact grow on trees is the explicit meaning expressed by that phrase. Just as an expressive sound can express both direct and indirect meanings, a consciousness can both explicitly and implicitly realize objects. ⚡

[28] Someone might object, "If that direct perceiver is a valid cognizer with respect to lack of vase, and [yet] is neither a direct perceiver nor an inferential cognizer to lack of vase, then it absurdly follows that valid cognizers are not numerically limited to the two, direct perceivers and inferential cognizers." [To this we respond that] the meaning of "valid cognizers are numerically limited to the two: direct perceivers and inferential cognizers" is, if something is a valid cognizer, it must be either a direct perceiver or an inferential cognizer. However, if it is the case that whatever is a valid cognizer must be either a direct perceiver or an inferential cognizer, this does not mean that if something is a valid cognizer to a particular object, it must be either a direct perceiver or an inferential cognizer to that object.

If there was pervasion, then—the subject, an object of knowledge: it follows that if something is an object of that phenomenon, it must be either the appearing object, object of apprehension, determined object, or object of engagement of that phenomenon, because if [something] is an object, it is necessarily one of those four. The pervasion and the sign have been accepted.[13] If accepted, then it follows that the subject, the sound and meaning generalities of vase, are one of the four—the appearing object and so forth—of the spoken sound *vase*, because they are that sound's object.

⁊·Khedrup Jé is making the point that just because something is an object of a particular consciousness it need not be the appearing object, object of apprehension, determined object, or object of engagement of that consciousness, just as something being the object of an expressive sound, like the spoken word *vase*, does not entail that it is the appearing object, object of apprehension, determined object, or object of engagement of that sound. Therefore, a phenomenon can be implicitly realized by a consciousness and thereby be an object of that consciousness without being included in those four types of objects of that consciousness. These four types of objects are explained in the section "Mode of Apprehension" below.

Since Khedrup Jé mentions meaning generalities here, and some understanding of them is necessary to grasp the following section, it will be helpful to explain them now. All conceptual consciousnesses need to depend on a mental image in order to generate apprehension of an object. This mental image is called a "meaning generality." Imagine you see a stunning house. At that time, when you actually see it, the house directly appears to your eye consciousness clearly, rich with all its detail and unmixed with mental fabrications. Then imagine that later on you remember this house. At this time the appearance of the house is most likely not as clear and rich with details as when you actually saw it. Although the eye consciousness actually seeing the house and the memory consciousness remembering the house both apprehend the house, and to both of them the house does appear, the way the house appears to them is very different. The appearance of the house to the eye consciousness, which is a non-conceptual consciousness, is unmitigated by a meaning generality, whereas the appearance to the memory consciousness, which is conceptual, is entirely dependent on a meaning generality. This meaning generality of the house is not the actual house itself but a mentally fabricated image that appears to conceptual consciousness as if it were the house. Whereas house is an impermanent phenomenon because it changes or disintegrates moment by moment, the meaning generality of house is a permanent phenomenon because it does

not disintegrate momentarily. Also, whereas house is a positive phenomenon in that the thought or terminological expression of house does not
directly negate anything, the meaning generality of house is a negative
phenomenon because it is an appearance of the elimination of all that is
not house. The standard description of the meaning generality of house is
that appearance of the opposite of not house that, although it is not house,
appears to the conceptual consciousness grasping at house as similar to
house. Because everything that exists is an object of conceptual consciousness, every existent has a meaning generality. If someone describes a particular house that one has never seen before, the image of this house that
appears to one's mind based solely on the description is a sound generality.

Purbu Chok says that the realization of selflessness by a yogic direct
perceiver is an implicit realization because the aspect of the object—the
selflessness of persons—does not actually appear to this direct perceiver
since it is a permanent phenomenon and permanent phenomena cannot
appear to direct perceivers.[14] It realizes the selflessness of persons implicitly through realizing a compounded phenomenon, such as the aggregates
that are devoid of a self of a person, explicitly. So there is a difference
between realizing an object by means of a direct perceiver and realizing
it explicitly.

**As for the third [the meaning of explicit realization and implicit
realization for a valid inferential cognizer]:**
Eliminating superimposition with regard to its object of comprehension by means of that object's meaning generality explicitly appearing is
the meaning of *explicit realization for an inferential cognizer.* An example is, by means of the meaning generality of sound being impermanent
explicitly appearing to it, the inferential cognizer realizing sound to be
impermanent eliminating the superimposition of holding sound to be
not impermanent.

The elimination of superimposition with regard to another object whose
meaning generality does not appear to it through the force of eliminating
superimposition by the meaning generality of its object of comprehension explicitly appearing: this is the meaning of *implicit realization for an*

inferential cognizer. For example, although to a valid inferential cognizer realizing sound to be impermanent, the meaning generality of the lack of permanence existing on sound doesn't explicitly appear, still [this inferential cognizer] eliminates the superimposition of sound having permanence. Without relying on another valid cognizer, it will be ascertained that sound lacks permanence by merely turning the awareness toward it [i.e., the lack of permanence on sound]. Here also, one should know as before the reason that this inferential cognizer is neither a direct perceiver nor an inferential cognizer with regard to that lack of permanence existing on sound and yet still is a valid cognizer with regard to it.

❧ Although on the face of it this distinction between explicit and implicit realization may seem like a dry abstract issue, actually it is an essential element of nearly every realization on the spiritual path. For example, as one explicitly develops the realization that this fortunate human life has great meaning in that it affords one opportunities to reduce suffering and create well-being for oneself and others, one implicitly refutes the idea that one's life is meaningless. As one realizes explicitly that death is certain to happen to oneself, one implicitly eliminates the idea that this life will last forever. As one explicitly realizes that other sentient beings are the same as oneself in wanting happiness and wanting to be free from suffering, one implicitly eliminates the apprehension that other sentient beings are totally foreign and fundamentally unlike oneself. Bringing this analysis looking at explicit and implicit realization into contemplation on aspects of the path helps to clarify how opposing pairs of concepts and perceptions work against one another. By discerning what states of mind are beneficial and constructive, we naturally see how to refute those that are destructive.

1.3 SPECIFICALLY AND GENERALLY CHARACTERIZED PHENOMENA

In the Sautrāntika all existing phenomena are divided into phenomena that are permanent, meaning not momentarily changing, and those that are impermanent, meaning changing or transforming moment to moment without pause. They also accept that specifically characterized phenomena are synonymous with impermanent phenomena because they have their own uncommon aspects or characteristics such as size, shape, color, and so forth. Further, they accept that generally characterized phenomena are synonymous with permanent phenomena that don't have these uncommon aspects or characteristics but are mere imputations by conceptual consciousness. The Sautrāntika also says that whatever is an object of comprehension of a valid cognizer is necessarily either a specifically or a generally characterized phenomena because whatever is an object of comprehension is the appearing object either of a valid direct perceiver or of an inferential valid cognizer; whatever is the former is necessarily a specifically characterized phenomena, while whatever is the latter is necessarily a generally characterized phenomena. Khedrup Jé first proves how valid cognizers are established as being definitely two, direct and inferential, due to the objects of apprehension in dependence upon which they realize their objects of comprehension being definite as two, specifically and generally characterized phenomena; after which he explains the etymology of these two phenomena, describes the definitions, and gives examples. ⊰

A presentation of specifically characterized phenomena and generally characterized phenomena

[31] Now a presentation of the two objects of comprehension, specifically characterized phenomena and generally characterized phenomena, will be made. There are three parts:

- Explaining the meaning of valid cognizers being established as definitely two, direct and inferential, due to objects of comprehension being definitely two, specifically and generally characterized phenomena.
- Explaining the meaning of the two terms, specifically characterized phenomena and generally characterized phenomena.
- Settling on the individual entities of specifically and generally characterized phenomena.

Explaining the meaning of valid cognizers being established as definitely two, direct and inferential, due to objects of comprehension being definitely two, specifically and generally characterized phenomena

Concerning the first, the meaning of the line from Dharmakīrti's *Exposition of Valid Cognition*, "Because of two objects of comprehension, two valid cognizers,"[15] stating that the sign, object of comprehension being definite as two, specifically and generally characterized phenomena, establishes that there are definitely two valid cognizers: direct and inferential cognizers. This should be known from the following lines from the same text:

> As for that, it is by the entity of self and other,
> realized, and thus the object of comprehension is accepted as two.[16]

[If someone says]: This is so because it pervades that the object of comprehension with regard to which a consciousness becomes a valid direct perceiver is a specifically characterized phenomenon and the object of comprehension with regard to which a consciousness becomes an inferential valid cognizer is a generally characterized phenomenon.

[Our system responds with]: Being definite as two, specifically and generally characterized phenomena, is not posited as a sign to [establish that] valid cognizers are definite as two, direct and inferential valid cognizers. This is because an inferential valid cognizer realizing that sound is impermanent is an inferential valid cognizer with regard to a specifically characterized phenomenon, sound being impermanent.

The pervasion that whatever is an object of comprehension of a valid direct perceiver is necessarily a specifically characterized phenomenon and whatever is an object of an inferential valid cognizer is necessarily a generally characterized phenomenon is also not explained [as the reason that valid cognizers are definitely divided into two types]. This is because some generally characterized phenomena, such as the lack of vase in a place devoid of vase, can be an object of comprehension of a valid direct perceiver; and some specifically characterized phenomena, such as sound being impermanent, can also be an object of comprehension of inferential valid cognizers.

Hence, valid cognizers being definite as two, direct and inferential, is established by the sign that the mode of apprehension is definite as two. [The two modes of apprehension are]:

- Realizing an object of comprehension through taking a specifically characterized phenomenon as the object of apprehension
- Realizing an object of comprehension through taking a generally characterized phenomenon as the object of apprehension

This is the meaning of "Because of two objects of comprehension, two valid cognizers."[17] This is because it is explained that:

As for that, it is by the entity of self and other,
realized, and thus the object of comprehension is accepted
as two.[18]

Therefore, the meaning of:

Because of being capable of performing a function and incapable of it,[19]

and so forth as well is that comprehension of objects of comprehension is definite as two in terms of taking phenomena that are able to perform a function as an object of apprehension and taking phenomena that are not so able as an object of apprehension.

꒜ Whatever sign establishes valid cognizers as being distinctly two types must distinguish the two in a way that excludes the one from being the other. The two signs put forward by two opponents do not do this. The first opponent's sign does not effectively distinguish the two types of cognizers because some inferential valid cognizers, such as that realizing sound to be impermanent, become inferential cognizers with regard to a specifically characterized phenomena, and not only with regard to a generally characterized phenomena. The second sign does not work because some valid direct perceivers have objects of comprehension that are generally characterized phenomena and some inferential valid cognizers have objects of comprehension that are specifically characterized phenomena.

Instead of relying on just objects of comprehension, the objects realized by a valid cognizer, Khedrup Jé turns to objects of apprehension, the objects *appearing* to valid cognizers, as a means to exclusively distinguish the two types of valid cognizers. The four—appearing object of a direct perceiver, object of apprehension of a valid direct perceiver, functioning thing, and specifically characterized phenomenon—are synonymous. The appearing object and object of apprehension of an inferential valid cognizer, permanent phenomenon, and generally characterized phenomenon are all synonymous. Therefore, since objects of *apprehension* are of two exclusive types, specifically and generally characterized phenomena, and all valid direct perceivers realize their objects of comprehension through taking only a specifically characterized phenomenon as an object of apprehension, while all inferential valid cognizers realize their objects of comprehension through taking only a generally characterized phenomenon as their object of apprehension, this distinction can serve as the basis for delineating the two kinds of valid cognizers through the force of the existence of two kinds of phenomena.

To establish this interpretation of Dharmakīrti's statement, "Because of two objects of comprehension, two valid cognizers," Khedrup Jé cites another statement by Dharmakīrti:

> As for that, it is by the entity of self and other,
> realized, and thus the object of comprehension is accepted as
> two.[20]

Gyaltsab Jé explains these lines as meaning that, as for specifically characterized phenomena, when they are *manifest*, as is a campfire on a forested mountain pass for the person sitting next to it, they are realized through appearing to direct perceivers by the force of their *own* uncommon entities and not through the force of some *other* entity, specifically, a meaning generality. Furthermore, they appear clearly, without being mixed with meaning generalities that are necessarily appearing aspects projected by conceptual consciousness and are generally characterized phenomena. Conversely, when specifically characterized phenomena are *hidden*, as is a campfire on a forested mountain pass for a person standing down in the valley, they need to be realized by an inferential valid cognizer. In such cases they cannot appear by force of their own entity, or in their own right, but need to appear as mixed with the entity of other phenomena, meaning generalities. Thus, it is due to this distinction that manifest versus hidden objects are able to be realized only through, respectively, a specifically or generally characterized phenomena acting as the appearing object or object of apprehension to the mind explicitly realizing them and that valid cognizers are definitely corelated as two, direct and inferential.[21]

Second, explaining the meaning of the terms

It may be asked, "Why are they called specifically characterized and generally characterized?" Specifically characterized phenomena are so called because they are phenomena that have a nature characterized by their entity appearing through its own power without depending on negations and other objects. Generally characterized phenomena are so called because their entity is not self-powered and they have a merely general nature.

"Able to perform a function" is the definition of a functioning thing. All functioning things are impermanent phenomena. "Unable to perform a function" is the definition of a non-functioning thing. All non-functioning things are either a permanent phenomena or non-existents.[22] Purbu Chok also says that specifically characterized phenomena and impermanent phenomena are synonymous, while generally characterized phenomena and permanent phenomena are synonymous. He gives "a phenomenon that is established by way of its own character without being merely imputed by a term or conceptual consciousness" as the definition of specifically characterized phenomenon and "a phenomenon that is merely imputed by a term or conceptual consciousness and is not established by way of its own character" as the definition of generally characterized phenomenon.[23] He also states that whatever is impermanent is necessarily the appearing object of a direct perceiver, and whatever is permanent is necessarily the appearing object of a conceptual consciousness. After explaining the meaning of valid cognizers being established as definitely two, direct and inferential, due to objects of comprehension being definitely two, specifically and generally characterized phenomena, Khedrup Jé now explains the meaning of specifically and generally characterized phenomena.

With regard to specifically characterized phenomena above, "without relying on negations" is mentioned to draw a contrast with generally characterized phenomena that rely on a negation, their own meaning generality, to appear to the primary awareness taking them as an object, the conceptual consciousness that apprehends them. Appearance to a conceptual consciousness can only happen by depending on a meaning generality, a mental image of a particular object, which is the appearing object of that conceptual consciousness. In order to appear to a direct perceiver no such reliance on a meaning generality is required. After the general description of the two phenomena Khedrup Jé explains them now individually. ⚶

The third, settling on the individual entities of each, has two parts:
- Settling on specifically characterized phenomena
- Settling on generally characterized phenomena

Settling on specifically characterized phenomena
The first has two parts:
- Presentation of the definition
- Identification of illustrations

Presentation of the definition

As for the first, others assert that the definition of specifically character-ized phenomena is that which abides as unmixed [with regard to being an] object, in time, and in nature; or that which is capable of performing a function and so forth. These are not acceptable. [33]

The Madhyamaka Prāsaṅgika school[24] asserts that a specifically charac-terized phenomenon is the main object of negation of the reasoning ana-lyzing the ultimate. Therefore they assert that the negation of the meaning isolate of specifically characterized phenomenon as asserted by proponents of true existence[25] is an ultimate truth. Because of that, whatever is asserted by the proponents of true existence as the meaning isolate of specifically characterized phenomenon is asserted by the Madhyamaka Prāsaṅgika as not established even conventionally. However, the Madhyamaka Prāsaṅgika also accept that which is unmixed [with regard to] place, time, and nature[26] and that which is capable of performing a function and so forth. It is for this reason that it follows that, although those are illustrations of specifically characterized phenomena at this occasion, they are not the definition.

As for our own school, the definition of specifically characterized phe-nomena is: a functioning thing that is not imputed by conceptual con-sciousness and in its own right abides in its uncommon nature.

Second, identification of illustrations

All functioning things that are established as unmixed [with regard to] place, time, and nature are illustrations of specifically characterized phe-nomena. Furthermore, others assert the meaning of unmixed [with regard to] place, time, and nature to be as follows. They hold that, if something exists in the east then it does not exist in the west and so forth is the mean-ing of unmixed with regard to place. If something existed yesterday then it does not exist today and so forth is the meaning of being unmixed with regard to time. If something exists as mottled then it does not exist as black and so forth is the meaning of unmixed with regard to nature.

[49] Now our assertion: If someone asks, "What is the meaning of 'being unmixed with regard to place, time, and nature'?" [We reply], "It is

the opposite of the mode of apprehension of an awareness that apprehends place, time, and nature as mixed."

[First then, we must ask what it does and does not mean to falsely apprehend place, time, and nature as being mixed]. It is established by one's own experience that the mode of apprehension of the conceptual consciousness apprehending place, time, and nature as mixed does not consist of the following [three types of] apprehension: if something exists in the morning, it necessarily exists in the evening; if something exists as mottled then it exists as pale yellow; and if something exists in the east then it exists in the west. That being so, [the following] is not the meaning of place, time, and nature being unmixed: as for a single specifically characterized phenomenon, if it exists in the morning, it doesn't exist in the evening; if it exists in the east, it doesn't exist in the west; and if it exists as mottled, it doesn't exist as pale yellow.

Therefore the mode of apprehension of conceptual consciousness apprehending place, time, and nature as mixed does consist of the following [three types of] apprehension: (1) the apprehension that the pillar that exists in the morning itself exists in the evening; (2) when a pillar is in contact with other things on its east and west [sides], [the apprehension that] that which contacts [the pillar] on the [pillar's] east side itself also contacts the pillar on the [pillar's] west side; and (3) when [considering] that ox is concomitant with all its instances, [the apprehension that the ox] that is mottled in color is itself also pale yellow in color and so forth.

Subsequently, the meaning of being unmixed, then, is as follows. That the pillar of the morning does not exist in the evening is the meaning of being unmixed with regard to time. That if the pillar exists in the morning, it must not exist in the evening is not the meaning of parts in time being unmixed. The meaning of a place being unmixed is, for instance, the thing or substance that contacts [pillar, for example] on the east does not also make contact on the west. A substance, if it contacts on the east side must not contact on the west side, and so forth, is not the meaning of being unmixed with regard to place. The meaning of being unmixed with regard to nature is that [for instance], the nature that exists as mottled is not pale yellow. It isn't that if a nature is present in mottled, it is absent in pale yellow.

Therefore there is no contradiction with respect to a vase, a thing, and so forth being concomitant with their instances and themselves being unmixed with regard to place, time, and nature. There is a pervasion that if it is a functioning thing, it is necessarily a specifically characterized phenomenon. Although something is a specifically characterized phenomenon, there is no contradiction in it being a generality that is concomitant with its particulars.

꒭ In the next section, Khedrup Jé explains the difference between a generality and a generally characterized phenomenon. Purbu Chok gives the following definition of *a generality*: a phenomenon that encompasses its manifestations.[27] An illustration is *object of knowledge*, which encompasses its manifestation, that is to say, its particular divisions and instances. Object of knowledge encompasses all of its divisions, like permanent and impermanent phenomena, and instances like table, house, and so forth. Another way of saying it encompasses these is to say that it pervades all of these phenomena in the sense that wherever or whenever any of them exist, object of knowledge also exists because each of them are an object of knowledge. In a similar way a specifically characterized phenomenon is a generality that encompasses its instances, like table and so forth. ꒫

Although there are many [wrong] reasons and texts that refute that generality is a functioning thing, no one among Dignāga father and sons[28] has stated a reason or [written a] text that says being a generality is contradictory with being a functioning thing. There isn't even a single word in any commentary or sub-commentary on the seven treatises on valid cognition that indicates that if it is a generality, it must not be a functioning thing.[29]

[50] One may ask, well then, how do you interpret [the following from Dharmakīrti's *Exposition of Valid Cognition*], "all meanings that a consciousness has,"[30] and so forth? Those passages indicate that the basis

of designation of the verbal convention "generality and common base" are the sound and meaning [generalities] that are objects of a conceptual consciousness; it does not indicate that if something is those [generality and common base], it is pervaded by not being a specifically characterized phenomenon, because functioning thing is also a generality that encompasses its manifestations, because if functioning thing did not encompass its manifestations, then it would absurdly follow that there are not multiple phenomena that are functioning things.

If something is a generality, it is not pervaded by being a generally characterized phenomenon. If it was pervaded, then if something was a generality, it would have to be a superimposition. In that case, since if something had multiple phenomena that are it, it would have to be a superimposition, and if something was substantially established, there would have to be no more than one thing in the world which was it.

⸙ Khedrup Jé's main point here is that the meaning of something being just a generality is totally different from something being a generally characterized phenomenon. Within this argument he is pointing out that generally characterized phenomenon is synonymous with superimposition. Here, to be *a superimposition* means that something is a phenomenon that is superimposed by conceptual consciousness—for example, one and different, definition and definiendum. Such things are superimpositions in that they are objects that are not established in their own right as existing from their own side but are established by the force of concepts projected onto the world by conceptualizing consciousness. For a thing to be one or different, to be a definition or a definiendum does not entail it being a superimposition; but such categories as one, and definition, and other superimposed phenomena themselves are superimpositions. Thereby, all superimpositions are necessarily generally characterized phenomena and permanent. ⸙

Moreover, given that the meaning of *generality* also connotes *common*, merely by encompassing two phenomena, something can be posited as their generality. The fact that generality and specifically characterized phenomena are not contradictory is attested to by the line, "because of being capable of performing a function and incapable of it,"[31] which shows that whatever is capable of performing a function is pervaded by being a specifically characterized phenomenon; and also because it is stated in the seven treatises on valid cognition not just once that *product* encompasses both vase—which is a concordant example for establishing sound as impermanent—and sound itself. Therefore the lines:

> As for that, it is said to be cause and result.
> As for that, it is asserted as self-characteristic [i.e., a specifically
>   characterized phenomenon][32]

indicate that result is also a specifically characterized phenomenon. The lines:

> Because of encompassing the object of establishment, a result.
> To also be established through a generality[33]

indicate that result is also a generality.

❖ Khedrup Jé is saying that something can be a generality without being a generally characterized phenomenon because whenever something encompasses several other phenomena, in the sense that there are several other phenomena that are instances of it that are not mutually pervasive with it, then that thing is a generality of those phenomena. He then gives two examples of functioning things or specifically characterized phenomena that are generalities. The first is product. He points out that product is a generality that encompasses both vase and sound; vase and sound are both instances of product, and there are other instances of product that are not them. The second example is cause. He cites two passages indicating first that cause is a specifically characterized phenomenon, and second that it is a generality. Now we turn to the meaning of *generally characterized phenomenon*. ❖

The meaning of *generally characterized phenomenon* is: a possessor of characteristics that is not realized through its own entity but must be realized through a generality. Therefore it follows that if something is a generally characterized phenomenon, it must be a superimposition. Being a generally characterized phenomenon is contradictory with being a functioning thing. [The line from Dharmakīrti's *Exposition of Valid Cognition* cited above]:

> Because being capable of performing a function and incapable
>   of it[34]

also indicates that if [something] is a generally characterized phenomenon, it must be incapable of performing a function.

[The third verse of this same text],

> As for others, [they] exist conventionally[35]

and so forth explains that an ultimate existent is an illustration of a specifically characterized phenomenon, and a conventional existent is an illustration of a generally characterized phenomenon.[36]

[51] Therefore, although *generality*, *coarse*, and *continuity* are generally characterized phenomena that are superimpositions and not substantially established, there is no contradiction in something being a generality, a coarse thing or a continuity, and its being substantially established, a specifically characterized phenomenon. There is no pervasion that such things are generally characterized phenomena. Therefore know that vase, for instance, is a generality; is also a coarse thing, a continuity, and a specifically characterized phenomenon; and is not a generally characterized phenomenon.

A reason for harming the assertion by non-Buddhists that a generality is a functioning thing is that because the Sāṃkhya school[37] asserts that the very fundamental principal that is the nature of blue is also the nature of yellow, and that this fundamental principal is a permanent substance, they must accept that the nature of blue and the nature of yellow are partless and singular. For that reason, the faults that (1) it absurdly follows that blue and yellow arise and cease simultaneously, and (2) that blue and yellow do not appear as different to a non-mistaken awareness, and so forth, come about. Thus the lines:

> If that which is different did not exist, generation and cessation
> would happen simultaneously[38]

and so forth from Dharmakīrti's *Exposition of Valid Cognition* should also be understood in this way. They don't show that if a generality and an instance of that generality were one substance, they would have to arise and cease simultaneously.

Also, as for a non-Buddhist [who accepts the following]: if at the time of asserting a coarse [substance] as substantially established, if he asserts that a coarse substance that is a part-possessor [i.e., has parts] is partless and is one substance with its parts, because the parts would also all [together] become a partless singularity, faults would arise such that it follows that when one part moved, every part would move, and so forth. If he asserts that all part-possessors are substantially different from their parts, the fault of it following that a part-possessor that doesn't depend upon its parts would come into being.

[52] In our own system, although a vase is a coarse substance, it has parts, is divisible, and because we assert it to be one substantial entity with the branches that are its parts, the aforementioned faults do not occur. Even though the day of the first date [of a month] is continuous and is substantially established, the faults such as analyzing whether, if that day's morning disintegrates, would that day disintegrate or not, or the absurd consequence of it becoming non-momentary and so forth do not exist, because: (1) Since from the morning of the first date, the first date has [only] begun, the first date exists [in the morning] but the first date hasn't been established completely. Although just prior to the morning of the

second date the first date has been established completely, from the second moment of that [time], the first date disintegrates, and (2) the very non-abiding at the second moment of one's establishment is the meaning of momentary. One should know to apply this [reasoning] to every continuous thing.

Settling on generally characterized phenomena

Second, the presentation of generally characterized phenomena has two [sections]:

- Presentation of the definition
- Identifying illustrations

Presentation of the definition

As for the first [definition]: that which is not an entity having a mode of abiding established from the object's own side but is established as a phenomenon merely imputed by conceptual consciousness.

Identifying illustrations

Second, the illustration: that which is the apprehended object of a conceptual consciousness that apprehends place, time, and nature as mixed. In order to realize this, it is necessary to know how an object appears to a conceptual consciousness and how a conceptual consciousness engages its object. Therefore I will explain this. If I may explain with an illustration: to the conceptual consciousness that apprehends a golden vase as a vase, a golden vase appears as a vase, and its directly apprehended object also appears as a vase.

Furthermore, there aren't two individual appearances that are the appearance of a golden vase as a vase and the appearance of its directly apprehended object as a vase. [Rather], these two [appearances] appear as mixed into one from the side of the appearance of the conceptual consciousness itself. [53] Because the two, the appearance and the imputation, are individually inseparable within the appearance, [we] say that "the appearance and the imputation are mixed into one."

Here "the appearance" refers to the vase that is a specifically characterized phenomenon, and "the imputation" refers to the sound and meaning generalities of a vase. If you wonder, "What are the sound and meaning generalities of a vase?": the appearance of a golden vase as a vase to the conceptual consciousness apprehending a vase is the sound and meaning generality; that very appearance itself as the opposite from not being a vase is also the sound and meaning generality.

❖ Purbu Chok defines *generally characterized phenomena* as phenomena that are merely imputed by terms and concepts and are not established as specifically characterized phenomena.[39] Like Khedrup Jé, he also gives a meaning generality, which is the directly apprehended object of a conceptual consciousness, as a primary example. In order to understand what a generally characterized phenomenon is through the example of a meaning generality, it is necessary to know more about conceptual consciousness. Purbu Chok defines *conceptual consciousness* as a determinative knower that apprehends sound generality and meaning generality as suitable to be mixed. He says "suitable to be mixed" because there are three possibilities of conceptual consciousness: (1) one that apprehends only a sound generality, (2) one that apprehends only a meaning generality, and (3) one that apprehends both, a sound and a meaning generality. An example of the first is a conceptual consciousness in the continuum of a person that apprehends a vase in dependence on merely the sound of the name *vase* without knowing the definition of a vase, a bulbous flat-based thing that is able to perform a function of holding water. An example of the second is a conceptual consciousness in the continuum of a person that apprehends a bulbous flat-based thing that is able to perform a function of holding water, without knowing that such a thing is called a vase. An example of the third is a conceptual consciousness in the continuum of a person who knows both the definition of a vase as well as that such a thing is called a vase.

The meaning generality of a vase is an appearance as opposite from non-vase to the conceptual consciousness apprehending vase. It arises and appears through the force of the conceptual consciousness apprehending vase conceptually eliminating everything that is not vase and thereby generating, or superimposing, a general idea of "vase." Recall from the section distinguishing generalities from generally characterized phenomena above that Khedrup Jé stated, ". . . if something is a generally characterized phenomenon, it must be a superimposition." Contrasting this way of existing with the way an actual vase exists illustrates how the meaning generality of vase is an example of a generally characterized phenomenon or something that is not an entity having a mode of abiding established from its own side, but is established as a phenomenon merely imputed by conceptual consciousness. Conversely, a vase is a specifically characterized phenomenon, thus having a mode of abiding established from its own side. As such, it has the power to appear to sense consciousness, whereas the meaning generality of vase does not.

Although the meaning generality of vase is not the actual vase, yet it appears to be so to the conceptual consciousness apprehending vase. The meaning generality of vase is an appearing object of the conceptual consciousness apprehending vase. In fact, it is the "directly apprehended object" mentioned in Khedrup Jé's explanation above. Because it is an appearing object of conceptual consciousness apprehending vase, and though it is not a vase it appears to that consciousness as a vase, therefore that consciousness is mistaken with regard to its appearing object. Whatever consciousness is mistaken with regard to its appearing object is a mistaken consciousness. All conceptual consciousnesses are mistaken with regard to their appearing object, a meaning generality, and thus are all mistaken consciousnesses. However, whatever is a mistaken consciousness is not necessarily a wrong consciousness. For example, the inferential consciousness realizing sound to be impermanent is mistaken with regard to its appearing object, the meaning generality of sound being impermanent, but correctly ascertains sound to be impermanent and thus is not a wrong consciousness. Conversely, the conceptual consciousness apprehending sound to be permanent is both mistaken and wrong. The difference between mistaken consciousness and wrong consciousness will be discussed further in chapter 2, Non-valid Awareness.

Just as a golden vase appears as a vase to the conceptual consciousness, a golden vase appears as the opposite from not being a vase. Just as its directly apprehended object also appears as a vase, this very appearance also appears as the opposite from not being a vase. However, these two appearances appear as mixed. Furthermore, although the conceptual consciousness doesn't separate the two appearances from the perspective of its appearance, it is not [as though] it holds that "these two are one" [that is to say, they appear as one but are not apprehended as one].

This conceptual consciousness is said to be mistaken to its appearing object because both the appearance of a golden vase as a vase and this consciousness's directly apprehended object appear as external objects and appear as the opposite from not being a vase although they are not either.

When engaging its object, although this conceptual consciousness is engaging an external object while adhering to the appearance of golden vase as a vase that does not exist as an external object, yet in regard to the mode of apprehension of that mind, there is an apprehension thinking "golden vase is a vase," and there is no adherence thinking that the sound and meaning generalities are vase or that the very appearance itself of a golden vase is a vase. Because of this there is no fault that is a mistake with respect to its determined object [but there is a fault with regard to its appearing object].

In brief, it should be known that a conceptual consciousness has both a mode of appearance and a mode of determination. With respect to the mode of appearance, the appearance of golden vase as vase and the directly apprehended object appear as external objects despite not being external objects, and they appear as the opposite from not being vase despite not being not the opposite of not vase. Therefore this conceptual consciousness is mistaken with regard to its appearing object.

With respect to the mode of determination, golden vase is determined "a vase"; such a determination also abides in fact. That very appearance as an external object, where there is no external object, is determined neither as "a vase" nor as "opposite from not being a vase." Hence, [the consciousness] isn't posited as mistaken with respect to the object of determination.

✢ Having written about settling on specifically characterized phenomena and generally characterized phenomena and on the differences between generality and generally characterized phenomena, Khedrup Jé now presents some related topics like concordant versus discordant type, same type and different type, and so forth. He uses the example of white parti-colored oxen and golden vases that are of different and discordant types from the point of view of their substantial cause,[40] but both are particular divisions or instances of their generality, impermanent. He further debates how differentiation is made by various persons. For example, a person who is not trained in nomenclature of the difference between a white parti-colored ox and a black ox will see both as the same type with respect to being oxen, while a person who is trained in terminology will classify them as different types. ✤

[62] Now I shall present some subsidiary topics that are useful on the occasions of the two—specifically characterized phenomena and generally characterized phenomena. It is like this [Dharmakīrti's *Exposition of Valid Cognition* says]:

> Why? Because all things inherently [naturally]
> abide in their own nature, [they]
> are dependent on things of concordant type and on the opposite
> from things of discordant type.[41]

This stanza says that specifically characterized phenomena are not mixed with any other phenomena of concordant or discordant type. [63] And since there also occurs, in regard to some superimposed phenomena,[42] the division of same type and different type, it may be asked, "How should one apprehend the meanings of *same type* and *different type*, *concordant type* and *discordant type*, and so forth?" In regard to this question, from within the classifications called "similar and dissimilar type," "concordant and discordant type," and "same and different type," similar type, same type, and concordant type can each be subdivided into pairs termed "similar,

same, and concordant substantial type" and "same, similar, and concordant isolate type."

As for positing concordant substantial type and so forth: since they
are posited by way of generation from one substantial cause, all different
things that are generated from one substantial cause are said to be mutually
of concordant, same, and similar substantial type. For that reason, since,
for instance, different barley grains coming from a stalk produced by a
single barley seed are generated from a single substantial cause and are
mutually different, they are said to be *of a concordant substantial type*. Conversely, although a white parti-colored ox and a black ox are, for instance,
similar in being oxen, because they are generated from different substantial
causes, they are said to be *of a discordant substantial type*. To give a clear
account of this subject, Shakya Lö explains extensively:

> That being so, as for all external and internal things, the presen-
> tation of different and non-different [substantial types] is made
> solely according to their substantial causes because without sub-
> stantial causes the generation of all things does not exist;[43]

and,

> Thus, as for the presentation of different continuities of con-
> cordant type and discordant type: it is made solely according to
> substantial cause.[44]

There are many such statements. This mode of interpretation should be
analyzed as to whether it isn't a faulty [interpretation of the] intent of [the
line in *Exposition of Valid Cognition*] "Different is from different cause."[45].

The meaning of *concordant isolate type* and so forth is this: non-
Buddhists such as the Sāṃkhya and so forth are similar [to Buddhists]
in holding that sandalwood, Asoka trees, oxen, and so forth are different substantial entities. However, they say that because a single type of
sound and mind engages sandalwood and Asoka trees, while a single type

of sound and mind does not engage sandalwood and oxen, therefore a single primordial nature of tree common to both sandalwood and Asoka trees exists, while one common to sandalwood and oxen does not. The Āchārya [Dharmakīrti] refutes this and instead asserts that the reason [sandalwood and Asoka trees are engaged by terms and awarenesses of the same type, while sandalwood and oxen are not] is that the tree type, which is an exclusion-of-the-other, commonly pervades[46] sandalwood and Asoka trees, whereas it doesn't pervade oxen. With that in mind, he says: [64]

> Although similar in being different,
> just this very engagement of some
> and not others by the near type
> is the cause of sound and consciousness.[47]

Furthermore, although finally the positing of white parti-colored ox and black ox as the same type rests upon the generality of ox commonly pervading both of them, if it is said, "Because the generality of ox commonly pervades them both, they are of the same type," that would be similar to [absurdly] saying, "It follows that permanent and impermanent [phenomena] are also of the same type because object of knowledge commonly pervades them both." If someone accepts [that such a statement is valid], since all phenomena would become of a concordant type, they would be forced to accept that discordant types do not exist.

Also, if one replies that "white parti-colored oxen and golden vases are of a discordant type because white parti-colored oxen are oxen while golden vases aren't oxen," it would be like saying, "It follows that white parti-colored oxen and black oxen too are of a discordant type, because the color of black oxen is black while the color of white parti-colored oxen is not black." Thus, finally one will have to accept that just about all phenomena are of a discordant type.

Therefore it should be known as like this: there are two, (1) the manner of being the same type for all positive phenomena that are functioning things such as vases and so forth, and (2) the manner of being the same type for all negative phenomena such as the non-existence of vase and so forth. From these the first one is: it is said that those two phenomena are the same type if when a person, be they trained in terminology or not, sees those two phenomena and, through just seeing them in an attentive manner, an awareness apprehending them to be similar is spontaneously generated. Things that are the opposite of that are not the same type. Therefore, because white parti-colored oxen and black oxen appear as similar to the innate awareness[48] of all people who merely see through directing their minds at them, be they trained in terminology or not, while white parti-colored oxen and vases do not, it is said that white parti-colored oxen and black oxen are of the same type while white parti-colored oxen and vases are not of the same type.

As for the reason that awarenesses to which such similarity and dissimilarity individually appear are generated: the internal condition is that habituation to the imprints of nomenclature apprehending white parti-colored oxen and black oxen as the same type since beginningless time are similar [with regard to white parti-colored oxen and black oxen]. That isn't the case for white parti-colored oxen and vases. [65] The external condition is that white parti-colored oxen and black oxen are similar in having a hump and so forth,[49] while white parti-colored oxen and vases aren't so. Hence the fault of it absurdly following that two phenomena become of the same type merely due to being similar as functioning things does not arise. This is because it is established by experience that (1) although white oxen and human beings are similar in being functioning things, an awareness apprehending them as the same type does not spontaneously arise, and (2) because white parti-colored oxen and black oxen—all those endowed with a hump and so forth—appear as the same type to the innate awarenesses of all beings, from children to scholars.

As for the same type and different type of all non-functioning negative phenomena [the second of the two categories mentioned above]: they are posited through their object of negation being of the same type and different type, because the different divisions of negative phenomena are not made by way of entity [of the negative phenomenon] but are divided according to their objects of negation. "If you realize it in this way, you won't become confused regarding the division of similarity and dissimilarity." Among the Snow Mountains, only the glory of the world himself,[50] having cleared his throat, proclaims this. Thus the presentation of specifically characterized phenomena and generally characterized phenomena has been extensively explained.

⚜ 1.4 CONVENTIONAL AND ULTIMATE TRUTHS

In the following section Khedrup Jé explains the division of objects from the point of view of the two truths. Khedrup Jé first explains the terminology of the two truths. The Tibetan word *kun rdzob*, from *kun rdzob bden pa*, is usually translated as "conventional" in the term "conventional truth." Here the more literal translations, "concealer" and "concealer truth," are alternately used in order to convey what is being expressed in this explanation of the etymology of this phrase. *Kun rdzob* is etymologized in three ways: (1) as convention (*thas nyad, vyavahāra*), (2) as mutual dependence (*phan tshun brten pa, parasparasambhavana*), and (3) as concealer (*sgrib byed, samantādvaraṇa*). In the context of the two truths, the third etymology is predominant in the Chittamātra and Madhyamaka (Middle Way) in the sense that non-ultimate phenomena seem to be truths for an ignorant consciousness that conceals reality and thus are "concealer-truths." In the Sautrāntika, concealer truth or conventional truth is synonymous with permanent phenomena and generally characterized phenomena. Ultimate truth is synonymous with impermanent, functioning thing and with specifically characterized phenomena. To obstruct direct apprehension of ultimate truth is to conceal it. For the Sautrāntika all generally characterized phenomena are truths for a concealer because they are true primarily in relation to conceptual consciousness. Conceptual consciousnesses are deemed to conceal the truth because they engage their objects only through the mistaken appearance of meaning generalities. This way of engaging specifically characterized phenomena obstructs taking them directly as objects of apprehension due to having an appearance of them that is mixed with an appearance of something that is in fact not them, their meaning generalities. ·⨍

Division in terms of entity; conventional and ultimate truths [65]
Next, the division of objects in terms of entity, the presentation of concealer, and ultimate truths will be explained. This has three parts:
- Etymologies of the two truths
- Definitions
- Identifying illustrations

Etymologies
As for the first [etymology, Dharmakīrti's *Exposition of Valid Cognition* states]:

> That which obstructs others' entities,
> obscurer. Although they are different selves, . . .[51]

The older translation reads,

> . . . concealer. Although they are different selves, . . .[52]

Most proponents of Buddhist tenets accord in asserting that *obscuring the seeing of suchness* is the etymology of *the concealer*. Therefore, taking conceptual consciousness apprehending a generality as the basis of positing the etymology of *the concealer*, it might be asked, why is that called "concealer"? Because it obstructs directly taking specifically characterized phenomena that are the suchness of things as explicit objects of apprehension, it is called "concealer." Thus, an awareness that apprehends generalities is the basis for the etymology of the concealer. Generally characterized phenomena are called "concealer truths" [or "truths for a concealer"] because they are true in the face of such an awareness that is the basis for the etymology of *concealer*. [66] However, while such a conceptual consciousness is labeled "a concealer" because of being the basis of the etymology of *concealer*, it isn't an actual concealer truth because, being a consciousness, it is ultimately established.

⁂ Because a consciousness that is the basis for the etymology of *concealer*, within the phrase *truth for a concealer*, is a consciousness, it is a functioning thing, impermanent, and therefore an ultimate truth or ultimately established. ⁂

We don't call something a "concealer truth" because of being both concealer and a truth. If that were the case, we would have to say that it was both false and true and thereby would draw contradictions.[53]

With respect to the etymology of *the ultimate truth*, some śhrāvaka schools[54] assert that something is called an "ultimate truth" because of being true in the sense of being able to withstand rational analysis. Sautrāntikas following reason,[55] [as presented in] the seven treatises on valid cognition, and Chittamātra proponents are concordant on this point. Furthermore, taking an unmistaken consciousness as the basis of the etymology of the ultimate, something is called "ultimate truth" on account of being true in the face of such a consciousness. On account of being established as the object of apprehension of such a consciousness, something is called "ultimately established." However, although Sautrāntikas and Chittamātras are similar in asserting that an awareness that takes the ultimate as its direct object is an unmistaken consciousness, they are discordant regarding what is an illustration of such an unmistaken consciousness. For example, Chittamātras assert that all other knowing direct perceivers are mistaken consciousnesses, while Sautrāntikas assert that these are unmistaken consciousnesses.

⁂ In general, *direct other-knowers* include all direct perceivers other than self-knowing direct perceivers. However, here the term is used to refer to those direct other-knowers in the continuum of an ordinary being. Direct other-knowers in the continuum of ordinary beings consist entirely of sense consciousnesses perceiving forms and sounds and so forth, the five sense objects. According to the Chittamātra, these sense objects appear to such sense consciousnesses as externally existent while in fact they are not. Therefore for followers of Chittamātra all such direct other-knowers are mistaken in that the way their appearing objects appear and the way those objects in fact exist are discordant. For followers of Sautrāntika sense objects do in fact exist externally and thus the way sense objects appear to sense consciousnesses and the way they exist are concordant; hence such sense consciousnesses are unmistaken.

The Chittamātra school doesn't accept external existence. Apprehended objects and apprehending subjects appear as different substantial entities, and thus apprehended objects appear as external objects. If analyzed, the apprehended objects and apprehending subjects are empty of being different substantial entities, just as the objects that appear in dreams are found to be mere appearances to, and thus not different substantial entities from, the dreaming mind when analyzed after waking. For the Chittamātra, both object and subject, a vase and an eye consciousness apprehending vase, for instance, arise simultaneously through the power of the same latencies that are their substantial cause. A sense consciousness does not arise by the power of an external object. This is where the Chittamātra and Sautrāntika differ. The emptiness of the apprehended object and apprehending subject being different substantial entities is the emptiness of phenomena as described by the Chittamātra. Sometimes it is called "emptiness of duality." Khedrup Jé will further explain these points below in the section "Identifying illustrations."

The four different schools of Buddhist philosophy give different definitions of these two truths. In his *Presentation of Tenets*, Jetsun Chökyi Gyaltsen[56] gives the following definitions according to the Sautrāntika. The definition of an ultimate truth is "a phenomenon that is ultimately able to perform a function"; and the definition of a conventional truth is "a phenomenon that is not ultimately able to perform a function."[57] Khedrup Jé defines them as follows: ⚡

Definitions

Second, definitions: the definition of an ultimate truth is "a phenomenon that is not merely imputed by conceptual consciousness but is established from its own side." The definition of a conventional truth is "a phenomenon that is established as merely imputed by conceptual consciousness."

⸙ By comparing these two definitions with those of specifically characterized phenomena and generally characterized phenomena given above, we see that they are very similar. Indeed, in the tenet system presented here, ultimate truth is synonymous with specifically characterized phenomena, and conventional truth is synonymous with generally characterized phenomena.

In the next section Khedrup Jé explains the different types of teachings the Buddha gave, which can be condensed into the three turnings of the wheel of Dharma. These three turnings are sometimes called: "the first, second, and third turnings," or "the first, middling, and last turnings." During the first turning the Buddha mainly taught the four noble truths. During the second, the Buddha mainly taught the perfection of wisdom sūtras wherein it is stated that not just persons but all phenomena are empty of a self. During the third turning the Buddha taught mainly the three natures according to the Chittamātra: other-powered, thoroughly established, and imputed phenomena. Khedrup Jé further debates as to which of the sub-schools Dharmakīrti's seven treatises on valid cognition belongs to. Although many of the presentations of awareness and knowers are in accordance with the Sautrāntika, the seven treatises on valid cognition also contain many points from the Chittamātra, as one can see below. These treatises on valid cognizers are therefore often described as a presentation common to the Sautrāntika and Chittamātra. ⸙

Identifying illustrations [73]

Regarding illustrations of the two truths according to our own system: From the three turnings of the wheel of doctrine by the Endowed Transcendent Destroyer, in the first teaching, desiring to take care of those of the śhrāvaka lineage who were temporarily unsuitable as vessels for the direct teaching of selflessness of all phenomena, the Buddha mainly gave a presentation depending on the existence of external objects and taught merely a selflessness of persons although wishing to show the self-lessness of phenomena.[58] In the middle and last teachings, desiring to take care of those belonging to the lineage of the Mahāyāna, the Buddha wished to teach the selflessness of phenomena. However, according to the last teaching, His statements that "all phenomena are characterless" in the middle teaching are interpretable because they were spoken with an alternative intent and so cannot be accepted literally. Because the final teaching can be accepted literally without having to seek an alternative intention, it is definitive. This is the explanation accepted by the Āchārya, father and son.[59]

Therefore, in these texts [the seven treatises on valid cognition] too, there are two modes of explanation. First, for the purpose of compassionately caring for those belonging to the śhrāvaka's lineage, a presentation accepting external objects in the view of others is made from the perspective of showing the selflessness of persons by following the first teaching. Second, in order to indicate our own system's Mahāyāna path, by following the final teaching, external objects are refuted from the perspective of delineating selflessness of phenomena. As well, consciousness free of the two extremes having settled on suchness,[60] the middle teaching is explained to have an intention behind it. From these two modes of explanation, when accepting external objects, Dharmakīrti is making assertions according with the system of the Sautrāntika. Śhāntarakṣita's *Ornament for the Middle Way* states that there are also three divisions of the Sautrāntika: (1) *Non-Pluralists*, who accept that many aspects appear to a single consciousness; (2) *Half-Eggists*, who accept that only a single aspect appears to a single consciousness; and (3) *Proponents of an Equal Number of Consciousnesses*, who assert that when many aspects appear, many consciousnesses also arise. From these three, here, when Dharmakīrti is accepting the presentation of the Sautrāntika, he relies upon the Non-Pluralist system.

[74] The Chittamātra school has two divisions: (1) *True Aspectarians*, who assert that a consciousness's aspect of its apprehended object is substantially established, and (2) *False Aspectarians*, who assert that the aspect of the apprehended object is a superimposition.[61] True Aspectarians also have three divisions—Non-Pluralists and so forth, as were mentioned above [in the context of divisions of the Sautrāntika]. False Aspectarians have two divisions: (1) For *Untainted* [*False Aspectarians*], because all conventional appearances appear through the power of latencies of ignorance, if those [latencies of ignorance] are overcome, [false mistaken appearances are also] reversed. Therefore, they assert that a buddha does not have [these] false appearances. (2) For *Tainted* [*False Aspectarians*], because conventional appearances have no relation whatsoever with ignorance, even when that [ignorance] is overcome, [conventional appearances] are not reversed. Therefore, they assert that a buddha has conventional appearances.

Āchārya Devendrabuddhi and Shākyabuddhi interpreted the thought of the Āchārya Dharmakīrti to be that of True Aspectarians. The author of the *Ornament for the Middle Way*, Shāntarakṣita, interpreted the thought to be that of Untainted False Aspectarians; and Dharmottara interpreted it to be Tainted False Aspectarians. However, just as my teachers have stated that the tenets of the True Aspectarians are more extensive than those of the False Aspectarians, and that the thought of Dharmakīrti was also based on just that, through many scriptures and logical arguments I have also come to know that the ultimate thought of the seven treatises is that of the Non-Pluralist True Aspectarians. I will briefly show the reasons for these assertions along with a presentation. The following lines of Dharmakīrti's *Exposition of Valid Cognition* indicate the mode of interpreting the statement "all phenomena are characterless" in the second teaching:

> This separate abiding of things is
> dependent on their separateness to that.
> Since that is polluted,
> their separateness is also polluted.

Other than the aspects of apprehended and apprehender,
there isn't any other character.
Thus, because empty of character,
lack of inherent existence was thoroughly explained.

Through the instances of aggregate and so forth,
all definitions are agents.
These possessors of attributes do not exist in suchness.
For that reason too, these are devoid of characteristics.[62]

The meaning of the first two verses is as follows. Differentiations of phenomena into pairs, such as cause and effect, definition and definiendum,
producer and object produced, and so forth, are made by conceptual
consciousness, to which apprehended objects and apprehending subjects
appear as different substantial entities. Since reason refutes that apprehended objects and apprehenders are different substantial entities, that
conceptual consciousness is established as mistaken. Therefore, since all
presentations of differentiations of phenomena into pairs, such as definition and definiendum and so forth, are established as mere conventions
that are posited by mistaken awareness, they are not ultimately established.
For this reason it is said, "[The Buddha] explained that all phenomena are
characterless and lack inherent existence."

[75] The meaning of the latter verse is as follows. Taking the definition
of the form aggregate, that which is suitable as form and so forth, all these
definitions actively define, and so we say "definition," and thus they are
qualified. Form and so forth, all these definiendums are defined, and so are
called "definiendum," and thus they are qualified. If their [i.e., definition
and definiendum's] factor of being agent and recipient of action was truly
established, they would become truly different, and thus definiendum—
form and so forth—and definition—suitable as form and so forth—would
have to be different substantial entities. For that reason, because (1) all
phenomena are included in definition and definiendum, and (2) definition
and definiendum are qualified by being action and agent, and (3) the factor
of being action and agent is not ultimately established, it is said, "[The

Buddha] explained [in the second turning of the wheel] that all phenomena are characterless and lack inherent existence."

Someone says, "The latter verse applies to the Sautrāntika system." This is incorrect, because (1) most śrāvaka sects—the Sautrāntika and so forth—do not accept Mahāyāna sūtras as the words of the Buddha, so it isn't definite that they must interpret the thought of the middle turning of the wheel of doctrine. (2) Further, the word "too" in the phrase "that reason too" [in the last line of the passage from *Exposition of Valid Cognition* cited above] includes the former [two stanzas—that is, it indicates that the school referred to as accepting this latter interpretation also accepts the former one, which is unquestionably uncommon to Chittamātra]. Therefore, both the former and latter interpretations of the verses above are different elucidations by the Vijñānavāda[63] themselves.

Like that, in the seven treatises, both the presentations (1) accepting the tenets of the Sautrāntika as seen by others and (2) accepting the system of the Vijñānavāda as our own system, have no difference in asserting that (1) if something is a specifically characterized phenomenon, it must be an ultimate truth, and (2) if something is a functioning thing, it must be a specifically characterized phenomenon. Hence, there is also no discordance with respect to the definition of ultimate truth. However, they are discordant with respect to the illustrations of the two truths. Although they are similar in asserting that if something is a specifically characterized phenomenon it must be an ultimate, and if something is a generally characterized phenomenon it must be a conventionality, the Sautrāntika accepts external objects as specifically characterized phenomena and ultimate truths, while the Chittamātra asserts that external objects do not exist. Therefore, since there is no discordance with respect to the assertion that if something is a functioning thing, it must be an ultimate truth, and if something is a phenomenon that is a non-thing,[64] it must be established as a mere conventionality, illustrations of the two truths should be known like that. [76] Whatever is able to perform a function is pervaded by ultimately being able to perform a function, because if something is able to perform a function it is necessarily substantially established without being merely imputed by conception. The two Āchāryas, Devendrabuddhi and Śhākyabuddhi, also said not just once that phenomena that are devoid of all ability to perform a function are conventionalities, and that whatever is able to perform even a slight function is a specifically characterized phenomenon and an ultimate existent.

Someone might object, "Well then, if whatever is an ultimate is necessarily a functioning thing, it absurdly follows that selflessness is a superimposition. If you accept that, since it would become impossible for a direct perceiver to explicitly comprehend selflessness, ārya beings would not directly realize selflessness." To this we respond that although we accept selflessness as a superimposition, here "superimposition" isn't the superimposition of "while it is not that, it is superimposed to be that." Instead, we apply the label "superimposition" to that which is an imputed existent. The reason for selflessness being an imputed existent is that its entity, not being independent, must appear to an awareness through the mere elimination of an object of negation. If something is a substantial existent, its entity necessarily can appear to an awareness without relying on the mere elimination of an object of negation because its entity arises from causes. Therefore, even the exalted wisdom of meditative equipoise of an ārya learner[65] directly sees all functioning things as merely momentary phenomena devoid of self. As for the non-affirming negation[66] that is the mere negation of self, it is implicitly comprehended by this exalted wisdom but is not explicitly realized by it. The reason why non-things are unsuitable to be realized explicitly by the direct perceiver of an ordinary being is that non-things have no capacity to cast their aspects to the direct perceiver of an ordinary being. If they had such a capacity, there would be no way to refute the existence of direct perceivers of ordinary beings that have non-things acting as their observed object condition.

Someone might ask, "Well then, does the exalted wisdom of a fully enlightened buddha realize non-things explicitly or implicitly?" To this we respond that the realization of all phenomena by the exalted wisdom of a fully enlightened buddha occurs by the power of irreversibly abandoning the obscurations to omniscience—which obstruct all objects of knowledge[67]—along with their latencies. Hence, even the realization of non-things isn't an implicit realization by the power of having directly eliminated superimposition on functioning things as such, but is an explicit realization by the power of having exhaustively abandoned the obscurations to omniscience. [77] Someone might object, "Well then, the aspects of non-things would appear, and in that case non-things would have the ability to cast their aspects to [a buddha's] consciousness apprehending them because it isn't acceptable for them to appear [to a buddha's consciousness] by the power of latencies in the same way as they appear to conceptual consciousness."[68] We respond by saying, "The aspect of non-things that appears to the exalted wisdom of a buddha is neither an aspect cast from the object nor an aspect appearing by the power of latencies; it is an aspect appearing by the power of abandoning obscurations."

⚡1.5 MODE OF APPREHENSION

In this section Khedrup Jé explains briefly the four different types of objects: appearing objects, apprehended objects, determined objects, and objects of engagement. Appearing object and object of apprehension are synonymous. Whatever is an existing phenomenon is necessarily an appearing object because whatever is impermanent is an appearing object of a direct perceiver and whatever is permanent is an appearing object of a conceptual consciousness. *Appearing objects* and *apprehended objects* refer to the objects that are actually appearing to a specific consciousness, although such objects may or may not be comprehended by the consciousness to which they appear. *Object of engagement* refers to the object that consciousness comprehends, actually gets at, or engages in. According to Purbu Chok, the object of engagement of a direct perceiver and the object of the mode of apprehension of a direct perceiver are synonymous.[69] Determined object of conceptual thought, object of engagement of conceptual thought, and object of the mode of apprehension of conceptual thought are synonymous. Thus, only conceptual consciousnesses have determined objects. Khedrup Jé gives the following explanation. ⚡

Classification of objects in terms of the way they are apprehended by object possessors [78]

Now, the means of classifying objects, dividing them in terms of the way they are apprehended by object possessors and so forth. The four objects to be explained are appearing object, apprehended object, determined object, and the object of engagement.

[82] Appearing object and object of apprehension are synonymous. As such, all phenomena that have become an object of a non-conceptual consciousness through their aspect clearly and directly appearing to that consciousness are an appearing object and object of apprehension of non-conceptual consciousness. In that case, in the context of non-conceptual consciousness, all external objects and consciousnesses are its appearing object and object of apprehension. Most non-conceptual other-knowing consciousnesses and all self-knowing consciousnesses are object possessors [of either external objects or consciousnesses].

Someone might ask, "Well then, do mistaken sense consciousnesses also have an object of apprehension?" To this we reply that there are two types of mistaken sense consciousnesses. (1) There are those, such as [an eye sense consciousness to which] falling hairs mistakenly appear, for which the appearance of its object's aspect is produced merely by an empowering condition, a corrupted sense power, and the proximity of an immediately preceding condition. These do not depend on the proximity of an external object. (2) Additionally, there are those, such as an eye sense consciousness to which one moon appears as two, which arise in dependence not only on a corrupted sense power but also on the proximity of an external object.

The first does not have an object of apprehension. This is because the appearance of its object's aspect does not rely upon an object but instead is produced merely from a corrupted sense power that is its empowering condition. Therefore, if other conditions are complete, although there is no object, it is a sense consciousness to which the aspect of falling hairs and so forth appears.

The second one has an object of apprehension. This is because, when a person squeezes their eyes with their fingers, if the single moon is not present, [83] it is impossible for the impression of two moons to appear. Furthermore, because when the single moon is present, if other causes and conditions are complete, the appearance of two moons arises. Therefore, this appearance of the aspect of two moons depends upon the presence of the single moon as an object. Experience establishes this. Therefore, it pervades that when the single moon is seen as two, the single moon also appears. However, that the aspect of the single moon does not appear in the way it actually exists is due to the sense power being corrupted.

For these reasons, all sense consciousnesses to which things, such as falling hairs and so forth, appear without relying on an object do not have an apprehended object. It is with this in mind that it was said, "Hair appearing, it is without an object."[70] All mistaken sense consciousnesses that depend upon the presence of an object that gives an aspect, such as the appearance of a colored orb at the tip of a butter lamp or the appearance of two moons and so forth, have an apprehended object. It is with this in mind that it was said, "Merely because of the butter-lamp, therefore it exists."[71]

If something is the object of apprehension of a non-conceptual consciousness (*rtog med shes pa'i gzung yul*), it does not pervade that it is an apprehended object (*gzung don*), because if something is an apprehended object it must be an external object. This is stated in many root texts and commentaries, such as, "Because it arose through the force of the object . . ."[72] and so forth.

❧ For example, the eye consciousness apprehending vase is the object of apprehension of the self-knowing direct perceiver that is concomitant with it and that is a non-conceptual consciousness. However, this eye consciousness is not an apprehended object because it is not an external object and because it is an apprehender. ☙

For all conceptual consciousnesses, whatever object appears as if being right in front of it is an object of apprehension of conceptual consciousness. In addition, whatever object appears [, it appears] without being obstructed by a meaning generality. [The meaning generality appears as being the actual object, which is not the reality; therefore conceptual consciousness is mistaken with regard to its appearing object. But] in the context of conceptual consciousness only sound and meaning generalities are appearing objects and objects of apprehension.

Through something being an object that is apprehended by a consciousness, it does not necessarily become an object of apprehension of that consciousness. If this were the case, then it would [absurdly] follow that the subject, sound, is impermanent and is an object of apprehension of the inferential valid cognizer realizing that sound is impermanent, because it is an object apprehended by that cognizer. If you accept [this position], this both directly contradicts your earlier position that it is not an apprehended object [of conceptual consciousness] and is harmed by many scriptural citations and reasonings.[73]

Some posit a division into direct and indirect objects of apprehension; this is pleasing to the gods.

Whatever is the object of the mode of determination of the conceptual consciousness that apprehends it is a determined object. For example, vase itself is the object of the mode of determination of the conceptual consciousness that apprehends by thinking "vase." Thereby, all conceptual consciousnesses whose mode of determining is concordant with fact, such as the apprehension that sound is impermanent, have a determined object. All those whose mode of determining is discordant with fact, such as the apprehension that sound is permanent, do not have a determined object.

[84] Whatever phenomena abide exactly as has been explicitly realized by a valid cognizer is an object of engagement. As for object possessors [of objects of engagement], there are the two valid cognizers [inferential valid cognizers and directly perceiving valid cognizers] and people who have these in their continuum.

CHAPTER TWO

Non-valid Awareness

A FTER THE DISCUSSION of various objects of awareness above, this and the following chapters explain consciousnesses that apprehend those objects. According to Khedrup Jé, consciousness, mind, awareness, and knower are synonymous and belong to the category of consciousness within the threefold division of functioning things—matter, consciousness, and non-associated compositional factors.[74] According to Buddhist teachings, mind is not the brain, nor is it an emergent property of the brain or "what the brain does," but different types of consciousness depend in different ways on the physical brain. Individual moments of knowing are mind, and the continuum of these that constitutes the stream of consciousness is also an instance of mind. Purbu Chok defines *consciousness* as that which is clear and knowing.[75] The entity of the mind being "clear" refers to three things: (1) the mind is not material and thus has no obstructive character, (2) any object can clearly appear to the mind just as any visible object can be reflected in a mirror, and (3) the mind is not fundamentally tainted or obscured by mental afflictions. The subjective function of mind is described as "knowing" and refers to the ability to experience, apprehend, or know its object.[76] For an object to be known does not necessarily mean that it also has to appear, as explained in the case of implicit realization in the previous chapter.

There are six types of consciousness: the five sense consciousnesses of eye, ear, nose, tongue, and body, and mental consciousness. In addition to these six types of main minds, there exist different classifications of mental factors that accompany these main minds. The *Compendium of Knowledge* by Asaṅga, which is the main textual basis for the presentation of this subject for all the four schools of Buddhist philosophy, enumerates fifty-one mental factors. A complete list of these mental factors, together with their classification and how they relate to primary consciousness, is given in appendix 2.

An infinite variety of minds can be divided in multiple ways in order to clarify their differences by contrast and comparison. One of the major modes of division is the division into the following seven types:

- direct perceivers
- inferential cognizers
- subsequent cognizers
- correctly assuming consciousness
- awareness to which the object appears but is not ascertained
- doubting consciousness
- wrong consciousness

The first two types will be explained in chapters 4 and 7, respectively. The last five of this sevenfold division are non-valid awarenesses, the subject of this chapter. This sevenfold division is used as a basis for explanation by many modern Tibetan masters in accordance with the earlier scholar Chapa Chökyi Sengé.[77] Khedrup Jé doesn't mention this division in his text and therefore doesn't explain correctly assuming consciousness and awareness to which the object appears but is not ascertained. However, since the sevenfold division is widely used in modern texts on awarenesses and knowers, a brief explanation of correctly assuming consciousness and awareness to which the object appears but is not ascertained will be given at the end of this chapter.

Purbu Chok[78] defines *valid awareness* as a knower that is new and incontrovertible, and by contrast defines *non-valid awareness* as a knower that is not new and not incontrovertible. *Knower* refers to consciousness, and *new* to an initial moment of that consciousness that is *incontrovertible* with regard to its object that it ascertains or realizes. *New* also eliminates subsequent cognizers from being valid cognizers. So *new* indicates the fact that valid cognizers newly realize their object by their own power, as opposed to the realization of an object being induced through the force of a valid cognizer that preceded them.

The three terms of the definition—*knower*, *new*, and *incontrovertible*— are also used in the explanation of valid awareness presented in the next chapter. Khedrup Jé explains non-valid awarenesses by dividing them into a twofold division: conceptual and non-conceptual. He will explain wrong conceptual consciousness and doubt before defining subsequent cognizers and non-conceptual wrong consciousness. ⚡

Presentation of awarenesses that know

With respect to the presentation of awarenesses that know, awareness, consciousness, mind, and knower are synonymous. [84]

Definition

The definition of awareness is: that which is generated as experience.

Divisions

The divisions include two means of classification. The first means of classification, when divided in terms of functionality [there are two]:
- non-valid awareness
- valid awareness[79]

With respect to the first, there are two:
- conceptual consciousness
- non-conceptual wrong consciousness

⚡2.1 CONCEPTUAL WRONG CONSCIOUSNESS AND DOUBT

In general, there are both valid and non-valid instances of conceptual consciousness. Valid conceptual consciousnesses are all inferential cognizers and will be explained in chapter 7. Non-valid conceptual consciousnesses fall into two types, those that ascertain their objects and those that do not. Both will be explained here. In the first paragraph below Khedrup Jé defines conceptual consciousness in general, after which wrong conceptual consciousness and doubt will be discussed.

As explained in the previous chapter, *conceptual consciousness* is defined by Purbu Chok as a determinative knower that apprehends sound and meaning as suitable to be mixed.[80] *Determinative knower* is a conceptual consciousness that thinks, "This is such and such," "That is such and such." *Sound* refers to *sound generality* and *meaning* refers to *meaning generality*. The meaning of *sound and meaning generalities as suitable to be mixed* is as follows. If someone describes an object that one has never seen before, the image of that particular object that appears to one's mind is not the actual object but an image that is generated based on the description alone and therefore a sound generality. When one sees a particular object for the first time without having been told the name of that particular object, then the image that appears to one's mind is a meaning generality. The sound generality and meaning generality that appear to one's mind are mental images and not the actual object. Although these mental images are not the actual object, they appear to actually be that object, and thus appear to be mixed with that object in that they do not appear as different from the object although in fact they are. This is one explanation of the meaning of sound and meaning generalities being mixed. Another explanation is that having seen a particular object for the first time, subsequently when someone mentions the name of that particular object, sound and meaning generalities appear to one's mind as associated and mixed.

The definition also mentions *suitable*, because there are persons, like young children, who have not trained in nomenclature of, for example, labeling a table as "table," and thus they do not have the sound and meaning generalities as mixed, but as suitable to be mixed. They generate a mental image of a table after having seen a table with the eye consciousness. The difference between seeing a table—as is done by the direct sense perceiver, the eye consciousness—and thinking about the table—as is done by a conceptual mental consciousness—is as follows. The eye consciousness is generated in dependence on contact with the actual color and shape of the table, whereas the conceptual consciousness is produced only in dependence of the mental image of the table. According to Purbu Chok, there are conceptual consciousnesses that apprehend only a sound generality, those that apprehend only a meaning generality, and those that apprehend both a sound and a meaning generality, as was explained in the previous chapter. Khedrup Jé explains this issue in a slightly different way with a twofold division: conceptual consciousnesses that affix names, and conceptual consciousnesses that affix meanings. He explains that sound and meaning are not individually separated as sound generality and meaning generality because conceptual consciousness directly affixes nomenclature to the appearance of sound and meaning. ⁂

Explanation of non-valid conceptual awareness [85]
Conceptual consciousness has two [parts]:
- definition
- divisions

Definition of conceptual consciousness
In our own system, the definition of conceptual consciousness is: an awareness that apprehends sound and meaning. Here, with reference to the sound and meaning, they are not individually separated as sound generality and meaning generality. Sound and meaning are posited as the appearing object of conceptual consciousness. This is so because the sound and meaning is expressed in [Dharmakīrti's *Exposition of Valid Cognition* as]:

> The three, sound, meaning, and phenomena, are what is expressed here.[81]

[Qualm]: If that is the case, [85] someone might ask how you interpret [the citation of Dharmakīrti's *Ascertainment of Valid Cognition*] then:

> A conceptual consciousness is a consciousness that has an appearance of suitability to be mixed with expression.[82]

[86] [Answer]: [There is no contradiction because] the meaning is: sound and meaning appear to conceptual consciousness and [conceptual consciousness] directly affixes nomenclature to the [appearance of] sound and meaning. Therefore, the meaning is: suitable to be mixed with expression. The [above citation] says that conceptual consciousness has the appearance of expression suitable to be mixed with expression. It doesn't say that [conceptual consciousness] has the appearance of sound generality and meaning generality suitable to be mixed.

Divisions of conceptual consciousness
If divided by virtue of necessity there are two [86]
  • conceptual consciousness that affixes names
  • conceptual consciousness that affixes meanings

The definition of the first, conceptual consciousness that affixes names, is: a consciousness that apprehends by affixing a name and a meaning. For example, a conceptual consciousness that apprehends its object within thinking "the white mottled one is an ox."
    The definition of the second, conceptual consciousness that affixes meanings, is: a conceptual consciousness that apprehends its object within affixing attributes to a substratum. For example, an awareness that apprehends its object within thinking, "this person has a stick."
    These two are not mutually exclusive because an inferential cognizer that realizes sound as impermanent is both.
    If conceptual consciousnesses are divided in terms of different kinds of awareness there are two:
  • conceptual consciousness that does not realize its object
  • ascertaining consciousness

The definition of the first, conceptual consciousness that does not realize its object, is: an awareness whose object of conception can be directly negated by a valid cognizer.

If divided there are two:
- wrong conceptual consciousness
- doubt

Wrong conceptual consciousness
The first is mutually inclusive with conceptual wrong consciousness. The definition of [wrong conceptual consciousness] is a conceptual consciousness whose object of the mode of determination is not established even conventionally. This is also mutually inclusive with superimposition. An example is conceptual consciousness that apprehends sound as permanent.

If someone says "All wrong conceptual consciousnesses possess an aspect that is definite as a one-pointed mode of apprehension." This cannot be accepted because it would follow that the conceptual consciousness thinking "sound is probably permanent" would not be a wrong conceptual consciousness. Therefore a wrong conceptual consciousness and doubt are not mutually exclusive.

❧ Wrong doubt, doubt tending toward the non-factual—for example, the doubt that thinks sound is probably permanent—is a wrong thought, a wrong conceptual consciousness. But not all forms of doubt are wrong consciousness. Doubt tending toward the factual, for example, the doubt that thinks sound is probably impermanent, is not a wrong form of consciousness. Although the doubt thinking that sound is probably impermanent doesn't realize sound to be impermanent, it does bring one closer to understanding this reality. Khedrup Jé defines and divides doubt in the following way. ❧

Doubt
The definition of doubt is: an awareness whose mode of apprehension has the aspect of qualms to two extremes.

When [doubt] is divided [there are three]:
- Doubt with qualms to both sides equally—for example, doubt that wonders whether sound is permanent or impermanent.

- Doubt tending toward the factual—for example, doubt that thinks sound is probably impermanent.
- Doubt tending toward the non-factual—for example, doubt that thinks sound is probably permanent.

⚜2.2 SUBSEQUENT COGNIZERS

In the next section Khedrup Jé describes ascertaining conceptual consciousness within a twofold division: inference and subsequent cognizers. Inference is a valid cognizer and will be explained in chapter 7. Conceptual subsequent cognizers are non-valid consciousnesses that will be defined here.

Although subsequent cognizers ascertain or realize their object, they are not valid awareness because the way they realize their object depends on and is induced by a previous valid cognizer. For this reason, they are not *new* in the sense indicated in the definition of valid cognizer as explained in the introduction to this chapter. Purbu Chok gives the following definition for *subsequent cognizer*: a knower that realizes what has already been realized.[83] He gives the following division of conceptual subsequent cognizers:

- Conceptual subsequent cognizers that are induced by direct perceivers—for example, a conceptual ascertaining consciousness ascertaining blue that is induced by a sense direct perceiver, like the eye consciousness apprehending blue.
- Conceptual subsequent cognizers that are induced by inferential cognizers—for example, the second moment of an inferential cognizer realizing sound to be impermanent.

Khedrup Jé, following the view of Sakya Paṇḍita, doesn't accept that either the second moment of an inferential cognizer or the second moment of a direct perceiver are subsequent cognizers. He also asserts that all subsequent cognizers are remembering consciousness and thus conceptual.

This will be discussed directly below in a debate in the section "Refuting others' systems."

According to Purbu Chok, a subsequent cognizer doesn't have to be conceptual. The second moment of an eye consciousness apprehending blue is an example of a non-conceptual direct perceiver that is a subsequent cognizer. In a similar way, the following directly perceiving subsequent cognizers are classified by Purbu Chok:

- Sense direct perceivers: such as the second moment of an eye consciousness apprehending blue.
- Mental direct perceivers: such as the second moment of clairvoyance knowing another's mind.
- Self-knowing direct perceivers: such as the second moment of a self-knowing direct perceiver experiencing an eye consciousness.
- Yogic direct perceivers: such as the second moment of an uninterrupted path of seeing [realizing selflessness directly].[84]

After defining ascertaining consciousness, Khedrup Jé gives a definition for subsequent cognizers that is similar to Purbu Chok's. ⸙

Ascertaining conceptual consciousness [87]
The second [from the division of conceptual consciousness in terms of different kinds of awareness, ascertaining consciousness, has two parts, definition and divisions].

Definition
The definition of ascertaining consciousness is: a valid cognizer, or an awareness that is induced by the power of a valid cognizer, that apprehends its objects by ascertaining [its object].

Division:
- inferential valid cognizer
- subsequent cognizer

The first [inferential valid cognizer] will be explained below [in chapter 7]. Second, [the presentation of] subsequent cognizer [is as follows].

With respect to subsequent cognizers [there are] two [sub-headings]:
- refuting [others' systems]
- positing [our own system]

Refuting others' systems
As to the first: some say the first moment of an inferential cognizer is a valid cognizer, but the inferential cognizer's second moment and thereon are subsequent cognizers because they are awarenesses apprehending an object that has been apprehended and not forgotten by a previous valid cognizer. This is incorrect, because that awareness that realizes sound as impermanent produced after the inferential valid cognizer realizing sound as impermanent by the reason of [it being] a product is not an inferential cognizer. This is because it is a mere ascertainment induced by the force of an inferential valid cognizer, rather than having been directly produced by recollection of the ascertainment of the reason's three modes by way of a valid cognizer. Otherwise, should something become an inferential cognizer by being merely an awareness produced indirectly through recollection of the three modes [of a correct reason], it would [absurdly] follow that even an ārya's wisdom of meditative equipoise realizing the aggregates as selfless would become an inferential cognizer.[85] Therefore, since the awareness realizing sound as impermanent produced subsequent to the inferential valid cognizer realizing sound as impermanent is not an inferential cognizer, a subsequent cognizer that is an inferential cognizer is impossible.

Some assert the inferential valid cognizer realizing sound as impermanent as being a subsequent cognizer with respect to impermanence. This too is incorrect, because instead of ascertaining impermanence by means of recollecting that very ascertainment completed earlier, [that cognition] ascertains impermanence [88] by means of newly ascertaining only that not ascertained earlier with relation to sound.

Some accept even the latter moments of direct perception as subsequent cognizers. This is an oversight, since subsequent cognizers are awarenesses that recollect an object that has been ascertained earlier, and if something is a recollecting awareness, it is necessarily a conceptual consciousness. Otherwise, should [something] become a subsequent cognizer merely by apprehending that which has been apprehended by an earlier valid cognizer, it would [absurdly] follow that the all-omniscient wisdoms from the second moment thereon would be subsequent cognizers. Moreover, it would [absurdly] follow that a valid direct perceiver realizing selflessness would be impossible and so forth—the refutations are limitless, but I will demonstrate [the others] below.

Positing our own system
With respect to the verse [of Dharmakīrti's *Exposition of Valid Cognition*]:

> As for a conventional [recollection] that
> apprehends the apprehended [object].[86]

In commentaries by Devendrabuddhi, Śhākyabuddhi, and Prajñā-karagupta, they equally explain the entity of a subsequent cognizer to be recollection. Because Sakya Paṇḍita also says [in his *Treasury of Reasoning*]:

> Subsequent cognizer
> remembers past [objects],[87]

Thus we, the majority of logicians, are unanimous regarding the assertion that the entity of a subsequent cognizer is recollection. Therefore, the definition of a subsequent cognizer is said to be an awareness that ascertains by recollecting again a meaning that has already been ascertained by the prior valid cognizer that induced it.

๛2.3 Non-conceptual Wrong Consciousness

A wrong consciousness doesn't have to be conceptual. An eye consciousness that sees snow mountains as blue is a wrong non-conceptual sense consciousness. In a similar way, a dream consciousness that sees horses in a dream as actual horses is a wrong non-conceptual mental consciousness. After defining non-conceptual wrong consciousness, Khedrup Jé gives seven examples of these types of mind. ๛

Explanation of non-conceptual wrong consciousness [88]
The definition of non-conceptual wrong consciousness is: an other-knowing consciousness that has a clear appearance [of its object] through an affected sense power that is its empowering condition.

๛ *An other-knower*, as was explained in the first chapter, is a consciousness that is turned outward; it engages external objects, not instances of internal consciousness that are concomitant with it. Purbu Chok gives the following examples of other-knowers: sense direct perceiver, mental direct perceiver, yogic direct perceiver, and conceptual consciousness.[88] Conversely, *a self-knower* is a consciousness that is directed inward and experiences the internal consciousnesses that it is simultaneous with. The eye consciousness apprehending blue is an other-knower, and the consciousness that is concomitant with and experiences that eye consciousness is a self-knower. Chapter 4 will give a more elaborate explanation of this distinction. ๛

When non-conceptual wrong consciousness is divided, there are [seven]:
- Non-conceptual wrong consciousness that is mistaken with regard to shape—for example, an eye consciousness to which a wheel appears through [observing] a quickly whirling firebrand.
- Non-conceptual wrong consciousness that is mistaken with regard to color—for example, an eye consciousness to which a white conch shell appears as yellow.

- Non-conceptual wrong consciousness that is mistaken with regard to action—for example, by force of sitting in a boat [someone generates] an eye consciousness that sees trees as moving.
- Non-conceptual wrong consciousness that is mistaken with regard to number—for example, an eye consciousness that mistakes one moon for two. [89]
- Non-conceptual wrong consciousness that is mistaken with regard to nature/entity—for example, an eye consciousness that perceives hairs falling [through the force of cataracts or an eye disease].
- Non-conceptual wrong consciousness that is mistaken with regard to time—for example, a dreaming consciousness that sees the sun shining at midnight.
- Non-conceptual wrong consciousness that is mistaken with regard to measurement—for example, an eye consciousness that sees a small object as big when looking from far away in a forsaken area.

Among these, dreaming consciousness is a mental consciousness and the rest are sense consciousnesses.

ᛧ2.4 CORRECTLY ASSUMING CONSCIOUSNESS

Correctly assuming consciousness is a conceptual consciousness that is a correct mode of thought but does not realize its object, and thus is a non-valid cognizer that is not incontrovertible. Purbu Chok defines it as a factually concordant determinative knower that is controvertible with regard to determining its object.[89] Correctly assuming consciousness goes a step further than doubt tending toward the factual in the sense that the aspect of having qualms to two extremes is not present. It is a mind that one-pointedly determines its own true object.[90] In his *Treasury of Reasoning*, Sakya Paṇḍita divides it into three types: (1) not depending on a sign or reason, (2) depending on a facsimile of a sign, and (3) depending on a correct sign.[91] An example of the first is the thought assuming that sound is impermanent without relying on any reason at all. An example of the second is the thought assuming that sound is impermanent based on the reason that sound is an existing phenomenon. Although sound is an existing phenomenon, there is not a valid pervasion that whatever is an existing phenomenon is necessarily impermanent, because some existing phenomena are permanent. Thus this sign is a facsimile of a sign. These two types of correctly assuming consciousnesses are not very stable forms of understanding, and they can easily turn into doubt about what they assume to be the case. The third type of correctly assuming consciousness is more stable because of being founded on correct reasons that when realized with a valid cognizer are the basis for generating a valid inference. An example of the third correctly assuming consciousness is the thought assuming that sound is impermanent based on the reason of being a product without having actually ascertained or realized that sound is a product, and the pervasion that whatever is a product is necessarily impermanent. Here not only is it true that sound is a product, but more important, there is a valid pervasion that whatever is a product is necessarily impermanent. This correctly assuming consciousness is the basis for a valid inference to arise realizing that sound is impermanent. This process helps to illustrate how we may gradually eliminate wrong views.

How can wrong views be eliminated and transformed into accurate realizations of reality? This process can be understood in the following way. A person first has a wrong conceptual consciousness, thinking that, for example, sound is permanent. Through hearing explanations about how sound momentarily changes and is produced by specific causes and reflecting on these facts, they come to see that sound is impermanent because of being a product. First a person starts to doubt their initial view and then gradually they come to a realization. The three types of doubt mentioned before arise in the following sequence: First there is the doubt tending toward the non-factual; this doubt thinks sound is probably permanent. Then doubt with qualms to both sides equally arises—for example, doubt that wonders whether sound is permanent or impermanent. Next doubt tending toward the factual, doubt that thinks sound is probably impermanent, arises. Subsequently, one becomes more confident in the doubt tending toward the factual and, if it is based on valid reasons, it transforms into the third type of correctly assuming consciousness mentioned above. As the person reflects on the reasons supporting this correctly assuming consciousness further, a correct valid sign will be generated when the person realizes incontrovertibly that sound is a product and that whatever is a product is necessarily impermanent. Based on this, inference arises, and thus sound is realized to be impermanent. Chapter 7 will explain this last process of inference in more detail.

2.5 Awareness to Which the Object Appears but Is Not Ascertained

Although the next chapter explains valid direct perceivers, not every direct perceiver realizes its object. There are direct perceivers that are not a wrong consciousness and also not a valid awareness. Awareness to which the object appears but is not ascertained is such a direct perceiver. Purbu Chok enumerates the following *three types of awareness to which the object appears but is not ascertained*: (1) sense direct perceivers of which attention is directed to something other than a particular object, (2) mental direct perceivers whose duration is too brief to be noticed, and (3) self-knowers experiencing those mental direct perceivers.[92] An example of the first is when, during an intense conversation with person A, a cursory eye consciousness to which person B appears walking by is generated although one doesn't consciously register that person B has passed by. Person B appears to the eye consciousness but is not realized or ascertained due to one's attention being focused intently on the conversation. An example of the second is a mental direct perceiver in the continuum of an ordinary person apprehending form. At the end of any instance of a sense direct perceiver apprehending an object, there exists a short moment of a mental direct perceiver to which that form, which was realized by the sense direct perceiver, appears but is not ascertained because the moment is too short for that ordinary consciousness to generate realization. An example of the third is a self-knower experiencing such a mental direct perceiver apprehending a form in the continuum of an ordinary being. It is not clear from the current text whether Khedrup Jé accepts the properties of this kind of consciousness as Purbu Chok has presented them. ⤙

CHAPTER THREE

Valid Cognizers

V ALID COGNIZERS ARE an indispensable element of spiritual practice. If our beliefs about the most fundamental basis of our spiritual path are not founded on sound reasons and unshakable realization of those reasons, then when we face difficult experiences and opposing arguments that challenge our beliefs, our conviction will waver. We risk becoming as if rudderless, adrift on a sea of doubt. Therefore we should value a wholesome skepticism from the outset and critically analyze assertions we encounter to see whether they are true or false without blindly accepting things on mere faith alone. As the Buddha said,

> O bhikshus and wise men,
> just as a goldsmith would test his gold by burning, cutting, and
>   rubbing it,
> so you should examine my words and
> accept them not merely out of reverence for me.[93]

Specifically, in the context of Buddhist practice, without establishing the truth of the Buddha's teachings for oneself, one will not be able to generate a lasting uncontrived wish to turn away from habitual destructive emotions and afflictions and strive for liberation. Based on what an ordinary person can perceive directly with their senses, *manifest phenomena*, one can use valid reasoning to extrapolate the existence of *hidden phenomena*, things that an ordinary person must come to know in dependence on a valid sign (like subtle impermanence, selflessness, liberation, and so forth).

Through prolonged habituation with these subjects and through meditative concentration, one will eventually be able to perceive even these hidden phenomena with direct perception. Initially however, inferential cognizers are an essential tool for entering the path of practice.

As explained in the previous chapter on non-valid awareness, from among the seven classes of mind—valid direct perceiver, inferential valid cognizer, subsequent cognizer, correctly assuming consciousness, awareness to which an object appears but is not ascertained, doubt, and wrong consciousness—the first two are valid cognizers. The Sanskrit term *pramāṇa* that is here translated as "valid cognizer" is a compound of *pra*, meaning first or best, and *māṇa*, meaning comprehend. A valid cognizer is the first and best—in the sense of freshly, newly, or independently—type of mind comprehending an object. To be *a valid cognizer*, a mind must fulfill two qualifications; it must (1) newly realize its object and (2) be incontrovertible.

"Newly realize its object" refers to the first moment of direct perception or an inferential valid cognizer. The first moment of a realization is the *best* in that it realizes the object by its own power. Subsequent moments of the cognition still realize the object, but do so through the power of the valid cognizer that induced them, not through their own power. Subsequent cognizers are *valid* in the sense of being correct and incontrovertible, but not valid in the sense of newly realizing an object, and thus are not classed as *valid cognizers* as explained in the previous chapter. As the Indian commentator Dharmottara says in *Explanatory Commentary on [Dharmakīrti's] Ascertainment of Valid Cognition*: "The first moment of a direct perceiver and of an inferential consciousness are valid cognizers, but later moments, which do not differ in establishment and abiding and are continuations, have forsaken being valid cognizers."[94]

"Incontrovertible" indicates certainty. The definition of an incontrovertible consciousness given by Purbu Chok is a knower that attains its object of analysis. To "attain" an object here means to eliminate relevant superimpositions or wrong views with regard to it. If one has directly experienced something unmitigated by concepts, and in such a way that there is no room for doubt that the experience arose due to faulty senses or a distorted mental consciousness, there is certainty, as in the case of a valid direct perceiver. Or if one has thoroughly established an understanding through faultless reasoning, as in the case of an inferential valid cognizer, then others' disputes will not shake one's confidence in the realization. In the case of a correctly assuming consciousness, such as believing in past and future lives, although there are valid reasons establishing what one holds to be true, one is either not aware of those reasons or is aware but has not come to an unshakable personal conviction of their veracity. If somebody argues well for a contrary position, one may abandon this assumption. In this example, if one generates a valid cognizer through direct perception of past lives, or through thorough reasoned analysis establishing past and future lives, then one has irreversible conviction regarding them. The only way such conviction will disappear is if one gradually forgets the direct experience or reasoning.

According to the Sautrāntika and the Chittamātra, a valid cognizer needs to newly realize its object. Candrakīrti—following the Prāsaṅgika Madhyamaka—accepts subsequent cognizers to be valid cognizers. Subsequent cognizers are no less inconvertible than the valid cognizers that induce them but lack the quality of newly realizing their object.

Khedrup Jé first explains the definition of valid cognizer, after which he explains that valid cognizers are of two types: direct perceivers and inferential cognizers.

3.1 DEFINITION OF VALID COGNIZERS

In this section Khedrup Jé explains the meaning and definition of a valid cognizer, after which he concludes by dividing valid cognizers into two, valid direct perceivers and inferential cognizers, which will lead to the next section in the text, "Division of valid cognizers."

Explanation of valid cognizers
With regard to valid cognizers, there are two [headings]: [89]
- definition
- divisions

Definition
The presentation of our own system has two parts: [97]
- The actual definition
- Explanation of valid cognizers that ascertain the definition

First, the definition of a valid cognizer:
A consciousness that is incontrovertible with regard to its object of comprehension, which is thoroughly realized by its own power.

Moreover, [Dharmakīrti] says in *Ascertainment of Valid Cognition*,

> Since these [*valid cognizers*] engage by thorough realization, therefore [they] are incontrovertible with regard to the activity [of their] object.[95]

Also, [Dharmakīrti] indicates this very point by saying [in his *Exposition of Valid Cognition*],

> *Valid cognizer* is an incontrovertible consciousness.[96]

⚡ In the next section Khedrup Jé proves again that a subsequent cognizer is not a valid cognizer because it is not *new*, as has been explained in the section on subsequent cognizers in the previous chapter. Although a *new realizer* and *valid cognizer* are mutually inclusive, *new*, in the sense of a consciousness realizing an object by its own power, differs slightly from *realizing a previously unrealized object*, which Khedrup Jé also refers to in the next paragraph. If an awareness newly realizes an object that was apprehended by a previous consciousness but not ascertained, then this newly realizing awareness is also a valid cognizer. To realize an object is much more than just to apprehend an object. Wrong consciousnesses apprehend their main objects but do not of course realize anything. ⸖

Likewise, [this commentary] says:

> As for a conventional [recollection] that apprehends what has been apprehended....[97]

This passage refutes that a subsequent cognizer, which remembers the object comprehended by the valid cognizer that induced it, is a valid cognizer. This passage does not indicate that being a valid cognizer that apprehends [an object] already apprehended by a preceding valid cognizer is mutually exclusive with being a valid cognizer.

⸖ In the next section Khedrup Jé elaborates on the fact that a valid cognizer need not newly realize something that has not been realized before in general. He explains that a valid cognizer is the clarifier of an unknown object in the sense that it has the potential to realize an unknown object; it is not that it has to newly know an unknown. He illustrates this by using the example of light dispelling darkness. ⸖

As for [the statement in Dharmakīrti's *Exposition of Valid Cognition*]:

> It is also the clarifier of an unknown object.[98]

This states that [a valid cognizer] is the means to know an unknown object in the sense of merely having the potential to know the unknown. Otherwise, if it refers to an awareness that knows the unknown, [then the following problem would ensue]. Either a knower would have to be produced by clarifying an unknown [object] within the present continuum [of a person], or it must know a previously unknown object. In that case it would follow that also for illumination that dispels darkness, one would have to posit that illumination either dispels darkness existing now or dispels a previously un-dispelled darkness. It would absurdly follow that when illumination appears in one particular place, its second and subsequent moments would not dispel darkness.

⸙ All instances of light illuminate, meaning dispel darkness. This is true in the sense that they all have the potential to dispel darkness. If this meant that every instance of light actively eliminates currently existing darkness or previously existing instances of darkness, then it would absurdly follow that the second moment of light in a specific place does not illuminate that place. Similarly, all valid cognizers have the potential to know an unknown. ⸙

Therefore, although the passage stating

> It is also the clarifier of an unknown object

indicates that whatever is a valid cognizer is pervaded by having the potential to act as a means of knowing an unknown object of comprehension, [this citation] is not an indicator of the definition of valid cognizer.

In this regard, the object of engagement of a valid cognizer has two aspects: [98] (1) Because the valid cognizer is the desired result sought after by the person who possesses it in her continuum, therefore, being the object of the action of engagement by the person in whose continuum it exists, it is an object of the action of engagement. (2) Because something is an object that a valid cognizer thoroughly realizes, it is called "the object of engagement of a valid cognizer." It is not in order to achieve a result of the object that it is engaged. Rather, whichever object the activity of a valid cognizer engages for the purpose of thoroughly realizing that object, that is also the object of engagement of a valid cognizer.

[Whatever] is the first [i.e., the desired result sought after by the person who possesses it in his continuum] is necessarily a specifically characterized phenomenon, because no thinking person would ever engage in non-functional phenomena for the purpose of achieving a result. In consideration of this point, [Dharmakīrti] said [in his *Exposition of Valid Cognition*]:

> From examining if it exists as the object of comprehension that
> is a specifically characterized phenomenon, it is the desired that
> will be established.[99]

And:

> The one who desires [as a] result that which is established by
> positing the presence of something's essence: this being will
> engage.[100]

And:

> That which is not a functional thing,
> what purpose is there to consider aiming for it.[101]

Being the latter object of engagement [described above] is not pervaded by being a specifically characterized phenomenon, because all objects of comprehension are objects engaged by valid cognizers in the activity of thoroughly realizing.

Therefore, the object of engagement of an inferential cognizer that comprehends [uncompounded] space to be a non-functioning thing is the composite of space and non-functioning thing. From this one can understand all [other] inferential cognizers that are contingent upon [i.e., generated in dependence on] a sign of negation.[102]

Here, with regard to [the stanza]: "A valid cognizer is an incontrovertible consciousness," the meaning of "incontrovertible" is twofold, because the object of engagement to which [it is] incontrovertible has two [types], as just explained above.

Furthermore, in this way, as for the [meaning of] "incontrovertible" by virtue of the first object of engagement: in just the way valid cognizer performs the function of comprehending an object, so too things abide in performing functions. This meaning is indicated by [the stanza]: "That which abides as a functioning thing is incontrovertible."

As for the meaning of "incontrovertible" in relation to the second object of engagement, it is the valid cognizer's having the ability to know the unknown mode of abidance of that object. This meaning is indicated by [the stanza]: "also, the clarifier of an unknown object." Therefore, the meaning of [the word] "also" [in the above stanza] is this: "not only is abiding in the ability to perform a function a meaning of incontrovertible; elucidator of an unknown object is also a meaning of incontrovertible."[100]

᳓·Next, Khedrup Jé explains that the nature of valid cognizers being incontrovertible is established by self-knowing cognizers. This reliance on self-knowers to ascertain valid cognizers is one reason the Chittamātra asserts that the ascertainment of all phenomena is said to depend on self-knowers.[103]·᳓

Second, the explanation of valid cognizers that ascertain the definition:
Presentation of our own system:
The nature of all valid cognizers, being incontrovertible with regard to [their] object of comprehension, is established by self-knowing cognizers. Therefore, [Dharmakīrti] stated [in *Exposition of Valid Cognition*]:

> From self [knowing cognizer], one's entity is realized.[104]

As for realizing that a knower that is incontrovertible with regard to the object of comprehension that is thoroughly realized is a valid cognizer, this is contingent upon correctly ascertaining to what bases are applied the conventions of *valid* and *non-valid*. Therefore, [Dharmakīrti] said [in his *Exposition of Valid Cognition*]:

From conventions, valid cognizers.[105]

Also, [as for] correctly ascertaining in that way to what bases are applied the conventions of *valid* and *non-valid*: all persons are incapable of ascertaining [it] by their own power—otherwise, it would [absurdly] follow that nobody would be ignorant with regard to the distinction of valid and non-valid [cognition]. Hence, as a method for correctly realizing to what bases are applied the conventions of *valid* and *non-valid*, [Indian pandits] composed treatises expounding the definition of valid cognizer. For that reason, [Dharmakīrti] said [in his *Exposition of Valid Cognition*]:

> The treatise is a dispeller of ignorance.[106]

Our own system is the only one that sees that, through the establishment of self-knowing cognizers, valid cognizers being incontrovertible to their object of comprehension is proven as the correct explanation of the meaning of these texts. Previously, no others have seen this.

[101] Therefore, I am going to explain the intentions of the great commentators [on Dharmakīrti's *Exposition of Valid Cognition*]. The explanations of an inferential valid cognizer by Devendrabuddhi and Śhākyabuddhi: An awareness that, based on seeing the light of a jewel, thinks "there is a jewel in that direction" is explained as an inferential cognizer, but [an awareness] that apprehends the light of a jewel as a jewel is not said to be an inferential cognizer. Therefore, [Devendrabuddhi and Śhākyabuddhi] explain that an awareness that realizes the presence of fire in that direction by having seen smoke there is similar [to an awareness that realizes a jewel by having seen its light] in being an inferential cognizer. [They don't mean that the two, an awareness that apprehends the light of jewel as a jewel and an awareness that apprehends smoke as a fire, are similar in being inferential cognizers.] Otherwise, one [absurdly] would have to accept that an inferential cognizer that realizes fire by [having seen] smoke and an awareness that apprehends smoke as a fire are similar in being inferential cognizers.

In chapter 1, in the section "Explicit and Implicit Realization," a related discussion was brought up with regard to the same example. In relation to an inferential cognizer realizing that fire exists on a distant mountaintop from which smoke is rising, fire is a hidden phenomenon and not a manifest phenomenon. For that inference, the existence of fire on the distant mountaintop has to be realized through the reason of the existence of smoke. Such a fire is too far away to be seen by the eye consciousness of the person possessing this inferential cognizer. However, for a person actually on the mountaintop that perceives fire at close range, fire is a manifest phenomenon and not a hidden phenomenon in relation to their eye consciousness perceiving the fire. Here, the distinction is made that such an inferential cognizer realizes fire in dependence on the sign smoke, not that such a cognizer realizes that the sign smoke is fire. Since smoke is in fact not fire, any consciousness apprehending smoke to be fire would be an invalid consciousness, not a valid one.

With regard to the meaning of the statement by the author of *Ornament* [*for Valid Cognition*, Prajñākaragupta]:

> Thus, the mind, apprehending a jewel,
> [arisen] from [seeing] the light of a jewel,
> is definitely either a direct perception
> or an inferential cognizer.[107]

[102] The eye consciousness, seeing the light of a jewel, which induces the awareness that apprehends a jewel, is a direct perceiver. [An awareness that] realizes a jewel [by seeing] the light of a jewel is explained as an inferential cognizer. Therefore [the awareness that] sees the jewel is the valid [cognition] that establishes the property of the subject, and the [awareness] that apprehends the jewel is said to be the inferential cognizer.

A correct proof by which one would generate an inferential cognizer realizing that there is a jewel in a specific place by the sign, the light of a jewel, could be stated like this: In the darkened corner of a room from which the light of a jewel glitters, there is a jewel because there is the light of a jewel. Here, there is an eye consciousness that realizes the property of the subject, that there is the light of a jewel in the darkened corner of a room from which the light of a jewel glitters. This eye consciousness cannot see the jewel itself, but it induces or acts as a primary condition for the production of an inferential cognizer realizing that there is a jewel in the corner of the room based on seeing the light of a jewel and knowing the forward pervasion, that wherever there is the light of a jewel a jewel must also exist.

3.2 DIVISIONS OF VALID COGNIZERS

As seen above, valid cognizers can be divided into valid direct perceivers and inferential cognizers. Valid direct perceivers are valid cognizers free of conceptuality. As explained in the previous chapters, conceptuality refers to the mixing of a generality of sound and/or meaning with the realized object. If one imagines thinking of Tibet, although one may correctly ascertain aspects of it, the appearance to one's mind is actually a meaning generality of Tibet appearing as the real Tibet. One may have heard many accounts of life in Tibet, and these create a vivid mental picture, but place, time, and nature appear mixed into a more-or-less fixed image, *a meaning generality*. If one knows the term "Tibet," that name, a "sound generality," also appears as one with the meaning. Dharmakīrti argues that such a generality appears primarily through mental negation of what the object is not: what actually appears to the mind is the opposite of not being Tibet. Above in section 2.1 Khedrup Jé explained it in a twofold division: conceptual consciousness that affixes names and conceptual consciousness that affixes meanings. He explained that sound and meaning are not individually separated as sound generality and meaning generality because conceptual consciousness directly affixes nomenclature to the appearance of sound and meaning.

In the case of direct perception, the actual object appears, unmixed in terms of place, time, and nature. That is, rather than a conglomerate of various related concepts of Tibet appearing as Tibet by means of negating what is not Tibet, actual functioning things, such as mountains and valleys, undergoing momentary change, appear to one's sense consciousness. Of course, for this to occur one would have to be in Tibet. Such an appearance has far greater detail, encompassing an infinite variety of subtle features, many of which an ordinary person fails to notice. Thus a valid direct perceiver, in terms of vividness and detail, is superior to a conceptual cognizer. To check this we may compare in our minds the experience of looking at a flower firsthand verses the experience of just thinking of a flower or recalling one we've seen. Furthermore, all conceptual consciousnesses are said to be based on direct perceivers. One forms concepts and ideas, however abstract, based on what one has seen, heard, smelled, tasted, and touched. If we have never seen a flower, or even heard of one, it would be difficult to have an accurate concept thinking of one.

Although a valid direct perceiver is superior in terms of clarity, initially one's direct perception is very limited. One can only know what appears to one's limited range of sight, sound, smell, taste, and touch. Therefore, using one's perceptions as a springboard, one must use reasoning to extrapolate the existence of other objects. In a mundane sense, one employs such extrapolation all the time—one flees a house when one smells smoke before one even sees fire, or one knows it won't rain anytime soon because there are no clouds on the horizon. Using accumulated experience and abstract reasoning, one can extend one's inference to more subtle phenomena, such as to future fluctuations in the weather, to anticipate how various experiences will trigger emotional reactions in oneself or others, and even to ascertain the possibility of enlightenment. In spiritual practice, one must initially use these same tools to understand the Buddha's teachings on hidden phenomena like subtle impermanence and selflessness, explained in chapter 1, as well as karma, advanced meditative states, and other important subjects that do not appear to one's immediate sense perceptions.

Khedrup Jé proves in the following that valid cognizers are exhaustively divided into two types: valid direct perceivers and inferential cognizers.

The next chapter will explain direct perceivers, and chapter 7 will explain inferential cognizers. ᢶ

With respect to the explanation of the divisions of valid cognizers: [102] Mere valid cognizers is the basis of division.
Enumeration of divisions:
  • direct perceiver
  • inferential cognizer

The reason for the enumeration being definite. Valid cognizers are definite as two, direct perceivers and inferential cognizers, because they are definite as:
  • Valid cognizers that comprehend their object of comprehension by taking a generally characterized phenomenon as their apprehended object.
  • Valid cognizers that comprehend their object of comprehension by observing an apprehended object that is a specifically characterized phenomenon.

Or:
[Valid cognizers] are definite in two, direct perceivers and inferential cognizers, because they are definite in:
  • [valid cognizers] that comprehend their object in a manifest manner
  • [valid cognizers] that comprehend their object in a hidden manner

Furthermore, in general [the term] *definite enumeration* has [a variety of uses]:
  • Definite enumeration that is the elimination of a direct contradiction, [thereby] dispelling a third possibility. For example: definite enumeration of objects of knowledge into permanent and impermanent [phenomena].
  • Definite enumeration that has a purpose. For example: definite enumeration of inferential cognizers into inference for oneself and

inference for another. Although whatever is an inferential cognizer is pervaded by being inference for oneself, by virtue of purpose they are explained as definitely [enumerated] into those two [inference for self and inference for other].

- Definite enumeration of inclusion in types. Although in terms of substance something is not definitely enumerated as that set [of types], if in terms of being included in those types it is definitely included, then, with this in mind, it is said to be definitely enumerated as that set. For instance, it being said that all the paths to buddhahood are definitely enumerated as the six perfections is an example of definite enumeration of inclusion into types.

- Definite enumeration regarding the elimination of wrong ideas is to eliminate the wrong concepts of those opponents who say that something is not suitable to be divided into two. The definite enumeration of valid cognizers into two [direct perceiver and inferential cognizer] is an example.

Of those, regarding the definite enumeration of eliminating a direct contradiction: if a phenomenon is definitely enumerated as two, the existence of something that is that phenomenon [but] neither of those two is a fault. For the other [kinds of definite enumeration], there is no definitude that such a [thing that is neither of the two] must not exist.

☙ In this last section Khedrup Jé defines different ways in which phenomena can be divided. Having these kinds of divisions helps to get a better understanding of a particular classification and answers the question of what it means for a certain phenomenon to belong to a particular classification. The first classification mentioned above, definite enumeration that is the elimination of a direct contradiction, indicates that whatever is an existing phenomenon must belong to one of the two types of this division and there is no third possibility. For example, something that exists must be either permanent or impermanent, there is no other possibility. Nothing can be found that is both an existing phenomenon and is neither permanent nor impermanent. The aspect of *direct contradiction* means that whatever is impermanent is necessarily not permanent, and vice versa; these two phenomena are mutually exclusive. With regard to any existent phenomena, like a book, we can make a twofold division of all phenomena into being that or not being that: all phenomena either are a book or are not a book. These two possibilities directly contradict each other; book is opposite to not book, and no third possibility is possible. This is a very important and powerful tool in reasoning.

Other enumerations are given for the purpose of giving a clarification to a particular classification without the need for eliminating a direct contradiction; examples are the "enumerations that have a purpose" and "enumeration of inclusion in types" given above. "Definite enumeration regarding the elimination of wrong ideas" is given to show that a particular class of phenomena can be divided into various types in order to dispel wrong ideas holding that either the class of phenomena cannot be divided at all, does not possess divisions that actually do exist, or can be divided into more types than are actually possible. ⚜

CHAPTER FOUR

DIRECT PERCEIVERS

PURBU CHOK DEFINES direct perceivers as knowers that are free from conceptuality and non-mistaken.[108] "Free from conceptuality" means that they apprehend objects without depending on a mental image or meaning generality; they directly apprehend objects without the involvement of conceptual thought. For example, an eye consciousness apprehending a table sees the table directly, and the table appears clearly to that mind. A conceptual thought of a table needs to generate a mental image, a meaning generality of the table, in order to apprehend it. The table doesn't appear as clearly to this conceptual consciousness as it does to the direct eye sense consciousness. "Non-mistaken" means that direct perceivers are non-mistaken with regard to their appearing object. This eliminates conceptual consciousnesses that are always mistaken in regard to their appearing object, as explained above in the section on conceptual consciousness, and also eliminates those sense consciousnesses that are mistaken. As an example of the latter, an eye consciousness perceiving the color of a white cloth as yellow due to the eyes being afflicted by a disease like jaundice is a non-conceptual consciousness but is not a direct perceiver because it is mistaken with regard to its appearing object, the white color of the cloth. Therefore not all sense consciousnesses are direct perceivers, because those that are *non-conceptual wrong consciousnesses*, as explained in chapter 2, are sense consciousnesses that are not direct perceivers.

After explaining the definition of direct perceivers, Khedrup Jé divides direct perceivers into four: sense direct perceivers, mental direct perceivers, self-knowing direct perceivers, and yogic direct perceivers.

Valid direct perceivers [103]
Thus, valid cognizers have two divisions: direct and inferential. Of these two, there is the following presentation:
- definition
- divisions
- presentation of the results [of valid direct perceivers is given in chapter 6]

Definition

First, the definition of a valid direct perceiver is: a consciousness free of conceptuality and not made mistaken by an adventitious cause of mistake.

With regard to the conception of which it is free, in the statement "free of conceptuality": it is a conception apprehending sound and meaning, because it is explained [by Dignāga, *Compendium of Valid Cognition*]:

> [A mind] that is free of conceptions that joins
> names, classes, and so forth is a direct perception.[109]

Although a non-mistaken mind is pervaded by being free of conceptuality, as for saying both ["free of conceptuality" and "unmistaken"]: it is based on the minds of certain non-Buddhists who accept sense consciousnesses that have conceptuality [so in their view, something could be non-mistaken but still have conceptuality]. In order to negate their wrong views, [the definition] is stated in this way.

If [the definition] didn't state "non-mistaken," then there would arise the [unwelcome] consequence that all non-conceptual wrong consciousnesses would be direct perceivers, so it mentions both ["non-conceptual" and "unmistaken"].

Also, if you take the meaning of "free of conceptuality" to be "free of the substance of conceptuality," then the self-cognizer experiencing a conception would become not a direct perceiver. If you take it as "free of the isolate [of conception]," then an inferential cognizer would become not a conception [because it is not the isolate of conception]. So take it as "its essence is not generated as a conception."

❧ Here, Khedrup Jé brings in a little debate referring to the isolate of a phenomenon, in this case the isolate of conception. The concept "isolate" is used in the epistemology of debate to describe a particular phenomenon and isolate it from any other existent phenomena. For example, whatever is the isolate of vase must be one with vase and thus can only be vase itself. That which is one with vase must have as its verbal expression the sound *vase* as well as having the same meaning of "vase." If something has either a different meaning from vase, like pillar, or has even just a different sound expressing it from precisely the sound *vase*, like pot does, then it is different and hence not one with vase; due to being not one with vase such things are not the isolate of vase. Glass vase, for example, is a vase but is not the isolate of vase. In the debate above it is highlighted that although inference is conceptual, it is not the isolate of conception because it is not one with conception, and thus inference is free of the isolate of conception. Inference is not one with conception both because its meaning is not completely the same—whatever is a conception is not necessarily an inference—and because the verbal expressions of *inference* and *conception* are different. ❧

As for *unmistaken*, its meaning is not being made mistaken by an adventitious cause of mistakes, because [Dharmakīrti] explains in *Ascertainment of Valid Cognition*:

> It is not made mistaken by eye disease, quickly spinning, sitting in a boat, mental disturbance, and so forth.[110]

Thus this definition pervades both the tradition of the Sautrāntika and that of the Chittamātra school. [104] In the Chittamātra all sense consciousnesses [of ordinary persons] are mistaken consciousnesses because their object of observation, though not [existing] external to them, appears to be external through the power of imprints of dualistic appearance that have existed in relation to them since beginningless time. However, this school accepts that all direct perceivers are not produced as mistaken due to adventitious causes of mistake, such as eye disease and so forth [as explained in the section "Non-conceptual Wrong Consciousness" in chapter 2], so [the above definition holds true for the Chittamātra as well].

[106] **Divisions**
When valid direct perceivers are divided, there are four: sense direct perceivers, mental direct perceivers, self-knowing direct perceivers, and yogic direct perceivers. This is a common division of both the Sautrāntika and Chittamātra schools.

⁜4.1 Sense Direct Perceivers

Sense direct perceivers consist of the five sense direct perceivers: the eye, ear, nose, tongue, and body sense consciousnesses. The distinction between the five types of sense consciousnesses is made with respect to their own uncommon empowering conditions being different physical sense powers. These different sense powers are needed to enable the individual sense consciousnesses to realize the outer forms that are their respective objects—namely, color and shape, sounds, scents, tastes, and tactile sensations. The sense powers are subtle physical clear matter located within the sense organs. Except for the Vaibhāṣhika, all schools of Buddhist philosophy assert that forms appear to the sense powers, but the sense powers do not see, hear, taste, feel, or apprehend forms. The Vaibhāṣhika school asserts that the sense powers apprehend and can realize the forms that appear to them; the eye sense power, for example, sees and apprehends shape and color. Other Buddhist schools, like the Sautrāntika, say that in order for something to apprehend an object, it must be conscious, it has to be a knower. Since sense powers are matter they are not conscious and thus cannot apprehend objects. Purbu Chok, following the Sautrāntika, therefore defines a sense direct perceiver as a new incontrovertible knower that is free from conceptuality and arises in dependence on a physical sense power that is its uncommon empowering condition.[111]

For a sense direct perceiver to come into existence and function it depends upon three conditions: (1) its own empowering condition, just explained; (2) an observed object condition, the object the sense consciousness is engaged in; and (3) an immediately preceding condition, the previous moment of consciousness that produces the sense consciousness. The immediately preceding condition is a prior consciousness that is not interrupted or cut off from the awareness for which it acts as an immediately preceding condition by other consciousnesses and that primarily produces that consciousness as being an experiencer that is clear and knowing. For example, an immediately preceding condition of an eye consciousness apprehending a vase is the preceding moment of eye consciousness that is its direct cause. This could be an eye consciousness apprehending hand or table or any visible object other than a vase.

Below Khedrup Jé brings up a few doubts regarding how a subtle consciousness can produce more coarse forms of mind; like how a subtle mind of meditative absorption can produce the coarser mind of the subsequent state arisen from the meditative equipoise. This sheds an interesting light on the continuity of consciousness.

After explaining the term *sense direct perceiver* and the definition of this direct perceiver, Khedrup Jé explains the division of the five sense direct perceivers and their three conditions. Khedrup Jé's explanations in this text are mainly based on the Sautrāntika and Chittamātra schools of Buddhist philosophy. These two schools have different views regarding the observed object condition of a sense perceiver. According to Sautrāntika, the forms perceived by sense consciousness *exist externally* as different entities from the mind that perceive them and are pre-existing conditions acting as causes for those minds. For example, they hold that the external color blue that appears to the eye consciousness perceiving blue is a causal condition for that eye consciousness to arise. Conversely, the Chittamātra accepts form but does *not accept that form exists externally*, different in entity from the mind that perceives it, because nothing exists "out there" without being one entity with mind. All objects of the senses are in the same nature as the sense consciousness that perceives them. This is argued based on the reason that the sense consciousness and the appearance of an object to that consciousness come into being simultaneously by the power of a mental imprint, an assertion that the Sautrāntika does not accept. For the Chittamātra, instead of external forms, these mental imprints or latencies are the observed object conditions for sense consciousness. ⚜

An explanation of valid sense direct perceivers [107]

First, there are four parts to [the explanation of] sense direct perceivers:
- etymology
- definition
- divisions
- presentation of the three conditions

Etymology

It may be asked, "Why is [sense direct perceiver] called *sense direct perceiver*?" [To that we reply], "It is called *sense direct perceiver* because it is a direct perceiver that is produced in dependence upon a sense power that is its empowering condition." Direct perceivers apprehending forms and so forth [i.e., those apprehending form (color and shape), sounds, scents, tastes, and tactile sensations] are all similar in being produced from three conditions [: empowering condition, observed object condition, and immediately preceding condition].

It may be asked, "What is the reason that the so-called sense consciousnesses and so-called eye consciousness are labeled in terms of [their] empowering condition and not labeled in terms of [their] observed object condition and so forth?" [To this we reply], "Since all sense consciousnesses and mental consciousnesses have common objects, their uniqueness cannot be understood if they are designated in terms of [their] objects. Because the empowering conditions of all individual [sense and mental consciousness] are definite, if they are designated in terms of this [empowering condition] their uniqueness can be understood. Therefore they are designated in terms of that [their empowering condition] and not in terms of their object." Hence, [Dignāga's *Compendium of Valid Cognition*] states:

> Because it is an uncommon cause, sense powers take its designation.[112]

Definition

As for the definition [of sense direct perceiver]: it is a consciousness that is an other-knower, free from conceptuality and non-mistaken, directly produced from its empowering condition as a sense power from among the two sense and mental powers.

⚑ *An other-knower* is a consciousness that is directed outward, engaging in external objects. Self-knowing consciousnesses, on the other hand, are directed only inward as they perceive a consciousness within the continuum of the person who has this knower. They do not engage in external objects. This will be further explained in section 4.3, "Self-knowing direct perceivers," below. "Free of conceptuality" can mean that a consciousness's essence is not generated as a conception, as Khedrup Jé glossed above, or according to Purbu Chok, that if a consciousness is a sense direct perceiver then there are no conceptual consciousnesses that are it. "Non-mistaken" means that it is non-mistaken with regard to its appearing object. As explained before, conceptual consciousness is mistaken with regard to its appearing object because its appearing object, which is a meaning generality, appears to be the actual object primarily engaged although it is not. This is not the case for direct perceivers. Non-mistaken also eliminates mistaken forms of sense consciousness like the eye consciousness seeing the color of a white snow mountain as yellow due to jaundice. ⚑

Others, without differentiating between the systems of Sautrāntika and Chittamātra, posit the definition [of sense consciousness] as an other-knower that is free from conceptuality and non-mistaken and that is directly produced from its empowering condition, a physical sense power. Having stated this, they accept that in the Chittamātra system a previous consciousness of concordant type and potencies on those and so forth are sense powers that are the empowering condition of sense knower. This is contradictory.

॰ If someone accepts that, for the Chittamātra, the empowering condition for a sense direct perceiver is not a physical sense power but a previous consciousness of similar type and potencies on that consciousness, and yet includes in a definition of sense direct perceiver meant to be acceptable for both Chittamātra and Sautrāntika that it is produced from its empowering condition, *a physical sense power*, this is contradictory.

In Purbu Chok's definition of sense direct perceiver noted above, he makes it clear that whatever is a sense direct perceiver is produced in dependence on "a physical sense power that is its uncommon empowering condition." Although unlike Khedrup Jé, Purbu Chok specifies that the uncommon empowering condition for a sense direct perceiver must be a physical sense power, he is explaining the Sautrāntika system and not giving a definition meant to be acceptable for both Sautrāntika and Chittamātra schools, so there is no fault.[113] Also, by using the phrase "uncommon empowering condition" in his definition of sense direct perceiver, the uniqueness of each individual empowering condition for each of the six types of consciousness is asserted more strongly. If, as Khedrup Jé does in his definition, the empowering condition of sense direct perceiver is stated merely as a sense power without qualifying it as a physical sense power, such a definition can be used for sense direct perceiver in both the Chittamātra and the Sautrāntika. In general, the different schools of Buddhist philosophy assert varying "empowering conditions." These different views regarding the three conditions will be explained in more detail below. ॰

Divisions
When divided there are five, from sense direct perceivers that apprehend form up to sense direct perceivers that apprehend tangible objects [i.e.,

sense direct perceivers apprehending forms (shape and color), sounds, odors, tastes, and tangible objects]. Their respective definitions are: a consciousness that is an other-knower that is free from conceptuality and non-mistaken and that is produced directly from its own empowering condition, an eye sense power and so forth [i.e., ear, nose, tongue, and body sense powers].

Presentation of the three conditions [108]
The presentation of the three conditions has two parts:
- Analyzing whether or not the causal collection of sense consciousness is definite as the three conditions.
- Settling on the nature of three conditions.

[111] Analyzing whether or not the causal collection of sense consciousness is definite as the three conditions
In our own system, all the direct causal collections of sense consciousness are definite as three conditions. Therefore, [in Dharmakīrti's *Exposition of Valid Cognition*] it says:

> In addition to that, the sense power, object, or awareness,
> as well as the mental engagement that existed earlier;
> apart from this collection of causes and effects,
> others that are related do not exist.[114]

Whatever is a cause of a sense consciousness is not definite as [one of the] three conditions.

❧ For example, the person who made the vase that is perceived by an eye consciousness apprehending vase is an indirect cause of that eye consciousness but is not included in the three conditions of that eye consciousness. In this system, only direct causes of a sense consciousness are included in the three causal conditions of that consciousness. ❧

As for the three conditions, with respect to the one sense consciousness that is their effect, they are only mutually exclusive.

Settling on the nature of sense consciousness's three conditions has two parts:
- the Sautrāntika
- the Chittamātra

The first [settling on the nature of sense consciousness's three conditions according to the Sautrāntika] has three parts:
- the empowering condition
- the observed object condition
- the immediately preceding condition

Empowering condition
The empowering condition of sense consciousness is defined as: a sense power that especially empowers the uncommon features of its resultant sense consciousness.

In addition, the eye consciousness, for instance, has three features:
- The factor of its entity being clear and knowing experience.
- The factor of being produced as possessing the aspect of form.
- The feature of definitely apprehending only form, and it being utterly impossible for it to apprehend sound and so forth.

As for the first [feature], it is indeed produced primarily by the immediately preceding condition of eye consciousness. Further, that is not an uncommon feature that is dissimilar from those of other [consciousnesses] because all consciousnesses are similar in having a nature of being clear and knowing experience.

As for the second [feature], it is produced primarily by the observed object condition of eye consciousness. Further, that is not an uncommon feature that is dissimilar from those of other [consciousnesses] because some mental consciousnesses are also produced as possessing the aspect of form.

As for the third, this is an uncommon feature of only eye consciousness. [112] Further, because this [feature] is produced primarily by the empowering condition, the eye sense power itself, that is what primarily produces eye consciousness's uncommon feature. Therefore [the eye sense power] is called "that which especially empowers eye consciousness." By taking this illustration, nose sense power and so forth should be understood.

❧ The third feature listed above is the uncommon feature clearly distinguishing the five sense consciousnesses from one another in the sense that they can only perceive their particular objects because of their uncommon empowering conditions. The eye consciousness, by depending on its own uncommon empowering condition, the eye sense power, can only perceive color and shape and not sound, for example. Among the sense consciousnesses, the ear consciousness can only perceive sound, nose consciousness only scent, tongue consciousness only taste, and body sense consciousness only tangible objects. ❧

It may be asked, "What is the entity of eye sense power?" [To this we reply], by the sign that at times eye consciousness is not produced although an immediately preceding condition and observed object condition are complete, it is established that there is a cause of eye consciousness that is neither of these two. Such a cause definitely produces eye consciousness as an apprehender of only form because it is certain that a primary cause that produces an eye consciousness as definitely apprehending only form exists. Also, it is incorrect [to assert that] immediately preceding condition and observed object condition are such a cause. Therefore, that cause that is other than the immediately preceding condition and observed object condition of eye consciousness, which is the main cause that produces eye consciousness as apprehending only form, is called the "eye sense power." Insofar as it has produced the uncommon feature of the eye consciousness that is its effect, it "especially empowers." That itself [i.e., eye sense power] is accepted as matter because if it was consciousness, then it would be incorrect for it to be a conceptual consciousness and so it would have to be accepted as non-conceptual consciousness. Because it would be incorrect for it to be non-conceptual wrong consciousness, it would have to be accepted as a valid direct perceiver. [The tenet that] sense powers are valid cognizers is said to be unique to the system of the Vaibhāṣhika.[115] Therefore, understand this [explanation of eye sense power] as also illustrating the entity of ear sense power and so forth.

Observed object condition

Second, as for the observed object condition, [its definition is]: whatever directly produces the consciousness apprehending it as having its aspect.

The observed object condition and apprehended object of sense consciousness are synonymous. Further, there is no contradiction between being an apprehended object of sense consciousness and being a gross form. However, [the statement] "It is impossible for the aspect of gross [form] to appear to sense consciousness" and so forth, how the aspect of objects appear to sense consciousness, and what would be illustrations of observed object condition and apprehended object have already been explained in the chapter on objects [of knowledge, chapter 1].

[113] [According to the Sautrāntika], it is incorrect [to assert] that all apprehended objects that produce the sense consciousnesses apprehending them as having their aspects and the sense consciousnesses apprehending them occur simultaneously [as the Chittamātra asserts]. If they occurred simultaneously, they would both be equal in being already established. Furthermore, since it is incorrect for something that has been established to be produced again, they would become not cause and effect.

෴ According to the Sautrāntika, since apprehended objects such as form, sound, and so forth exist externally, they precede and act as causal conditions of the sense consciousnesses that apprehend them. ෴

Because [the apprehended object] is a cause of the sense consciousness that apprehends it, it is also incorrect for it to exist in the time after that consciousness. Therefore, the apprehended object of each sense consciousness arises before that particular sense consciousness. However, there is no fault of the apprehended object not being an object of sense consciousness[116] because sense consciousness is generated as having the aspect of its apprehended object, and because having the aspect of a phenomenon that appears is the meaning of taking a phenomenon as an object.

If the apprehended object of a sense consciousness has not ceased at the time the sense consciousness that apprehends it is established, then it exists at the time of that consciousness and it must have been established at the same time as that sense consciousness. This is because such an apprehended object of a sense consciousness is an impermanent phenomenon, meaning that it is momentarily changing and thus does not abide as before in the very next moment after it is established. If it were not established at the same time as the sense consciousness that apprehends it, it could not exist simultaneously with that consciousness. If an apprehended object is established at the same time as the sense consciousness apprehending it, then of course it cannot be the cause of that sense consciousness.

This reasoning is thorny and may seem counterintuitive because we know that two things that are related to each other as cause and effect do exist at a specified time, such as the present time. For example, fire is the cause of smoke, yet at a specific time, while a campfire is blazing, or at the present time for instance, both fire and smoke exist. However, for any instance of smoke, the fire that exists at the same time is not the cause of it. The precise instance of fire that is the cause of any particular instance of smoke must cease at the time its resultant smoke is established. Since fire is the cause of smoke, it must exist in the time preceding smoke. It is in the time just before smoke is established that fire produces smoke. Similarly, because the object apprehended by a sense consciousness is a cause producing that consciousness, it must exist before it and cease to exist when the sense consciousness that is its result is established.

It may be asked, "Well then, at the time of the sense consciousness, has its apprehended object ceased or not? In the first case, it would not be apprehended at the time of the sense consciousness. In the second case, the apprehended object would not be a cause [of the sense consciousness that apprehends it]."

[To this we reply], "As for all sense consciousnesses, at the time they exist, their apprehended objects have ceased. However, there is not the fault that they do not apprehend [their objects] because the manner of positing all sense consciousnesses and their apprehended objects as objects and object possessors is in dependence on positing a period that possesses both the time during which a sense consciousness exists and the time during which its apprehended object exists as parts." This point and so forth are similar to the manner of being cause and effect explained earlier [in the beginning of this section].

Generally, there are four ways for aspects of an object to appear to consciousness, namely:
- Aspects that appear by the force of the object, as with the appearance to an ordinary being's direct perceiver of the aspect of its apprehended object.
- Aspects that appear through the force of an imprint, as with the appearance to conceptual consciousness of an object's aspect.
- Aspects that appear through the force of meditative stabilization, as with the appearance to *the clairvoyance of the divine eye* of the aspect of manifold gross and subtle forms that are cut off [from the observer by great distance or by another object like a wall and so forth].
- Aspects that appear through the force of having completed the two collections [of merit and wisdom], as with the appearance to *an exalted knower of all aspects* of the aspects of all phenomena. [114]

Furthermore, eye consciousness apprehending form, for example, has two [parts]:

- The part that is the appearance of the aspect of externally existent form.
- The part that is a clear knower that experiences its own entity [i.e., the entity of eye consciousness apprehending form].

The first is called the "aspect of the apprehended object" of eye consciousness. There is no difference between that and eye consciousness apprehending form and what is called the "aspect of form appearing to eye consciousness apprehending form." Therefore, the aspect of the apprehended object of eye consciousness is eye consciousness itself. The meaning of an aspect appearing to eye consciousness is that it [i.e., eye consciousness] is itself produced from its own causes in the aspect of its object. It is not that there exists an aspect that is something other than itself appearing to it.

Second, the portion of the clear and knowing experience of eye consciousness is said to be the *aspect of the apprehender* of eye consciousness. [115] There is no difference between it and the self-knowing direct perceiver that experiences eye consciousness.

⚺There is a clear distinction between apprehended and apprehender. *Apprehended* is referring to an object that is apprehended by consciousness. Consciousnesses that realize objects are *apprehenders*. While all phenomena are apprehended, not all are apprehenders; tree, for instance, is not an apprehender because it does not experience any object. Purbu Chok makes a similar distinction in the beginning of his text on *Awarenesses and Knowers* where he explains the division of objects and object possessors; an *object* is that which is known by an awareness, whereas a thing that possesses its respective object is an *object possessor*.[117] Here Khedrup Jé explains the difference between an *aspect of the apprehended* and an aspect of the apprehender in relation to the example of eye consciousness. Eye consciousness itself is an aspect of the apprehended that is produced as having the aspect of its object, a form. The self-knowing direct perceiver that apprehends eye consciousness is an aspect of the apprehender. These two, aspect of the apprehended and aspect of the apprehender, are mutually exclusive both in general and with regard to any specific awareness. ᠅

If it is asked, "What is the reason that the aspect of the apprehended object of the eye consciousness is eye consciousness itself?" It is explained that in this manner if the aspect of the apprehended object of eye consciousness is not eye consciousness, there is no other suitable [explanation]. If it [the aspect of the apprehended object of eye consciousness] has to be accepted as the object of eye consciousness, this is incorrect because it would follow that the subject, eye consciousness, is a self-knowing direct perceiver, because of being a direct perceiver that knows an object which is its [eye consciousness's] own self. Furthermore, it follows that it [the subject eye consciousness] is a self-knowing direct perceiver with regard to that [the aspect of the apprehended object of eye consciousness], because it is a direct perceiver with regard to that and it is not an other-knowing direct perceiver with regard to that. If it is said that it [eye consciousness] is an other-knowing direct perceiver, then it follows that the subject eye consciousness, the aspect of its aspect of the apprehended object appears to it, because it is an other-knowing direct perceiver with regard to its aspect of apprehended object. If this is accepted, then because it follows that the aspect of that aspect of its aspect of the apprehended object also appears, the aspects will become endless.

[117] If it is asked, "What is the meaning of [Dharmakīrti's *Exposition of Valid Cognition*, which states], 'Because there is the fault that, by its own entity, it would be a self of many [contradictory things]'?"[118]

To this, we reply as follows. The Sautrāntika accepts that the aspect that appears to sense consciousness is the aspect that has been given by the entity of the object itself. The Chittamātra responds, "In that case the following fault arises. Because the way an aspect appears must be present in the object, therefore it follows that the body of a single person would have many [contradictory] natures [such as] desirable and undesirable." Therefore, this is a text that indicates, "As for aspect, it is not an aspect given by the entity of the object itself, but rather an aspect that appears through the force of an imprint."

❧ The fault of the body of one person having the entity of being both desirable and undesirable arises in a situation where the body of one person is observed by two different people, a friend and an enemy. To the eye consciousness of the friend, the person's body appears as desirable, whereas to the eye consciousness of the enemy, the same person's body appears as undesirable. The Chittamātra explains this difference in appearance as arising due to the different imprints in the mind of the friend versus those in the mind of the enemy. According to the Chittamātra, the Sautrāntika accepts that the aspects of the body appearing as desirable and undesirable are produced not by imprints in the minds of the different observers but by the external object, the one body itself. Therefore they fault the Sautrāntika as falling into the contradiction that the body of a single person observed is itself both desirable and undesirable. According to the Sautrāntika only forms and shapes appear nakedly to the eye consciousness; the distinction of being desirable and undesirable is made by a conceptual consciousness, which arises subsequent to the eye consciousness.

The Vaibhāṣhika, on the other hand, accept that consciousnesses engage their objects by nakedly experiencing them without being produced in the aspect of their objects. They do not accept the existence of aspects. To refute this view, the Sautrāntika argues that by not accepting the role of aspects in the process of consciousnesses apprehending their objects, Vaibhāṣhika cannot explain why an eye consciousness, for example, sees visual forms but does not experience sounds. They argue that in the absence of aspects, an eye consciousness apprehending blue is the same with regard to both blue and sound in that it is not produced in the aspect of, or does not possess the aspect of, either blue or sound. Khedrup Jé continues here with a refutation of the Vaibhāṣhika view. ❧

[118] If the aspect of the apprehender of eye consciousness [which is synonymous with the self-knowing direct perceiver that experiences eye

consciousness] apprehended the aspect of the apprehended object of eye consciousness without an aspect, through being similar in that an aspect does not appear, it would not be feasible to differentiate between [the self-knowing direct perceiver that experiences eye consciousness] apprehending [some things] and not apprehending [others].

Thereby, it would follow that just as [the aspect of the apprehender of eye consciousness] apprehends the aspect of the apprehended object of eye consciousness, it would also apprehend the aspect of the apprehended object of ear consciousness. This being the case, [according to our own system] the aspect of the aspect of the apprehended object also appears to the aspect of the apprehender.

᠅ Here Khedrup Jé argues that if one does not accept that consciousness takes the aspect of its object, then it follows that not only is it difficult to explain why an eye consciousness sees visual forms but does not experience sounds, but it also becomes difficult to make a distinction between a sense consciousness and a self-knowing consciousness apprehending that sense consciousness. This leads to the absurd consequence that self-knowing consciousness also apprehends external objects and can no longer be distinguished as having just the aspect of the apprehender, the consciousness it experiences. Furthermore, it would become difficult to distinguish the self-knowing direct perceivers' experiencing one sense consciousness, such as eye sense consciousness, from those experiencing another, such as ear sense consciousness. ᠅

The meaning of an aspect appearing has already been explained with the statement "It is produced from its cause as the entity of the [object's] aspect." Although both the Sautrāntika and Chittamātra accept that this is the meaning of an aspect appearing, the Sautrāntika asserts that eye consciousness is produced as having the aspect of form by its cause, an external form. Alternatively, the proponents of Vijñānavāda assert that it [eye consciousness] is produced as the entity of [the object's] aspect by the force of imprints.

Immediately preceding condition [119]

Third, an immediately preceding condition is: A prior consciousness that is not cut off from [the awareness for which it acts as an immediately preceding condition] by other consciousnesses and that produces [that consciousness] as an entity of experience.

Furthermore, [immediately preceding condition] is called "immediately preceding" because it is not cut off [from the consciousness for which it acts as an immediately preceding condition] by other consciousnesses. It is called "condition" because it is a cause. It is called "concordant" because it is similar in being a consciousness. Therefore, we should understand the meaning of *concordant immediately preceding condition* in this way.

҈ This explanation of the term *concordant immediately preceding condition* becomes clearer if applied to a specific example. Take an eye consciousness apprehending vase. Its immediately preceding condition is the preceding moment of eye consciousness, which could be an eye consciousness apprehending hand or table or any visible object other than vase. This immediately preceding condition is called "immediately preceding" because it exists in the moment immediately prior to production of the first moment of eye consciousness apprehending vase. It is called "condition" because it is a *cause* of that eye consciousness apprehending vase. *Cause* and *condition* are synonyms in the parlance of Buddhist philosophy. This immediately preceding condition is also called "concordant" because it is similar to the eye consciousness apprehending vase that it produces in that it is also a consciousness. There are other causes of this eye consciousness apprehending vase, such as vase, the material that was shaped into a vase, and the person who crafted the vase. These things are not the immediately preceding condition of eye consciousness apprehending vase because they are not consciousnesses. Even indirect causes of this eye consciousness apprehending vase that are awarenesses are not the immediately preceding condition of this eye consciousness because they are cut off or separated from it by at least one other consciousness or moment of consciousness.

For a consciousness to be the immediately preceding condition of a particular awareness, it must be the direct cause of that awareness. ⟡

A concordant immediately preceding condition does not need to be a similar type in all aspects. This is because some non-conceptual consciousnesses act as the substantial cause for the concepts that are their effects.

⟡ For example, an eye consciousness apprehending vase is the immediately preceding condition for the conceptual consciousness apprehending vase, which is its direct effect. These two knowers are similar in being consciousnesses but are of dissimilar types in that the former is non-conceptual and the latter is conceptual. Below are two further debates concerning situations where an awareness of one type acts as the immediately preceding condition of an awareness of a different type.

This is a rough illustration of a point made above in the section discussing the empowering condition of sense consciousness. There, in order to establish the existence of an eye consciousness's empowering condition, it was stated that something other than the immediately preceding and observed object conditions of eye consciousness is required to explain how an eye consciousness arises, because there are cases where those two are present but an eye consciousness is not produced. For example, when an eye consciousness seeing blue gives rise to a conceptual consciousness apprehending blue that immediately follows it.

In the next section, Khedrup Jé explains how a contaminated mind arises immediately following an uncontaminated supra-mundane path. This happens on the path of seeing and the path of meditation. Together with the path of no-more-learning, these three paths are called "supramundane," "ārya," or "noble paths" because they exist only in the continuum of a noble being, a person who has generated a direct perception of selflessness.[119] This will be explained further in section 4.4 on yogic direct perceivers below. For now, to understand Khedrup Jé's discussion immediately below it is necessary to know that uncontaminated paths are meditative absorptions that realize selflessness directly. They are called "uncontaminated" because they belong to the class of minds that do not arise due to karma and afflictive emotions and instead act as antidotes to the view of a self, the ignorance that is the most fundamental cause of suffering. When a person on the paths of seeing or meditation comes out of this kind of absorption, they generate in their continuum minds that are contaminated. Such minds are contaminated because they belong to the class of minds that arise through the force of karma and afflictive emotions and do not act as antidotes to the view of self. An uncontaminated path is an antidote to the afflictions and therefore is called an "uncontaminated path." When progressing over the paths, the afflictions are eliminated in stages. Total elimination happens when the path of no-more-learning is achieved. This will be more elaborately explained in the next chapter on the four noble truths. ⸱⸙

[Qualm]: It may be asked, "Well then, what is the substantial cause of the first moment of the contaminated mind that exists just after arising from a consciousness that is meditative equipoise on an uncontaminated supramundane path?"

[Answer]: "As for that, the last moment of uncontaminated consciousness that is meditative equipoise is such [a substantial cause]."

[Qualm]: Someone may object, "Well then, it follows that that [last moment of uncontaminated consciousness that is meditative equipoise] is contaminated because the contaminated is held to be its effect." [120]

[Answer]: "Although it would be contaminated if it were the result of contamination, how could it become contaminated if the contaminated is held to be its effect? If that were the case, it would be said that by just having relation with a contaminated cause things become contaminated. Then it would [absurdly] follow that all paths of seeing that are produced from a supreme path of preparation in the continuum of an ordinary being would be contaminated."

⸙ In order to realize a hidden phenomenon like selflessness directly, as the meditative absorptions of the path of seeing and the path of meditation do, one first needs to realize it in a conceptual manner. This conceptual realization happens on the two mundane paths of ordinary beings, the path of accumulation and path of preparation. The path of preparation has four subdivisions: heat, peak, forbearance, and supreme path or path of supra-mundane qualities. The supreme path of preparation in the mind of an ordinary being is the substantial cause for the first moment of the path of seeing that follows it. However, that path of preparation is contaminated, whereas the path of seeing that is its substantial effect is uncontaminated. If whatever effect arose from a contaminated cause must be contaminated, then it absurdly follows that the first moment of the path of seeing is contaminated. This is absurd because the first moment of the path of seeing is an exalted wisdom of meditative equipoise directly realizing selflessness, which is the direct antidote to intellectually acquired grasping at self. Therefore, far from being contaminated, it is an antidote to contamination. Just as whatever is a substantial cause of an uncontaminated mind need not be uncontaminated, likewise, whatever is a substantial cause of a contaminated mind also need not be contaminated.

Next Khedrup Jé refutes doubts regarding the first moment of consciousness that arises after meditative absorption on cessation. The different Buddhist tenets define meditative absorption on cessation in various ways because the object of meditation is explained differently. They all accept, however, that these absorptions have ceased the gross types of consciousnesses, like the sense consciousnesses, and the gross forms of the mental factors feeling and discrimination. Only a subtle mental consciousness remains to realize its object. This current presentation is being made according to the Sautrāntika, and they do not accept mind-basis-of-all, so that cannot be posited as the consciousness present during meditative absorption on cessation. Since according to this school mind-basis-of-all does not exist, "afflicted mind" also cannot be held to exist, for afflicted mind must take mind-basis-of-all as its object of observation. Mind-basis-of-all and afflicted mind are exclusively accepted by the Chittamātra as being the seventh and eighth main minds. ⁜

[Qualm]: It may be asked, "What is the substantial cause of the first moment of consciousness that has just arisen from meditative absorption on cessation?"

[Answer]: As for myself, I respond as follows. "Undoubtedly it is to be accepted that within the continuum of a person who is engaged in meditative absorption on cessation there is a mental consciousness with an aspect of unclarity that slightly engages in a very subtle manner. This is because (1) here, it is improper to accept mind-basis-of-all,[120] and without mind-basis-of-all it is unfeasible for the afflicted mind having that as an object of observation to exist; (2) even those who accept mind-basis-of all do not accept the presence of afflicted mind during meditative absorption on cessation; (3) at that time the consciousnesses of the five doors[121] and grosser levels of mental consciousness together with their entire retinues cease; and (4) it is unfeasible to accept the absolute non-existence of consciousness during [meditative absorption on cessation]."

[Qualm]: Someone might ask, "Why is it unfeasible for there to be no consciousness [during meditative absorption on cessation]?"

[Answer]: "Because that would contradict the sūtra that says, 'The consciousness that is engaged in meditative absorption on cessation is not separate from a body.' Further, it would follow that [the person engaged in the meditative absorption on cessation] would not be a sentient being. It would follow that the body [of a person] engaged in meditative absorption of cessation would be similar to a corpse. It would also follow that at that time, if one abided for a long time without a consciousness animating the body, the body of one engaged in meditative absorption on cessation would decay and so forth." Also, this would contradict our own tenet system in which it is accepted that a person is a collection of four or five aggregates.[122]

Furthermore, (1) at the time [of meditative absorption on cessation], if the entity of meditative absorption is consciousness, it is unfeasible for it to be other than mental consciousness; (2) a body must be matter; and (3) even if a person is accepted to be something like a collection of body and mind, still consciousness would be established at that time. If this meditative absorption is not any of these three,[123] then one has to say that one agrees with the side that accepts that it is the imputed existent designated at the time of the body in which all gross feelings, discriminations, and so forth have been stopped.

❧ Having rejected the possibility that there is no consciousness during meditative absorption on cessation, the author then addresses the question, "If this absorption is not consciousness, what else could it be?" Khedrup Jé presents three options. It must be either mental consciousness, the material body, or the person that is a collection of these two. The first possibility has already been rejected by the hypothetical opponent, and the second possibility of a material body without consciousness has just been refuted above with the reason that it would be no different from a corpse. If the opponent accepts the third possibility, then they must accept the presence of consciousness during this absorption. If these three possibilities are rejected and instead the opponent asserts that the meditative absorption on cessation is something that is merely imputed on the body at the time when gross feelings and so forth have been stopped, then this absorption would be an imputed existent and the following error arises. ❧

In this case, one has to accept that meditative absorption is not a [functioning] thing, because at this time it is accepted that being a functioning thing is contradictory to being an imputed existent.

❧ Here, "at this time" means while the tenets accepted by the Sautrāntika are being taken as the basis for this presentation of the three conditions. According to this system, anything that is merely imputed by conceptual consciousness does not exist by means of its own characteristics and thus is permanent or not existent. Anything that is a functioning thing is established by means of its own characteristics and not merely imputed by concepts. Khedrup Jé is arguing that if the meditative absorption on cessation is not mind or body or the collection of these, then it must be something merely imputed by conception at the time the body of the yogi abides devoid of gross feeling, discrimination, and so forth. If that were the case, then it would be a permanent thing and many faults would ensue. ⸙

One would have to accept that whatever is a thing does not have the ability to engage in [the five paths that] abide in happiness in this lifetime.

⸙ The "five paths that abide in happiness in this lifetime" are enumerated in chapter 4 of Maitreya's *Ornament of Clear Realization* (*Abhisamayālaṃkāra*) among the thirty-four aspects of a knower of all aspects, which are similar to those possessed by bodhisattvas. The five are the four concentrations of the formless realm and the emancipation of cessation. The author is implicitly asserting that these five paths are similar to meditative absorption on cessation in consisting of a cessation of gross feeling, discrimination, and other gross minds. If it is accepted that during such a cessation there is no awareness present in the person's continuum and subsequently this type of absorption is a merely imputed phenomenon, then it absurdly follows that being a functioning thing and engaging in or being one of these five paths are mutually exclusive. In that case no person could engage in these paths. ⸙

[Qualm]: Someone might object, "Well then, if mental consciousness exists [during the meditative absorption on cessation], then the feeling and discrimination in its retinue must exist. In that case, it is contradictory to assert that all feelings and discriminations have been stopped."

[Answer]: "All gross feeling and discrimination have been stopped; I also do not assert the existence of gross consciousnesses [at this time]. If it is held that even unclear feeling and discrimination must not exist at that time, a fault would accrue to those who assert the existence of mind-basis-of-all during [meditative absorption on cessation] because they have asserted many times that feeling and so forth, the five omnipresent mental factors, are definitely in the retinue of the basis-of-all."[124]

❧ Any mental factor, such as the five omnipresent mental factors (feeling, discrimination, intention, contact, and mental engagement), that is in the retinue of a main mind must possess five aspects of similarity[125] with that main mind. One of these is the similarity of time, which means that at any time when the main mind, with which it is concomitant, is produced, that mental factor is also produced. For a complete list of the mental factors and explanation of the five aspects of similarity, see appendix 2. Those who posit the existence of mind-basis-of-all also assert that this consciousness possesses the five omnipresent mental factors in its retinue. This being the case, it would be contradictory for those who accept that mind-basis-of-all exists during absorption on cessation to reject the existence of any mental factors at all during that time. Khedrup Jé makes the distinction that while the grosser levels of main mind, feeling, and discrimination are stopped, their subtler levels remain. ❧

[Qualm]: Someone might ask, "In that case, what is the difference between [meditative absorption of cessation] and absorption without discrimination?"

[Answer]: "Although there is no difference in the five sense consciousnesses and gross mental consciousness together with their retinues being objects of negation [of these two absorptions], there are huge differences between these two in terms of the action of negating and so forth. [For the latter, the action of negating gross consciousnesses is performed by] mundane paths, and [for the former, meditative absorption on cessation, the act of negating is performed by] supra-mundane paths. There is also a difference in terms of the discrimination entering into the absorptions being erroneous or non-erroneous."

Second, settling on the nature of sense consciousness's three conditions according to the Chittamātra [127]

❧ Here Khedrup Jé explains the Chittamātra presentation of the three conditions that give rise to a consciousness. While the Chittamātra agree with the Sautrāntika that the immediately preceding condition is the immediately prior moment of consciousness, their presentations of the other two conditions differ in fundamental ways. The Chittamātra do not accept the existence of external objects that exist as a different nature from the direct perceiver experiencing them. Contrary to our everyday assumptions, there is no world "out there" existing independently from our experience. Great Indian proponents of the Chittamātra like Asaṅga frequently compare our everyday existence to a dream or a shared illusion.

The Sautrāntika consider the objects of sense experiences to be ultimate existents because they exist exactly as they appear to sense consciousness, without any conceptual overlay. It is only after our initial perception that we begin to conceptualize and fantasize about them, and then they appear to our thought consciousness in distorted ways. Things that are impermanent appear to be permanent, things that are in fact causes of suffering appear as stable sources of happiness, things that are unclean appear as pure, and so forth. The presentation of the Sautrāntika fits with our commonsense view of the world, but the Chittamātra challenges this view. Both the Chittamātra and the Middle Way schools assert that our misconceptions about reality are so thoroughly ingrained that their effects spill over into our sense impressions, distorting even direct appearances. The Chittamātra use the example of a mirror—although the details seen in the mirror, such as colors and shapes, are perceived correctly, the overall appearance of objects that are spatially distant from the mirror is mistaken because although such objects appear to be real faces or eyes or flowers and so forth, they are merely reflections of such objects. When we realize we are seeing a reflection, the paradigm through which we view the experience shifts irrevocably.

While the Chittamātra and Middle Way schools agree that the imprints of past misconceptions distort the appearance of sense objects, the Chittamātra part ways with the Middle Way school by pressing this reasoning to a stronger conclusion: appearances to sense consciousness are purely the result of imprints on the mind. There is no "stuff" out there acting as a trigger for sense experiences.

The Chittamātra break down our sense experience into various aspects. For an experience of a blue cloth, there is the appearance as blue, the appearance as a solid object, the appearance of depth and distance, and so forth. Each of these appearances is the result of a corresponding imprint on the mind. In the context of the three conditions that give rise to a sensorial experience, mainly we are concerned with the first appearance—the appearance as blue. The commonsense view, articulated by the Sautrāntika, is that the cloth reflects blue light rays, which contact the eye sense power, thereby generating an eye consciousness experiencing blue. In the Chittamātra system, the color blue does not exist prior to the consciousness that experiences it. Instead, blue and the eye consciousness experiencing blue are two simultaneous results of a common cause, an imprint on the mind carried over from the past. Just as the appearance of a mountain experienced in a dream is not itself the dream consciousness but still cannot be said to exist differently from that consciousness, and just as the dream mountain and the dream consciousness arise simultaneously as the result of an imprint on consciousness, so it is in wake-time with sense objects and sense consciousnesses.

Because blue does not exist prior to the eye consciousness experiencing blue, Chittamātra must posit something other than blue as the observed object condition, or the condition that causes the eye consciousness to be generated and arise in the aspect of blue. They posit that an imprint existing on the immediately preceding consciousness is that observed object condition, and that this imprint is the substantial cause of both—the appearance of blue, and the eye consciousness apprehending blue. This imprint has been carried over from previous existences, and it ripens as the present experience.

Regarding the empowering condition, Chittamātra agree with the Sautrāntika that there is an uncommon empowering condition for eye consciousness called an "eye sense power." However, Khedrup Jé asserts that this eye sense power is also an imprint carried on the immediately preceding consciousness rather than a physical form as asserted by Sautrāntika followers. Because both the observed object condition and the empowering condition are imprints on the immediately preceding consciousness, in this system all three conditions—the observed object condition, the empowering condition, and the immediately preceding condition—are in fact of one nature, different aspects of the same substantial entity. For example, a thumbprint on a stick of butter is not substantially different from the butter. Physically we cannot separate the thumbprint from the butter; the distinction is merely conceptual, the thumbprint is merely an aspect or property of the butter although it is not butter itself.

In the section below, Khedrup Jé explains the three conditions from the point of view of the Chittamātra in more detail. ❦

[127] Now I will explain the presentation of the three conditions according to the system of the Vijñānavāda. This presentation contains three parts: the identification of the
- observed object condition,
- empowering condition, and
- immediately preceding condition of a sense consciousness as posited in the system of the Vijñānavāda.

Observed Object Condition
The first [observed object condition] has two parts:
- the actual [presentation]
- as an ancillary topic, an explanation of the sign of definite simultaneous observation

The actual presentation
First, [the actual presentation]: If we take the eye consciousness apprehending blue as an illustration, from among the five, (1) the aspect of blue that appears to the eye consciousness apprehending blue, (2) the appearance as blue, (3) blue, (4) the previous consciousness that is the immediately preceding condition of that very eye consciousness apprehending blue, and (5) the potential, on that previous consciousness, to generate the eye consciousness apprehending blue as a possessor of an aspect of

the object [blue], which of these should we posit as the observed object condition of the eye consciousness apprehending blue?

[128] Blue, the appearance as blue, and the aspect of blue that appears to the eye consciousness apprehending blue are all unreasonable [to accept] as the observed object condition of the eye consciousness apprehending blue, because if something is that's [i.e., that consciousness's] observed object condition, it must be its cause, and the three [blue, the appearance as blue, and the aspect of blue that appears to the eye consciousness apprehending blue] are of the essence of the eye consciousness apprehending blue itself, so they are unacceptable as the cause of the eye consciousness apprehending blue.[126]

Accepting consciousness that serves as the immediately preceding condition [of the eye consciousness] as being the observed object condition is also unfeasible. If it were [the observed object condition], then similarly you would have to accept that very previous consciousness as the empowering condition as well.[127]

Then it would be impossible for a direct sense perceiver to have any direct cause other than the previous consciousness that is its immediately preceding condition. In that case, all of the lines of reasoning explaining that it is impossible for a single direct cause alone to generate a result would harm [that position], and it would not pervade that a substantial cause must rely on supporting causes to generate a result.

[131] Well then, what is the correct stance? I will explain. Āchārya Dignāga says in his *Investigation of the Object*:

> That which is the nature of an inner object of knowledge
> and appears as though it were an outer object
> is the object [of the five senses],
> because it is the nature of the object of the primary
>   consciousness.
> It is also its very condition.[128]

Of the two, the observed object described here, as well as the one described [by a later passage of the same work]—

... because you posit the capacity, they are sequential.[129]

—the meaning of the first is this: the blue and other objects that appear to sense consciousnesses as though they were external objects are the objects of those sense consciousnesses. Because they are both the observed object and the condition of their respective sense consciousnesses, they are the observed object condition.

Why are they the observed object?

... because it is the nature of the object of the primary consciousness.

This passage explains: it follows that it is the observed object condition, because it is the nature of the object of knowing of that's primary consciousness.

Why are they a condition?

... because it is only a part of and is unmistaken, it is [that's] condition.[130]

This passage explains: the blue that appears to a sense consciousness is a part that is of the essence of only that sense consciousness, so even though they exist at the same time, it is feasible for it to be a condition [of the sense consciousness]. The reason is that if the sense consciousness has the blue as its object, it arises, and it does not arise if it does not have it, so it unmistakenly follows after it or reverses [i.e., it exists if blue exists, and if blue does not exist, it does not].

Accepting that the system of observed object conditions taught in this text also allows for cause and effect to exist at the same time, and for cause and effect not to be pervaded by being substantially different, is merely the assertion of previous scholars like Vasubandhu, the Ācārya of Abhidharma, and others; it is not what the Sovereign of Reason [Dignāga] posits as the correct stance.

From the point of view of the Ācārya's [Dignāga's] teaching, regarding the observed object condition that he himself posits as the correct one, he says, "alternatively, the potential—because it determines—is sequential." How can we interpret the meaning of that? [132]

"Alternatively" is a connective phrase within the autocommentary. It means, previous scholars explained in such and such way; alternatively, I explain it in this way... The meaning of "the potential—because it determines—is sequential" is: "the potential" existing on every previous [moment of] sense consciousness to generate its result, a subsequent [moment of] sense consciousness possessing the aspect of a [particular] object, is the observed object condition of the subsequent sense consciousness in a "sequential" fashion [that is, the potential on each moment of sense consciousness is the condition for each subsequent moment of sense consciousness]. That is "because" it is the condition that "determines" the aspect of [which particular] object its resultant subsequent sense consciousness will have.

The phrase "because it determines" [alone] is to be taken as the proof; combining it as "because it determines the potential" and making that out as the proof is irrelevant, because if you thereby formulate it as "it is the observed object condition of the subsequent sense consciousness, 'because it determines the potential' for the subsequent sense consciousness," then the pervasion is unrelated [to what one is trying to prove]. If you formulate it as "it is the observed object condition of the subsequent [moment], 'because it determines the potential' for the previous [moment]," then you incur the fallacious consequence that the observed object condition of a sense consciousness is the indirect cause of that sense consciousness.

Furthermore, as for positing the potential on the previous sense consciousness as the observed object condition of the subsequent sense consciousness in this way: it is not posited as the observed object condition on account of being both the observed object and the condition of that subsequent sense consciousness. Rather, it is because it is the main condition generating the subsequent sense consciousness as possessing the aspect of its observed object. Therefore it is called the "observed object condition."

Again, in the system of the Chittamātra, all aspects of an object that appear to a sense consciousness are aspects appearing through the force of imprints on the mind. They are not cases of the object casting its aspect from its own side. For that reason, because the generation of a sense consciousness as possessing the aspect of a [particular] object is a generation through the force of imprints upon the previous [sense] consciousness, then that very potential, which is in essence an imprint of the similar class existing upon the previous [sense] consciousness, is the main condition generating its resultant subsequent sense consciousness as possessing the aspect of a particular object. And for that reason, this Chittamātra manner of positing it as the observed object condition of that [subsequent consciousness] is simply an extremely secure presentation issuing from their [fundamental] tenets.

⁑ The above-mentioned "imprint of similar class" refers to potencies producing later types of consciousness similar to the former consciousness that infused these potencies on the mind-basis-of-all when those former consciousnesses ceased. Therefore an appearance of blue to a later eye consciousness is produced by an imprint of a predisposition infused by a former eye consciousness; it is not produced by an imprint of a predisposition infused by a conceptual consciousness.[131] In addition to this imprint of similar class, the Chittamātra classify three other types of seeds or imprints: imprints of verbalization, imprints of the view of the self, and imprints of the branches of cyclic existence. The imprints of verbalization are created by conceptual consciousness; objects are established as referents of conceptual consciousness in dependence on language and conceptuality. A conceptual consciousness that thinks, "This is blue," leaves such an imprint of verbalization on the mind-basis-of-all when that consciousness ceases. When this imprint ripens, such a mode of imputed appearance can also appear to an eye consciousness apprehending blue. The *imprints of the view of self* refers to those imprints, posited by earlier instances of ignorance grasping at a self of persons or a self of phenomena, that produce both later instances of those wrong concepts and the appearance to them of a self of persons or phenomena. The *imprints of the branches of cyclic existence* refers to imprints posited by conceptual consciousnesses grasping at subject and object having different natures. Such imprints produce the appearance of subject and object having different natures in the face of later awarenesses. ⸔

Well then, what is the meaning of the statement in *Investigation of the Object Autocommentary*:

> An observed object condition needs to have two qualities.[132]

Within the camp that posits the color blue and so forth appearing to a sense consciousness as the observed object condition, the meaning is that it possesses the two qualities [133] of (1) being the observed object of that sense consciousness and (2) also being its condition. In [Dignāga's] own camp that accepts the potential as the observed object condition, the meaning is that the observed object condition of a sense consciousness possesses the two qualities of being (1) the determiner of the aspect of observation for a sense consciousness and (2) the condition of that sense consciousness. For that reason, [Dignāga] explained in *Investigation of the Object Autocommentary*:

> Sometimes, from the potential fully ripening, the consciousness arises in the very aspect of a [particular] object. At other times, from that aspect, a [new] potential [is posited on the mind]. As to whether those two are other from consciousness, or not other, say what you like. Thus the inner observed object [the potential on the mind], because it possesses two qualities, is accurate as the observed object condition.[133]

Therefore, know that for this system, if something is the observed object condition of a sense consciousness, it must be the generator of that sense consciousness as possessing the aspect of a [particular] observed object, but although something may be the generator of a sense consciousness as possessing the aspect of a [particular] observed object, it does not need to be the observed object of that sense consciousness.

Intermediate verse:

I, who observe with proper intellect all the observed objects of knowable things, have explained unmistakenly the observed object conditions of sense consciousness in accordance with [Āchārya Dignāga's] *Investigation of the Object*.

❧ Below, Khedrup Jé explains one of the many lines of reasoning that the Chittamātra employ to prove that sense objects are not external to the sense consciousness perceiving them. This particular reasoning, *the sign of definite simultaneous observation*, is especially favored by Dignāga and Dharmakīrti. Our common everyday assumption is that the color blue exists independently from and prior to the eye consciousness apprehending it. As discussed above, such an assumption must be called into question when reflecting upon the nature of experience. How can blue, or anything else for that matter, exist without a consciousness apprehending it? We are all familiar with the famous thought experiment, if a tree falls in the woods and nobody is there to hear it, does it make a sound? How can sound exist without somebody apprehending it? Are the waves of vibration moving through the air "sound," or is sound an experience generated when those vibrations contact the ear? Or, more radically, is the whole appearance of an external world of our shared experience just an illusory projection of our minds? The Chittamātra consider it axiomatic that blue can only exist at the time when there is an eye consciousness experiencing blue, because the criterion for existence is whether it is established by valid cognition. Other Buddhist schools accept this same reason but do not come to the same conclusion.

If blue and the eye consciousness experiencing blue always exist together, then it follows that there must be some relation between them. In general, when two things are related, they must be related as cause and effect or as being of the same nature. Chittamātra assert that this relation cannot be one of cause and effect because blue and the eye consciousness experiencing blue are experienced simultaneously. Whenever blue is experienced by the eye consciousness, at the very same time that eye consciousness is experienced by the self-cognizer that accompanies it. Because these two phenomena always exist together and simultaneously, their relationship must be one of being the same nature. Our conception of external existents gives rise to the illusion that the objects exist prior to and externally from the subjective experience of them, but that experience cannot be supported by reasoning. Thus sense objects do not exist independently of the sense perceiver apprehending them, and their appearance to that sense perceiver as distant is an illusion. This is similar to the people and events of dreams appearing as real as those of waking experience when in actuality they are not. Likewise, sense objects' appearance as "cut-off"—that is, unrelated to the subjective consciousness—is an illusion. ✤

An explanation of the sign of definite simultaneous observation [133]
Second, the explanation of the sign of definite simultaneous observation has three parts:
- explanation of the need for such a sign
- arranging the sign and identifying the three points
- establishing the [three] modes of the sign

Explanation of the need for such a sign
First, [explanation of the need for such a sign]: a Chittamātra challenger posits [the sign under discussion] for a defender who propounds external objects, in order to establish that the blue and so forth that appear to a sense consciousness as though they are external objects are not actually external objects. Thus the Chittamātra proponents establish consciousnesses and the objects they perceive as not being substantially different by means of the reason of "definite simultaneous observation." This is established because [it follows that if objects] are not established as not substan-

tially different from whatever consciousness apprehends them, they would definitely have to be accepted as external objects.

Furthermore, as for visual form, sound, and so forth: [134] if they were not established as not substantially different from the ordinary being's sense consciousness apprehending them, then one would have to accept that visual forms, sounds, and so forth are established just as they appear to an ordinary person's sense consciousness—that is, as distant and cut off from it. If they were established in that way, then one would have to accept that they are established as objects that are external to consciousness. So for that reason, we must utilize the sign of definite simultaneous observation to establish that those [sounds and so forth] are not substantially different from the ordinary being's sense consciousness apprehending them.

However, we cannot establish, for example, Devadatta's mind as not being substantially different from, for example, the clairvoyance that knows Devadatta's mind. But even though we cannot establish that, we don't incur the erroneous consequence that Devadatta's mind is an external object. So, for that reason, taking such a mind as a basis [example], there are some objects and object possessors for which the sign of definite simultaneous observation cannot establish being not substantially different.

. Likewise, even for blue and so forth, because if they were not established as substantially one with their object possessors—the eye consciousness apprehending blue, and so forth—we would have to accept them as external objects, therefore the sign of definite simultaneous observation establishes them as substantially one. However, it does not establish blue and so forth as substantially one with all object possessor consciousnesses that apprehend them. Otherwise, you would have to accept [absurdly] that blue and so forth are substantially one with the all-knowing exalted wisdom. Therefore, if you say—as do most contemporary logicians of the Snow Land in the Chittamātra system—"any [pair of] object and object possessors is pervaded by not being substantially different," then even the all-knowing exalted wisdom directly realizing selflessness would become not substantially different from self-grasping. In that case, being substantially separate would become impossible in the Chittamātra system.

❧ The main point here is that we cannot establish every pair of subject and object as substantially one. Although the color blue is substantially one with the eye consciousness apprehending it, it is not substantially one with every individual eye consciousness apprehending it, such as Devadatta's eye consciousness apprehending blue. That is because blue can exist without Devadatta's eye consciousness in a way that it is perceived by an eye consciousness in another's person's continuum. Likewise, blue is not substantially one with the Buddha's all-knowing wisdom, because somebody can ascertain blue without ascertaining the Buddha's all-knowing wisdom; they are not always observed simultaneously. Blue is also not of one nature with the inferential valid cognizer realizing blue. If it were so, then merely thinking of blue would cause it to exist. More important, in this system blue is in fact the cause of such an inferential cognizer, just as it is in the Sautrāntika. Inferential cognition uses sense evidence to determine what is hidden from the senses, and thereby necessarily arises subsequently to what it discovers. Furthermore, this sign is used only in relation to objects of the senses. Although things like uncompounded space are of one essence with the valid cognition that cognizes them, even if they were not so, they would not be classed as "external existents." "External" in this context implies an object of the senses that is substantially different and spatially separated from the sense consciousness perceiving it. Uncompounded space is not an object of the senses. ❧

Arranging the sign and identifying the three points
Second, arranging the sign and identifying the three points. Arranging the sign: "Whatever thing is definitely simultaneously observed with something else is not substantially different from that [thing]. For example, sound and object of hearing. The blue that appears to an eye consciousness apprehending blue and the eye consciousness apprehending blue are also definitely simultaneously observed."

As for this [sign's] three [points]—the sign, the predicate [of the pro-
bandum], and the subject [135]—our own system is as follows. The five
objects—forms, sound, and so forth—are themselves established concor-
dantly for both proponents of external objects and the Vijñānavāda as the
appearing [subject for the debate]. The basis of debate is whether [these
five] are established or not as objects external to the ordinary being's sense
consciousness apprehending them. As such, the two proponents of external
objects establish those very five objects as externals, while the Vijñānavāda
uses the sign of definite simultaneous observation to establish them as substantially one with the sense consciousness apprehending them.

So, the five objects—form and so forth—are the subject that the sign
of definite simultaneous observation establishes as substantially one with
the sense consciousness apprehending them. Therefore the object [blue]
is proven as not being substantially different from the eye consciousness
apprehending blue with the sign of definite simultaneous observation.
[140]

Well then, in our own system, how do we accept blue and so forth—as
consciousness, or as matter? If it were matter, it would be of the nature of
atoms, and as a consequence would be an external object. However, if it
were consciousness, the faults described above[134] would hit their mark. For
these reasons, we do not accept either of those positions.

It is like this: the blue and so forth that appear to an ordinary being's
sense consciousness as though distant and cut off are in actual fact substantially one with that ordinary being's sense consciousness apprehending
them. For that reason, we accept them as of the essence of the ordinary
being's sense consciousness apprehending them, but we do not accept
them as either matter or consciousness.

Well then, isn't blue one essence with the all-knowing exalted wisdom
as well? [The reasoning] is not similar. Regarding the blue that appears
to an ordinary being's sense consciousness, the sign of definite simultaneous observation establishes it as substantially one with that sense consciousness. But we are unable to establish blue and so forth as substantially
one with the all-knowing exalted wisdom, because if we posit the sign of

definite simultaneous observation, the property of the subject is not established, and also there is no other sign [that can establish it as such].

Whoever accepts that there does not exist a functioning thing that
is neither matter nor consciousness has not investigated properly. Most
proponents of tenets accept [the existence of] functioning things that
are neither matter nor consciousness [such as non-associated compositional factors]. Vaibhāṣhika accept space and so forth, Sautrāntika accept
beings and so forth, and Chittamātra accept the absorption of cessation
[as being non-associated compositional factors]. Furthermore, all of these
schools must accept many functioning things that are neither matter nor
consciousness, such as mental imprints and so forth. So saying "when you
divide functioning things, there are two—matter and consciousness" is
merely by reason of habituation to reciting that phrase many times from
childhood itself.

Now I will explain the point of the predicate of the probandum. Because
True Aspectarians and False Aspectarians accord in accepting blue and so
forth as substantially one with the eye consciousness apprehending blue
and so forth, and also because, as I have already explained, [141] you must
take blue itself, and so forth, as the subject. Then either of the two, (1)
establishing [blue and the eye consciousness apprehending it] as substantially one, or (2) establishing them as not substantially different, is not
incorrect. [In other words, the predicate can be either *substantially one* or
not substantially different; either is correct.] Whichever one establishes,
there is no difference in terms of establishing the subject one wants to
know about, because being either of those two is contradictory to being
an external object.

What is the point of the sign? [143] The meaning of "definite simultaneous observation" is this: *simultaneous* in this context means the same
time and place. "Observation" means observation by a valid cognizer. *Definite* means pervasion. So definitely understand it [to mean]: it pervades
that at a time when one is observed by valid cognition, the other is also
observed by valid cognition. And it pervades that at a time when the other
is observed by valid cognition, the first one is also observed by valid cog-

nition. For example, it pervades that as for blue, whenever a valid direct perceiver apprehending blue observes it, at the same time, with regard to the valid direct perceiver apprehending blue as well, it is observed by a direct valid self-cognizer experiencing it. And it pervades that whenever a direct valid self-cognizer observes the valid direct perceiver apprehending blue, then at that time the valid direct perceiver apprehending blue also observes blue.

[Qualm]: "Isn't this mode [of reasoning] similar in the case of the present taste and visual form of molasses? It is not similar, because if it were similar, then it would [absurdly] follow that if you saw the visual form of molasses, you would necessarily also experience its taste."

[144] Well then, what is the meaning of [Dharmakīrti saying in *Exposition of Valid Cognition*]:

> Because the consciousness is mistaken, one sees two moons as different, though they do not exist in that way?[135]

The meaning is in regard to the passage, "With regard to whatever object is definitely experienced simultaneously with a mind: how can you establish it as an aspect different from that [mind]?" Someone might ask, "If blue and so forth are not different from sense consciousness, what can we make of this appearance as distant and cut off?" This passage indicates [the response], that [appearance] is by virtue of a mistaken [consciousness]. In short, this passage is positing an example of how blue and so forth cannot be different from sense consciousness yet do appear to be different. It is not positing a concordant example establishing non-separation [because the two moons do not exist as non-separate, since they do not exist at all].

Establishing the three modes of the sign[136]
Third, establishing the [three] modes [of the sign]: [in the passage] "because they are definitely simultaneously observed," the property of the subject is established by a direct self-cognizer. Of the two pervasions,

regarding the mode of establishing the forward pervasion: whatever [two things] are definitely simultaneously observed are pervaded by not being substantially different. The reason is that with two mutually different things, if by observing one, one necessarily observes the other, then it pervades that a relation is established [between them]. And since you must observe them simultaneously—that is, at the same time—then one negates that it is a causal relationship. One thereby has established that if they are definitely simultaneously observed, they are related in the sense of being one essence. [Finally], [two things] being related in the sense of being one essence is contradictory to their being substantially different.

As for the way of establishing the counter pervasion: the passage "different things, like blue and yellow, do not have definiteness of being experienced [at the same time]"[137] demonstrates this mode. "If [two things] are substantially separate, it follows that it is contradictory for them to be definitely simultaneously observed, because if there were two substantially different things that were definitely simultaneously observed, they would be suitable to appear [to consciousness], but we don't observe anything like that." With *a sign of non-observation of that which is suitable to appear*, you negate that [two things] that are substantially different can be definitely simultaneously observed, and thereby you establish [the counter pervasion]. [145] Also, if such a thing existed, the reason that it would be suitable to appear is that if two things are definitely simultaneously observed, they are pervaded by simultaneously appearing to a valid cognizer.

Empowering condition and immediately preceding condition

[146] Now I will explain the empowering condition and the immediately preceding condition [according to the Chittamātra]. Know that the definition of the immediately preceding condition is just as I explained before in the context of describing the tenets of the Sautrāntika. Since it would thereby be redundant, I will not explain it again.

There is a difference in terms of how the Sautrāntika and the Vijñānavāda accept the empowering condition. It is this: both are similar in accepting the nature of the eye sense power, which is the empowering condition of an eye consciousness, as being something different from the other two conditions of the eye consciousness. Both accept that it is the main cause that causes the eye consciousness to engage as an apprehender of only visual form among the five sense objects, and that creates its uncommon distinction not to engage any of the other [four sense objects]. However, the difference is that the Sautrāntika accept that very [eye sense power] as being matter, whereas the Chittamātra accept it as being the nature of a potential existing on the previous [moment of] consciousness that is the immediately preceding condition of [the eye consciousness]. For that reason, Āchārya Dignāga said, "The cooperative power is the nature of a potential. It is also the sense power, and it is also not mutually exclusive with cognition."[138] I have finished explaining the presentation of the three conditions of a sense direct perceiver in the Vijñānavāda.

⚘4.2 MENTAL DIRECT PERCEIVERS

In this section, Khedrup Jé explains mental direct perceivers. We must be careful to distinguish between mental direct perceivers in particular and the broader category of non-conceptual mental consciousness. In general, self-knowing direct perceivers, mundane clairvoyances (like reading other peoples' minds, remembering previous lives, etc.), and yogic direct perceivers are all forms of non-conceptual mental consciousness. While they are all direct perceivers and not included in the five sense consciousnesses, they are not mental direct perceivers. In the context of the division into four kinds of direct perceivers (sense direct perceivers, mental direct perceivers, self-knowing direct perceivers, and yogic direct perceivers), the second division—mental direct perceiver—indicates something more limited in extent. Specifically, it refers to a subtle kind of mental direct perceiver that spontaneously arises, even in ordinary beings, immediately after a sense consciousness apprehends its object. This mental direct perceiver in turn induces conceptual consciousness grasping that object. Conceptual consciousness then thinks, for example, "pot," or "this is a pot," and so forth, labeling objects of the senses with names and thereby delineating them from other objects. The mental direct perceiver that arises between a sense perceiver and the conceptual consciousness it induces is called a "subtle kind of consciousness" because it exists for the shortest moment of time and thus can only be perceived by highly realized beings—āryas—who have direct perception of impermanence and selflessness.

Purbu Chok gives the following definition of a mental direct perceiver: that which is generated in dependence on a mental sense power that is its own uncommon empowering condition and is a consciousness that is an other-knower that is free from conceptuality and non-mistaken.[139] What it means to be an other-knower, non-mistaken, and free from conceptuality have all been explained above in section 4.1 on direct sense perceivers. The uncommon empowering condition of any mental direct perceiver is a mental sense power. Here, whichever of the six consciousnesses has immediately preceded a mental direct perceiver and served as its uncommon empowering condition is that mental perceiver's mental sense power. Mental direct perceivers explained in this chapter are induced by one of the five sense direct perceivers apprehending any of the five sense objects: forms, sounds, odors, tastes, or tangible objects.

[153] Now, secondly, the presentation of mental direct perceivers. This also has four parts:
- definition
- divisions
- the mode of generation
- [an] ancillary [topic], identifying the mental sense power

Definition
First, [the definition of a mental direct perceiver is]: a non-mistaken other-knowing mental consciousness that is directly produced from the mental sense power that is its own [uncommon] empowering condition.

Divisions

When [mental direct perceivers are] divided, there are five: mental direct perceivers apprehending forms and so forth [i.e., sound, odor, taste, and tangible objects].

❧ Khedrup Jé now explains the way a mental direct perceiver is generated. In general, there are three varying explanations by three Indian Buddhist scholars: Prajñākaragupta, Śhaṅkaranandana, and Dharmottara. They assert alternating generation, generation of three types, and generation only at the end of a continuum, respectively. Khedrup Jé follows the second assertion, generation of three types, as will be explained below. According to Śhaṅkaranandana's system, three types of phenomena—the second moment of a sense direct perceiver apprehending its object, the first moment of a mental direct perceiver apprehending that object, and the self-knowing direct perceiver experiencing those two—are generated simultaneously. Khedrup Jé supports his assertion with a quote from Sakya Paṇḍita that says that when the sense direct perceiver and the mental direct perceiver arise simultaneously, two types of externally directed object knower and one type of internally directed self-knower exist.

Alternating generation is as follows: First, the first moment of a sense direct perceiver apprehending its object is generated; then the first moment of a mental direct perceiver apprehending that object is generated; subsequently the second moment of a sense direct perceiver apprehending that object is generated; then the second moment of a mental direct perceiver apprehending that object is generated, and so forth. Between each moment of a sense direct perception, a moment of a mental direct perception is generated. The two are generated alternately.

Generation only at the end of a continuum is as follows: a mental direct perceiver is only generated at the end of a continuum of a sense direct perceiver. ❧

The mode of generation

First, a single moment of sense direct perceiver arises. After that, with (1) that very [sense direct perceiver] acting as the immediately preceding condition, (2) the physical sense power simultaneous with [that first moment of sense direct perceiver] acting as the empowering condition, and (3) the second moment of its apprehended object acting as the observed object condition, the second moment of sense direct perceiver arises. [154] Simultaneously with that, the first moment of mental direct perceiver [also] arises. The first moment of mental direct perceiver's immediately preceding condition and observed object condition are not different from [those of] the second moment of sense consciousness. The difference is that the mental direct perceiver is not generated from a physical sense power; it is generated from its [own uncommon] empowering condition, the mental sense power that is simultaneous with the first moment of sense direct perceiver. Therefore know it to be as [explained] before that the second moment of mental sense power and the second moment of sense direct perceiver exist from being [established] simultaneously until finally both cease simultaneously.

Except for it being merely renowned among former [Tibetan scholars] that this [above point] is the assertion of the great brahman [Śhaṅkaranandana], there isn't any source [for it] in any of his textual systems that have been translated into Tibetan. Nevertheless, it is clear that the thought of *Treasure of Reasoning* [composed by Sakya Paṇḍita Kunga Gyaltsen] corresponds with that very [assertion].

From the *Treasure of Reasoning*:

> To this mode of generation [we] apply the term "triple type of direct perceiver," because when the sense direct perceiver and the mental direct perceiver arise simultaneously, two types of externally directed object knower and one type of internally directed self-knower exist.[140]

Thus it is the thought [of Sakya Paṇḍita]. I haven't heard of an especially good reason to count how many types are there in this mode of generation, so it is not absolutely necessary to count how many types are there. If in any case we do count, we recognize the very application of three types in accordance with the assertion of [Sakya Paṇḍita] to be acceptable.

⸙ Next, Khedrup Jé gives a supplementary explanation of the *mental sense power* that is the uncommon empowering condition giving rise to a mental direct perceiver. All minds must have an uncommon empowering condition, this being the factor determining which kind of objects they can engage and in which of the six classes of consciousness they are included. While one can posit the five sense powers (eye sense power and so forth) as the uncommon empowering conditions for the five sense consciousnesses, respectively, positing the uncommon mental sense power is more complicated. Because any main consciousness's or main mind's immediately preceding moment of consciousness creates an opportunity for the arising of the subsequent moment of consciousness, the preceding moment of a main mind can in that way act as a mental sense power for mental direct perceivers to come about. This preceding moment of main consciousness is in fact necessary for any consciousness to arise, but for sense consciousnesses it is the common, not the uncommon, empowering condition, while for mental consciousness it is the uncommon empowering condition. Khedrup Jé first explains the view of the Vaibhāṣika, who hold that only mental consciousnesses have mental powers as a cause, and in order for a new instance of mental consciousness to arise, all the previously existing six collections of consciousness must cease. This is because a mental consciousness cannot exist in a person's continuum at the same time as the other five main consciousnesses, and in order for an instance of mental consciousness to arise, a mental consciousness that is its cause must cease. A cause cannot exist at the time of its effect. Khedrup Jé rejects this position and instead follows the views of Asaṅga and Sakya Paṇḍita, who hold that all main consciousnesses have causes that are mental powers, and that both mental consciousness and sense consciousness can exist in a person's continuum at the same time. Therefore, any among the six collections of consciousness on the verge of ceasing are capable of creating an opportunity for the generation of a subsequent main consciousness; and this does not depend on the cessation of all six collections of consciousness. Finally, he also proves that mental sense powers have a continuum with the reason that a mental sense power is synonymous with a main mind in the sense that every mental sense power is a main mind, and every main mind causes a subsequent main mind to come about. ⟡

Ancillary, identifying the mental sense power

Here I will present our own assertion [based on Vasubandhu's and Asaṅga's systems]. From [Vasubandhu's] *Treasury of Knowledge*:

> Whatever is the main consciousness that is the immediately preceding of [any of] the six [collections of consciousness] is [necessarily] a mental [knower]. To establish the base of the sixth, we accept constituents as eighteen.[141]

With respect to this system [the Vaibhāṣika, as taught in the *Treasury of Knowledge*], they assert that a mental sense power acts as the basis of only the sixth, the mental consciousness. From the point of view of creating an opportunity for the generation of the other five [sense] consciousnesses, they do not posit a mental sense power [as the empowering condition]. However, because they assert that multiple main consciousnesses of discordant types do not arise simultaneously in one continuum, they assert that all the previous six collections of consciousness must cease in order to generate a subsequent mental consciousness. [155] For that reason, they accept the mental sense power as the very force that creates an opportunity for the arising of a subsequent mental consciousness after the previous main consciousnesses of all six collections have ceased. Therefore, the quote [from *Treasury of Knowledge*]:

> Which immediately follows the cessation of the six[142]

is accepted as applying to the cessation of all six, not just to the cessation of any one of the six.

Also, although they [the Vaibhāṣhika] do not accept that the [state] of these [six] just having ceased is the mental sense power, even if they did accept that, because they are a disputant who asserts the past to be substantially established, the flaws of contradicting their own root system would not come about. If we accepted like that, then our root system would degenerate.

As for those who assert that many [distinct] consciousnesses of discordant types [can] arise simultaneously in [a single continuum]: just as Asaṅga applies the phrase *the mental consciousness that abides in the immediately preceding [moment]* to the mental sense power, [they also] posit as the mental sense power the property of creating an opportunity for the immediately following main consciousness to arise.

Therefore, since even any one among the six collections of consciousness being on the verge of ceasing is capable of creating an opportunity for the generation of a subsequent main consciousness, it does not depend on the cessation of all six collections of consciousness. This very point is also the thought of [Sakya Paṇḍita's] *Treasury of Reasoning*. Therefore, the property of creating an opportunity for the generation of a subsequent main consciousness after the previous main consciousness has just ceased is posited as the mental sense power.

I don't see the reason that a subsequent mental power is not generated by the mental sense power as establishing that a mental sense power must not have a continuum. Furthermore, I see [that assertion] as contradicting the statement made many times in the great scriptures that a mental sense power is synonymous with a main mind. Since a cause having or not having a continuum does not establish that [its] result does not have a continuum, it is not established that the mental direct perceiver doesn't have a continuum just because the mental sense power [that is its cause] doesn't have a continuum.

If it is necessary [that the cause and result must correlate in either both having a continuum or both not], then [it follows that] the mental direct perceiver should have a continuum because its observed object condition and immediately preceding condition [both] have continuums. The sense direct perceiver is a cause of the mental direct perceiver, and it [the sense direct perceiver] possesses a continuum; thereby the claim "the mental direct perceiver does not have a continuum" degenerates. [Hence,] many who fancy themselves experts on the topic of the mental sense power have become like blind men looking at forms.

⚘4.3 SELF-KNOWING DIRECT PERCEIVERS

A *self-knowing direct perceiver* refers to the part of a consciousness that is the mere awareness of both that consciousness itself and the aspect of that consciousness's object that appears to it. A self-knower only engages internal objects, objects that are within a person's mental continuum, as opposed to external objects. Thereby, the self-knower is distinguished from *other-knowers* or *outwardly focused knowers* that perceive external objects. For example, an eye consciousness apprehending a vase is an other-knower, whereas the consciousness that experiences that eye consciousness is a self-knower. The self-knower that experiences eye consciousness is not an eye consciousness, although it is also not a separate entity from eye consciousness. It is an aspect of eye consciousness that experiences eye consciousness itself.

Not all Buddhist schools accept the existence of self-knowers. The Vaibhāṣhika do not accept consciousness as operating through aspects at all—that is, they assert that an eye consciousness sees its object nakedly, without the mediation of aspects. They argue that if aspects existed they would be like a fence between the object and the consciousness. Other schools, with the notable exception of Chittamātra, whose explanation on this point is slightly different, assert that the object, such as a vase, casts its aspect toward the eye, and this aspect contacts the eye sense power. Through the force of the sense power, a sense consciousness is generated having the aspect of the object. At the same time as the consciousness is generated in the aspect of the external object, it is also generated in its own aspect as the knower of that object. The factor of awareness that real-izes the external object is the *other-knower*, and the factor of awareness that realizes the consciousness is the *self-knower*. The former, knowing the apprehended object, is also called "that which has the aspect of the apprehended [object]," and the latter, knowing the apprehender itself, is called "that which has the aspect of the apprehender." According to Purbu Chok, that which has the aspect of the apprehender is the definition of a self-knower.[143]

The reasoning that led Indian scholars to construct this paradigm grew from the question of memory. After seeing a vase, one not only remem-bers the vase but one also remembers the experience of seeing the vase. Since all memories are the recollection of previously realized phenom-ena, if at the time of realizing a vase there is no awareness realizing the awareness that realizes vase, how could there later be a memory of the awareness that realized vase? An interesting ancillary debate is whether this paradigm leads to the fallacy of infinite regression—the knower of the knower of the knower, and so forth. Thus, the concept of *self-knower* was born.

As mentioned above, Vaibhāṣika do not accept that consciousness functions via *aspects* at all, so they cannot posit a consciousness having the *aspect of apprehended* and *aspect of apprehender*. The Madhyamaka Prāsaṅ-gika school also rejects the existence of this kind of self-knower, but for different reasons. They state that if a consciousness needs a self-knowing consciousness to perceive itself, then it follows that a self-knowing con-sciousness also will need a self-knowing consciousness to be known, thus leading to an infinite regression. Instead, they assert that a consciousness not only perceives a particular object but also realizes the appearance of the aspect of that object to that particular consciousness directly, and thereby the consciousness itself indirectly. By the power of these two realizations, realizing the appearance directly and the consciousness itself indirectly, one can later—when that particular consciousness has ceased—remember that particular object and the experience of having seen that object. For a related discussion of aspects of the apprehended and apprehender see

the presentation of the observed object condition regarding sense direct
perceivers above in section 4.1. ⚘

Self-knowing direct perceivers

[163] All consciousnesses have two factors: (1) a factor of clarity and
knowing that experiences its own entity and (2) a factor that is the appearance of the aspect of its object. The first one is known as the aspect of the
apprehender. In both systems—the Sautrāntika and the Chittamātra—
this [factor] is asserted as the illustration of the self-knowing direct
perceiver. The latter [factor] is known as the aspect of the apprehended
object. It is asserted as the object of experience of the self-knowing direct
perceiver.

Thus, bearing in mind that the reason for applying the term *self-knower*
to the aspect of the apprehender is that it is the experiential factor of clarity
and knowing of all consciousnesses, [Sakya Paṇḍita] also says in *Treasury
of Reasoning*: "the self-knower is the mere opposite of matter."[144] However,
since turning away from matter [that is, not engaging it as an object] and
being generated as [the entity of] the knower is the qualifier of [i.e., the
defining feature of being] the self-knower [and just that is the meaning
of this quote], [he] isn't indicating that the self-knower doesn't have an
object. Otherwise, the reason of being generated as a knower would be
able to prove that [a consciousness] doesn't have an object, so you would
have to establish that by being a knower, something would thereby not
know an object, and if something were an object, it would not be known
by an awareness. Thus you would acquire the misfortune of holding as the
essence a merely mistaken system.

⚘ Though the Vaibhāṣhika also accept an experiential factor of clarity and
knowing of consciousness, still they don't accept it as the self-knower. The
reason is that, since they accept consciousness as without aspects, they
don't accept even in the slightest something called "the aspect of the apprehended object." [164] For that reason, they don't accept the experiential
factor of clarity and knowing of consciousness as a self-knower, as they

think it is incorrect [to accept] a self-knower without a known object or an experiencer without an object of experience. ⸙

Thus those who accept consciousness as having aspects have established the existence of the aspect of the apprehended [object]. As that very [aspect] is established as being not factually other than the experiential factor of clarity and knowing of consciousness, the self-knower is easily established. Thereby [*Treasury of Reasoning*] says, "the second mode also establishes the self-knower."[145] If it were not like that, if [instead] the factor [of] consciousness [that is] clarity and knowing were a self-knower but didn't need to know an object, there would be no contradiction in both accepting [a consciousness] not possessing the aspect of apprehended object and accepting the existence of the self-knower. And what relation would there be with having to establish the self-knower by establishing the aspect of apprehended object? Intelligent people, think over [this point]. Thus the experiential factor of clarity and knowing of consciousness is the experiencer, and that consciousness and its aspect of apprehended object are the objects of experience. For this reason scholars call this "self-knower."

⸙ Followers of the Sautrāntika assert a *self-knowing direct perceiver* because it is a direct perceiver that knows an object that is its own entity. The Chittamātra call it a *self-knowing direct perceiver* because of its being a direct perceiver that knows [its] object in a manner as non-dual from itself. [The Chittamātra] don't posit it as a self-knower because of its knowing an object that is of its own entity, because they assert that, although blue is also the entity of the direct perceiver apprehending blue, the eye consciousness apprehending blue is an other-knower with respect to blue. ⸙

Thus the followers of the Sautrāntika posit the difference between a self-knower and an other-knower by way of its object being factually other than it [the consciousness] or not. The Chittamātra posit [that difference] by way of [the consciousness] having dualistic appearance or not when apprehending its object. In this way, the Sautrāntika and Chittamātra definitions of self-knowing direct perceiver are also different, so they are distinguished and explained respectively.

According to the Sautrāntika, the definition of a self-knowing direct perceiver is: an unmistaken consciousness that is free from conceptuality and that directly knows its object that is its own entity. According to the Chittamātra, the definition of self-knowing direct perceiver is: an unmistaken consciousness that is free from conceptuality, and that directly knows its object of apprehension in the mode of freedom from dualistic appearance, and so forth. [165]

Thus you should say, "the entity of all consciousnesses is self-knower" and "all consciousnesses possess a self-knower." You should not say, "all consciousnesses are self-knowers with respect to the entity," or "all consciousnesses are self-knowers." Like that, whatever is called "that which the self-knower apprehends, the consciousness's aspect of the apprehended object" is referring to the consciousness itself. The meaning of *aspect appearing* refers just to something being generated as the aspect; it is not as though the aspect exists like a fence between the object and the consciousness. This very point, which was earlier settled through reason, is the established conclusion of both the Sautrāntika and the Chittamātra. Therefore in the chapter "Entering into Suchness of [Bhāvaviveka's] Blaze of Reasoning," when explaining the assertions of Proponents of Truly Existent Things who accept consciousness as endowed with aspects [i.e., proponents like Chittamātra and Sautrāntika], [Bhāvaviveka] explains it like this: "When consciousness engages the aspects of apprehended object and apprehending subject, appearance [of the] aspect of various objects, forms and so forth, strongly arising, refers to 'appearance'. If asked, 'What is the strong appearance of its various aspects?' it is consciousness completely becoming the aspect of the object, . . ."[146]

✠4.4 YOGIC DIRECT PERCEIVERS

Unlike the first three kinds of direct perceivers—sense direct perceivers, mental direct perceivers, and self-knowing direct perceivers—yogic direct perceivers do not occur naturally in ordinary beings but are the intended result of prolonged meditation. Yogic direct perceivers occur only in the continuums of āryas (superior beings) who, among the five paths of accumulation, preparation, seeing, meditation, and no-more-learning, have achieved the path of seeing or above. The way to progress on these five paths of liberation and enlightenment is outlined in appendix 5. In order to generate yogic direct perceivers in their continuum, a practitioner must first achieve calm abiding, the ability to maintain single-pointed concentration effortlessly for as long as one wishes. On that basis, he or she can achieve special insight, the ability to analyze an object of meditation within the space of calm abiding such that the analysis increases the stability of concentration, and the concentration increases the strength and clarity of analysis. A further development is the ability to apply such special insight to increasingly more profound objects like subtle impermanence and selflessness.

Initial meditation on selflessness is performed through conceptual consciousness on the basis of multiple reasonings. Such minds only engage selflessness through the filter of a meaning generality, a mere mental image of selflessness. Through repeated familiarity, their object appears with great clarity and vividness, requiring less effort to bring to mind. Eventually, through the force of familiarity and merit, the filter of the meaning generality falls away, and a meditator achieves a direct perception of selflessness. This experience is described as being "like water poured into water," because in the face of the yogi's awareness there is no distinction between the mind meditating and the object realized. When a person first generates a direct realization of selflessness, this mind is their first achievement of a yogic direct perceiver. At the very moment it arises the person achieves the first moment of the path of seeing. Subsequently the practitioner must cultivate and deepen this mind whose future continuity will eventually become the enlightened mind of the buddha that the practitioner becomes.

Although this mind of the yogic direct perceiver is direct, it does not arise suddenly or randomly. It is the definite result of a long process of intentional cultivation, and even after achieving it, a practitioner must make continual effort to strengthen and enhance it. The principal quality of this mind is that it acts as the direct antidote to afflicted states of mind, eliminating their seeds such that they cannot arise again in the continuum of the practitioner.

As for its own uncommon empowering condition, a yogic direct perceiver depends upon its own uncommon empowering condition: a meditative stabilization that is a union of calm abiding and special insight. This is clearly indicated in Purbu Chok's definition of a yogic valid direct perceiver: an other-knowing exalted knower in the continuum of a superior being that, in dependence upon its [uncommon] empowering condition, a meditative stabilization that is a union of calm abiding and special insight, newly and directly realizes either subtle impermanence or the coarse or subtle selflessness of persons.[147]

[166] Now, I will explain the fourth [division of direct perceiver], yogic direct perceivers. That also has three [sections]:
- definition
- divisions
- [extensive] presentation

Definition
First [the definition]: an exalted wisdom that directly realizes its object, an aspect of truth, on the basis of its empowering condition, a meditative stabilization.

Division
Second, as for divisions, there are three: śhrāvaka, pratyekabuddha, and Mahāyāna yogic direct perceivers. Alternatively, there are direct perceivers included in the path of seeing, the path of meditation, and the path of no-more-learning. As for the path of preparation, it is not a yogic direct perceiver. I have already explained this through scripture and reasoning

in other places [such as *Presentation of the Grounds and Paths Called "A Scholar's Delight"*].

꘎ Under the third heading above, extensive presentation of yogic direct perceivers, Khedrup Jé discusses yogic direct perceivers in the context of the four noble truths. This discussion is presented in the following chapter. ꘎

CHAPTER FIVE

THE FOUR NOBLE TRUTHS

AN UNDERSTANDING OF the four noble truths—the truth of suffering, the truth of its origin, the truth of cessation, and the truth of the path—is the foundation of the Buddhist path. An extensive explanation of the four noble truths is presented at this point in the text because they are the primary objects realized by yogic direct perceivers and because, of the four noble truths, the latter two are achieved by generating yogic direct perceivers, which act to abandon the first two. Because this topic is so central to understanding the Buddhist path and imbues all the other topics discussed in this text with deeper significance, we have taken the liberty of generously elaborating on Khedup Jé's presentation with extensive commentary.

The order in which the four truths are explained here—first that of suffering and its origin, followed by cessation and the path to it—corresponds to the order in which yogis typically realize them. In terms of a cause-effect relationship the order is different: the truth of suffering's origin gives rise to the truth of suffering, while the truth of the path gives rise to the truth of cessation.

The four noble truths are called "truths" because they abide in and accord with reality. Furthermore, meditation on them leads to the purification of mental obscurations. Asaṅga says in his *Compendium of Ascertainments*:

> If you ask, "What is the meaning of truth?" I say, the meaning that is the characteristic of not being discordant with the teachings, and the meaning that, when it is seen, becomes the cause of purification—these are the meaning of truth.[148]

They are called *noble* truths because only noble beings, those who have directly realized selflessness, directly perceive them. Asaṅga says in his *Shrāvaka Levels*:

> Although noble beings know and see perfectly meditation on those truths as being in accordance with reality just as it is, childish beings do not know or see it perfectly just as it is. Because of that, they are known as "noble" truths. Although for childish beings those [truths] are indeed by nature true, they do not realize it. For noble beings, they are true in both ways.[149]

Thus, while noble beings perceive directly the process of samsaric rebirth through realizing the first two truths, and the process of how to win liberation from this cycle of suffering through realizing the last two truths, ordinary beings are confused about the nature of the origins giving rise to suffering. As Śhāntideva describes in his *Entering the Bodhisattva Way*:

> Although they have the mind wishing to forsake suffering,
> they hasten quickly toward suffering itself.
> Although they want happiness,
> out of ignorance, they destroy their own happiness like an enemy.[150]

The way ordinary beings like us habitually relate to ourselves, others, and the physical world around us is fundamentally mistaken or deluded. This in turn brings about future samsaric suffering despite one's sincere wish for real happiness. It is only by understanding the full scope of the faults of the truth of suffering that a fully qualified wish to leave cyclic existence is generated. Seeing the process of how the origins of suffering cause one to be repeatedly ensnared in the cycle, one comes to understand the means to reverse it. Tsongkhapa writes in his *Songs of Spiritual Experience*:

> If you do not make effort to reflect on the faults of the truth of suffering,

authentic aspiration for liberation will not arise.
If you do not reflect on the origin, the stages of engaging in
    samsara,
you will not understand the means to cut the root of samsara.
Therefore, rely on the wish to definitely emerge from existence,
    knowing its misery,
and cherish the understanding of that which binds you in
    samsara.
I, the yogi, have practiced in this way;
you, who seek liberation, please cultivate yourself in this way.[151]

His Holiness the Fourteenth Dalai Lama emphasizes the importance of a sound understanding of the four noble truths in order to gain the faith of conviction in the Three Jewels as a valid refuge. Reasons unmistakenly establishing such an understanding are expounded in Dharmakīrti's *Exposition of Valid Cognition*, the source of Khedrup Jé's presentation here. From His Holiness's *Supplication to Seventeen Nālandā Scholars*:

> By understanding the meaning of the two truths, the basic mode
>   of existence,
> one ascertains with valid cognizers exactly how one engages in
>   and turns away from samsara by means of the four truths,
> thereby eliciting a stable faith in the three refuges.
> Bless me to establish the root of the path of liberation!

Through a thorough ascertainment of the two truths, conventional and ultimate truth, one understands how the ignorance grasping at an unrealistically exaggerated sense of self gives rise to attachment, anger, other afflictive emotions, and karma, and how those produce and perpetuate an unbroken continuum of rebirths that are in the nature of suffering—namely, samsara. By correctly analyzing the two truths one generates the wisdom that both eliminates the ignorance that is the root of samsara and leads to the bliss of nirvana. On this basis, one gains confidence in the four noble truths, thereby developing a firm faith of conviction in the Buddha as a valid guide, his teachings, and the community of practitioners who uphold them from generation to generation.

After manifesting enlightenment beneath the Bodhi tree in Bodhgaya, the Buddha expounded the four noble truths several weeks later in Deer Park, Sarnath, in what is renowned as his *first turning of the wheel of Dharma*.[152] At that time, from his own experience, he taught that the truth of suffering is to be known, the truth of origin is to be abandoned, the truth of cessation is to be actualized, and the truth of the path is to be meditated on. Though this teaching is usually understood as taught primarily for disciples seeking mere liberation from samsara, it can be used to understand the essence of the paths of each of the three levels of beings. Beings of the small scope are motivated primarily by a wish to obtain a good future rebirth. Beings of the middling scope are primarily motivated to achieve liberation from samsara. Beings of the great scope strive for the full enlightenment of buddhahood in order to perfectly work for others' welfare. Tsongkhapa explains in *Arranging the Path of Valid Cognition*:

> There are two sufferings—that of taking birth[153] in bad migrations and that of taking birth in happy migrations. The causes—the origins of those—are twofold, that which engenders bad migrations and that which engenders happy migrations. Therefore cessation and path also each become twofold. Accordingly, the stages of the path of persons of small scope are brought about by realizing as incontrovertible the four: both cause and effect in relation to bad migrations, as well as the path that abandons those and the cessation that ceases them. By realizing as incontrovertible those in relation to happy migrations, the path of middling-scope beings are brought about; and by coming to realize the subject, the stages of the path of great-scope beings are brought about.[154]

Here "the subject"[155] refers to the Buddha, signifying he is incontrovertible with respect to the four noble truths. By way of the truth of origin he realized how sentient beings continuously endure true sufferings, and he realized how, by leading them along the various stages of the true paths, they too can come to actualize the truth of cessation. Khedrup Jé arranges his presentation of the four noble truths in the following way. ᠅

[Extensive] presentation
Third, [extensive] presentation has two [divisions]: [166]
  • a general presentation of the object, the four noble truths
  • a specific presentation of the aspect of selflessness

The first [a general presentation of the object, the four noble truths] has three [subdivisions]:
  • the nature of the four noble truths
  • definiteness of number
  • definiteness of order

᠅ Corresponding with Khedrup Jé's outlines above, this chapter will be explained under four headings:
  • The Nature of the Four Noble Truths
  • The Four Noble Truths Are Definite in Number
  • The Four Noble Truths Are Definite in Order
  • The Aspects of Selflessness

5.1 THE NATURE OF THE FOUR NOBLE TRUTHS

When Shakyamuni first taught these four truths, he explained each individual truth as being characterized by four aspects, or attributes. Taken alone, such attributes may seem abstract, so it is important to be aware of the bases of which they are attributes and the wrong conceptions about these bases that meditation on the attributes counteracts. Dharmakīrti explains in his *Exposition of Valid Cognition*:

> With respect to the four truths, one superimposes permanence, pleasure, "I," "mine," and so forth—

the sixteen wrong aspects—
then thoroughly craves [after these projected qualities].[156]

Each of the four truths has a different basis:
- For the truth of suffering, the basis is the contaminated appropriating aggregates.
- For the truth of the origin, the basis is karmic formation and craving, respectively, the second and ninth links of the twelve links of dependent origination.[157]
- For the truth of cessation, the basis is the permanent extinction of delusion and suffering by means of an antidote.
- For the truth of the path, the basis is the exalted wisdom directly realizing selflessness.

Each of the four noble truths is also characterized by four attributes. These bases, along with the attributes qualifying them, will be described in greater detail below. Misapprehension of these four bases, either grossly on the basis of studying wrong tenets or subtly through past habituation, is what causes beings to unwittingly create the causes of suffering and avoid or even destroy the causes of happiness, and thereby to cycle in samsara. The gaining of an intellectual understanding of these attributes acts as an immediate antidote to the gross manifestations of wrong views. Subsequent cultivation of such understanding gradually diminishes the force that these misapprehensions exert on a practitioner's mind, until through yogic direct perception one gains the direct antidote that can permanently uproot even the subtle habituation to wrong views and afflictions, thereby extinguishing the causes that would create further cyclic existence. This very yogic direct perception eventually overcomes all previously accumulated negative karma and afflictions, thereby freeing one from cyclic existence and achieving liberation. Khedrup Jé explains the nature of the four noble truths separately by giving illustrations of each of these truths and explaining the four aspects of each truth.

The Truth of Suffering

No beings wish to suffer, but most are unaware of what causes suffering, or of exactly what is and is not suffering. Thus the Buddha taught the truth of suffering first in order to stimulate a wish to be free from samsara and to practice the means for attaining temporal and ultimate happiness for oneself and others. The Buddha propounded this truth by means of several different presentations, such as the specific sufferings associated with each of the six realms of existence individually, and the sufferings experienced in all or most realms of samsara in general. However, in the context of explaining the truth of suffering, the three levels of suffering—the suffering of suffering, the suffering of change, and pervasive compounding suffering—explained in the *Descent into the Womb Sūtra*[158]—are central.

The first of these three—the suffering of suffering—refers to painful sensations, such as the uncomfortable experiences associated with sickness. The second—the suffering of change—refers to contaminated happiness, sensations that look outwardly pleasurable but by nature are subtler kinds of suffering. For example, if, lingering in a shady spot, one becomes cold and decides to warm up in the sun, this immediately feels agreeable. But soon one becomes too hot in the sun; what was experienced as pleasurable at first soon turns into the suffering of heat. The pleasurable sensation experienced when first standing in the sun was the previous cold sensation's diminishing, which one tends to mistakenly view as something inherently pleasurable. If it were inherently pleasurable, no matter how long and under what circumstances one engages in it, it should remain pleasurable. The same is true for pleasurable feelings arising through enjoying food, entertainment, sport, music, dance, and so forth. Conversely, unpleasant activities such as hitting oneself with a hammer, for instance, never appear to become anything resembling pleasurable. As Āryadeva points out in his *Four Hundred Stanzas*:

> Pleasure, when it increases,
> is seen to change into pain;

Pain, when it increases,
does not likewise change into pleasure.[159]

The first two types of suffering, just explained, are reasonably easy to
identify. The third, pervasive compounding suffering, is more difficult to
realize. It is a state of being under the power of karma and afflictions. It is
sometimes compared to the predicament of a person who must carry an
agonizingly heavy burden a very great distance. His discomfort during the
actual act of shouldering the load is described as the suffering of suffering,
his delight on taking a temporary reprieve, the suffering of change, and
the overall task of carrying such a burden is like the pervasive compounding suffering associated with bearing the contaminated appropriating
aggregates.[160] "Pervasive" indicates that this suffering exists in the continuums of beings in all realms of samsara from the lowest hell to the most
refined states of the formless realm. "Compounding" means that this type
of suffering is distinguished as that which exists in conjunction with the
potential to give rise to or produce future suffering by the power of karma
and afflictions. Karma and afflictions are explained with more detail in
appendix 3. Pervasive compounding suffering is equivalent to the second
attribute of the truth of suffering, appropriately called "suffering." One's
aggregates of body and mind[161] are pervasive compounding suffering, so
until one can stop the uncontrolled appropriation of further samsaric
aggregates—that is, rebirth in cyclic existence—no place or experience
can provide us with lasting respite. Khedrup Jé also mentions similar illustrations for the truth of suffering, like the entire impure environment and
beings dwelling therein. ⚐

First, [the nature of the four noble truths]. [167] If presented elaborately
with respect to the truth of suffering, there are many illustrations that
could be extensively explained by way of what is included in the entire
impure world of environment and beings. Here, I shall explicitly present
only the contaminated appropriating aggregates as the illustration of the
truth of suffering.

❖ The truth of suffering, from the bodies within which beings cycle in samsara to the environments and external worlds that samsaric beings inhabit, arises out of contaminated mental states. As Asaṅga explains in his *Compendium of Knowledge*:

> If one asks, "What is the truth of suffering?" it is to be known by way of sentient beings' birth, and also the abodes where they are born . . . all that constitutes the world of sentient beings, and all that constitutes the environment they inhabit, arises through karma and afflictions. All of these things that arise by the power of karma and afflictions are called "the truth of suffering."[162]

Contaminated appropriating aggregates are *contaminated* because they are the result of past afflictions and karmic actions. They are called *appropriating* because they become substantial causes for taking rebirth under the power of karma and craving. These two factors, in turn, play a principal role in shaping the various characteristics of one's body, mind, outlook, and even the environment one comes to experience. Khedrup Jé explains now the importance of knowing this aspect of the aggregates. ❖

These very contaminated appropriating aggregates are such that if one does not realize them as in the nature of suffering, there is no method to generate (1) the renunciation that desires to forsake cyclic existence or (2) a fully fledged mind that seeks liberation. From realizing them as in the nature of suffering, a desire to forsake cyclic existence naturally arises. Therefore, mainly from the point of view of yogic practice, holding [these aggregates] as the illustration of suffering, [Dharmakīrti's *Exposition of Valid Cognition*] said:

> Suffering is the aggregates that cycle in existence.[163]

❖ In the same text Dharmakīrti also explains:

> Because of being the basis for faults, and
> also because of being under the power of the cause, [the aggregates] are suffering.[164]

Until one abandons these contaminated aggregates—that is, stops relentlessly appropriating them in future lifetimes—one has no choice but to experience unending suffering. In order to actually abandon them, one first needs to develop a fully qualified wish to do so. Producing such a wish, likewise, depends on a profound understanding of the faults of samsara. In the Lamrim tradition this situation is often compared to the situation of a deluded prisoner: failing to see the various faults of either the prison in which he is held or his powerlessness therein, and instead becoming enamored with small pleasures like food or conversation, he will never develop the authentic desire to be free that is necessary to inspire the various endeavors associated with actualizing his freedom.[165] Likewise, only a realization of all four aspects of the truth of suffering, which counteracts the four misconceptions or superimpositions, will induce a genuine mind aspiring for liberation that underpins the actualization of the path to liberation as Khedrup Jé explains below. ❧

There are four aspects of truth of suffering that are to be meditated upon [respectively] as antidotes to the [four] superimpositions of the appropriating aggregates as pure, pleasurable, permanent, and self.

❧ The superimposition of the aggregates as *pure* refers to seeing them as unsullied and clean, despite the fact that they are born from contaminated causes. *Pleasurable* refers to viewing the contaminated happiness of the aggregates as a basis for pleasure when in fact they are the principal vessels for the sufferings of birth, aging, sickness, and death. *Permanent* refers to the view of the aggregates as not changing from moment to moment, or, more grossly, to the belief that one will not die for years. *Self* is the conception of a substantially existent self, in the sense of being self-sufficient, who is either substantially distinct from, or one with, the aggregates, whereas in reality the person is empty of such a self. Realizing the four aspects described below counteracts these misconceptions.

These four [aspects] are:
- [The aggregates are] impermanent, because of disintegrating in every moment.
- [The aggregates are] suffering, because of being under the other-power of karma and afflictive emotions, or because of being discordant with [the nature of the] noble beings.
- [The aggregates are] empty, because of being devoid of a self that is factually other than themselves.
- [The aggregates are] selfless, because their nature is devoid of self.

Impermanent gives the meaning of the momentary changing nature of the aggregates. This counteracts the misconception of permanence. *Suffering* refers to the pervasive compounding form of suffering. Khedrup Jé explains that realization of this aspect counteracts both the conception of the aggregates as pleasurable and that of purity.[166] *Empty*, in this context, means not having a substantially existent self in the sense of being a self-sufficient person that is independent of the aggregates. Realizing this counteracts the conception of a self-sufficient self.[167] This is considered easier to realize than the fourth aspect, *selfless*, since the object of refutation is to be merely eliminated on the basis of phenomena factually different from one's aggregates. The realization of *selfless* refutes the existence of a self-sufficient substantially existent person that exists in the same nature as the aggregates.[168] Such a self-sufficient person, though it doesn't actually exist, appears in relation to the aggregates in a manner akin to the way a lord presides over his many subjects or a pilot controls an airplane and all the people on board. The subtleties of how the aggregates are to be established as selfless are covered in section 5.4 below, The Aspects of Selflessness.

If one doesn't realize, by way of ascertaining through valid cognizers, all four of these aspects of the truth of suffering, a fully characterized mind aiming for liberation will not arise. [The reason for that] is like this: although by realizing [the aggregates] as suffering, a desire to be free from cyclic existence arises, but if one doesn't realize them as impermanent, since one won't realize the certainty that one will be separated from the aggregates, one will be unable to stop craving for the aggregates.

꙳ Khedrup Jé explains that although the realization of the second aspect, suffering, is the crux here, the realization of the impermanence of the aggregates, as well as the various objects of one's attachment, is also essential to understand their fickle and unreliable nature, and thereby quell one's craving for them. ꙳

If one doesn't realize [the aggregates] as selfless, craving for what is mine, like the sense powers and so forth, will continue to be naturally induced. So although it might seem as though by realizing [the aggregates] as impermanent and suffering a mind desiring to be free from the mere aggregates has arisen, that self-grasping [mind] will definitely induce a mind seeking [to obtain] certain kinds of contaminated objects that [one believes] will accomplish one's happiness.

꙳ Likewise, the fully qualified realization of the first noble truth must be accompanied by the mind realizing selflessness, the fourth aspect. Why? Because if one cannot block the arising of its counterpart, self-grasping, craving for those things deemed to establish one's happiness arises of its own accord, and thus creates karma that impels further samsaric suffering. Khedrup Jé's conclusion: ꙳

Therefore, although by realizing [the aggregates] as impermanent one knows that [one will] definitely be separated from the aggregates, and by realizing [them] as suffering one develops the desire to be free, in order to generate a fully qualified [mind] seeking liberation that has turned away from desire for any contaminated thing, it is necessary to know the [fourth] aspect of the truth of suffering, the very lack of an inherent self.

The Truth of the Origin

Having recognized the suffering nature of the aggregates, one will generate the wish to be free of them, and thus will search for their cause. Through the realization of this second noble truth, one recognizes that suffering does not arise randomly or through the action of a creator god; it is, in essence, one's own creation, the result of one's own actions since it arises from previously accumulated karma and afflictions. By the power of (mental) afflictions one intentionally engages in mental, verbal, and physical actions and thus creates mental, verbal, and physical actions or karma. The root cause for afflictions to arise is ignorance or a misconception of a self of persons that is substantially existent in the sense of being self-sufficient. From Dharmakīrti's *Exposition of Valid Cognition*:

> If there is self [grasping], one discerns another,
> grasping at the side of self and opposing that of others.
> From thorough association with these,
> all faults come to arise.[169]

Khedrup Jé too will explain below that the afflictive ignorance obscured with respect to the nature of self in the continua of samsaric beings is the most fundamental example of the true origin of suffering and the root of samsara. Based on the sense of a concrete *I* or *mine* one becomes attached to things seen as pleasant and develops strong aversion toward things seen as unpleasant. In this way, one accumulates various karmic actions, which in turn deposit imprints on the mindstream. Due to meeting with the necessary conditions at the time of death—principally the craving for existence that activates them—these imprints propel further rebirth under the power of karma and afflictive emotions, thereby continuing the samsaric cycle. This process can be understood in greater subtlety from other sources presenting the twelve links of dependent arising.[170]

[168] The root of cyclic existence, the conception of self, all [afflictive emotions], attachment and so forth—which arise under that [conception's] power—and even all karmas that are accumulated under the power of afflictive emotions, are called "the noble truth of the origin" because of [each individually] being both a contaminated thing and the cause of its own result, the truth of suffering.

Therefore, as for [Dharmakīrti's] saying [in his *Exposition of Valid Cognition*]:

> Although unknowing is the cause of [cyclic] existence,
> it is not expressed [here]; only craving is explained.
> Because [craving] propels the continuity,
> and because [craving] is the immediate [cause of karma], karma
>   also is not [expressed].[171]

Though ignorance is the cause of [cyclic] existence, on this occasion of indicating the aspects of strong production and condition, it is not directly expressed; only craving is directly indicated. "Because [craving] propels the continuity, and because [craving] is the immediate" indicates the reason that, although karma is also a cause of suffering, at that time it is not directly expressed; only craving is directly indicated.

❧ In the previous passage, having defined the truth of the origin in rather broad terms, Khedrup Jé comes to address the doubt: If all of the samsaric delusions are the truth of origin, why does Dharmakīrti emphasize the delusion of craving so heavily? The reasons are, as above, that this craving is the most direct cause for the accumulation of karma discussed here—if it is present, its energy drives the machine of samsara, and if it is hindered, so too is the process of accumulating the causes of suffering. As Khedrup Jé's *Ocean of Reasonings: An Extensive Explanation of [Dharmakīrti's] Commentary on Compendium of Valid Cognition* elaborates:

The principal direct cause of these suffering aggregates is this very craving. If there is craving, it nurtures karmic imprints and, their potency having become powerful, brings that very consciousness possessing [those] imprints to the brink of taking rebirth. It also effects the accumulation of new karmas. If there is no craving for the aggregates, although there is karma, it has no capacity to establish its result, the aggregates of [karmic] maturation, since without craving, even kingdoms impelled by karma forsake objects of enjoyment in the same way they do grass.[172]

Thus, since craving powers the process of rebirth in cyclic existence in such important ways, it is held as the basis upon which the truth of the origin is presented here, much in the same way as the contaminated appropriating aggregates took a central position in the explanation of the first noble truth above. But Khedrup Jé also quotes the commentary of Dharmakīrti that karma and afflictions are the causes of samsara in the following section. ❖

[This passage] does not indicate that ignorance and karma aren't expressed [at all] as the truth of origin, because in other sections [of *Exposition of Valid Cognition*], multiple parts of the text—"if self exists, other is known...,"[173] "for that reason, an unobstructed wish to be free,"[174] and so forth—say many times that afflictions and their accompanying karma are the cause of cyclic existence. Not realizing the meaning of this [above passage], those who maintain that "in *Exposition of Valid Cognition*, only craving [for objects of] attachment, craving for annihilation, and the craving for existence are indicated as the noble truth of the origin" are merely denigrating most causes of suffering.

❖ Generally speaking, that which is the truth of the origin is the truth of suffering. While there is a great deal of philosophical debate about whether some instances of the truth of suffering, such as one's body and various physical sensations of samsaric happiness and suffering, are indeed to be considered the truth of the origin, what is very clear is that a primary cause of one's future suffering is the delusion of craving, for reasons discussed above.[175]

As in the truth of suffering, the truth of the origin has also four aspects that counteract four misconceptions or superimpositions. Khedrup Jé first mentions the four superimpositions, after which he explains the four aspects. ᛭

In order to counteract the four superimpositions of:
- holding suffering as without cause
- holding there being only one cause
- holding it as produced by the transformations of the sound-Brahma
- holding it as produced by the mind of [a god such as] Ishvara and so forth having first sent [an intention]

᛭ The view that "suffering as without a cause" was historically attributed to the followers of the Lokāyata (*rgyang 'phen pa*) from among the various schools of ancient Indian philosophical thought. The Buddhist commentaries composed in India often attribute to some Lokāyatas the view that the laws of karma and effect do not function, and the happiness and suffering beings experience arise not at all as a result of previous virtue or non-virtue but simply evolve in a natural, or perhaps random, fashion. The misconception of "there being only one cause" of suffering comes from the Vaiśheṣhika school of ancient India, which views that it arises from only one fundamental cause. According to the Buddhist texts, this school ascribes a view of an inherent or permanent sense of time out of which phenomena come to be born.[176] The view "holding it as produced by the transformations of the sound-Brahma" was held by the followers of Brahma, who repudiated the idea that suffering arises from karma and delusion, and reputedly asserted that the basis of production of the world's various environments and the beings therein was an essential sound-Brahma— the syllable OM—which was held as a permanent, unitary, physically and temporally partless entity that, due to the ignorance of beings, arises as the various inner and outer objects of the world.[177] The final misconception "holding it as produced by the mind of [a god such as] Ishvara and so forth having first sent [an intention]" assents to the view that an omnipotent god or quasi-omnipotent god establishes the moment-to-moment suffering and happiness of beings. This view was attributed historically to the followers of Ishvara, also known as Shiva. ᛤ

Four aspects of the noble truth of the origin are indicated:
- because of producing the entity of suffering, [the aspect of] cause
- because of being the source of all substantial kinds of suffering, [the aspect of] origin
- because of forcefully producing suffering, [the aspect of] strong production
- because of successively producing suffering many times, the aspect of condition

ᛤ The four aspects are: cause, origin, strong production, and (supporting) condition. *Cause* indicates that sufferings in general and especially the main illustration of the truth of suffering, the contaminated appropriating aggregates, need causes in order to come into being; there are no results without appropriate causes. Gyaltsab Jé explains in *A Guide on the Path of Valid Cognition* that they do not arise causelessly, since if they did they would not rely on other factors, and thus at the time when they are asserted to exist, they would cease to do so, and at the time they are asserted to not exist, they would come to exist. *Origin* indicates that this cause is not a single, independent cause, but rather a continuous network of causes that give rise again and again not only to the suffering aggregates but also to further causes, perpetuating the cycle. In *A Guide on the Path of Valid Cognition*, Gyaltsab Jé mentions that the meaning of this aspect is "giving rise to again and again in accordance with the cause, because from a single, partless [cause] there is no potential to produce such a result."[178] *Strong production* indicates that karma and afflictions like craving are strong enough in and of themselves to give rise to the suffering beings undergo. They do not require help from outside sources like a deity or omnipotent god. *Condition* indicates that craving, especially at the time of death, acts as the condition that helps the substantial cause, karmic seeds created through past intentional actions, to ripen into a future rebirth characterized by samsaric suffering. This *condition* gives rise to countless instances of suffering within the body of the future rebirth and impels the uninterrupted continuum of the aggregates. Likewise, this cause of suffering is influenced by various supporting conditions and only manifests as a result when these conditions are present, much as a seed only sprouts when sunshine, fertilization, and moisture are present.

The Truth of Cessation

Having recognized the origin of suffering, one will naturally wish to be free of that origin. If it were impossible to reduce and eventually win total freedom from the fundamental causes of suffering, then there would be no reason to engage in any kind of spiritual practice. For that reason, it is essential to train in the reasons analyzing the existence of such a cessation, and to establish its existence. His Holiness the Dalai Lama, in *Illuminating the Path to Enlightenment*, describes three premises that should be known in order to develop certainty about the possibility of cessation:

> You should develop the recognition of the possibility of a true cessation of suffering on the basis of these three facts:
> - The fundamental nature of consciousness is luminous and pure.
> - Afflictions can be purified and separated from the essential nature of mind.
> - There are powerful antidotes that can be applied to counter the defilements and afflictions.[179]

The truth of cessation is an analytical cessation or everlasting separation from a portion of or all afflictions induced by means of its corresponding antidote. Unlike the other three truths, which are functioning things, being impermanent, this truth is a permanent phenomenon. This is because it is a non-affirming negation,[180] because it is a mere absence of afflictions in the mind of somebody who has abandoned them. All non-affirming negations are permanent. The truth of cessation is achieved by meditating on the truth of the path and is therefore called "a result of the fourth truth." However, all results are impermanent, so, being permanent, it is not actually produced by the path in the way a sprout is produced by a seed. Rather, meditation on the truth of the path ceases the continuity of afflictions, thereby leaving this mere absence, stable and unchanging, in their place. It is similar to when we turn on a light in a room. The illumination of the room brings about a cessation of darkness in the room that did not exist before. But this absence of darkness is not a momentarily changing thing and does not function to produce effects. Thus, in Buddhist practice, freedom from samsara itself is not a place to go, an object to possess, or even a mental state to achieve, but the very absence of suffering mental states. Although the truth of cessation itself has no qualities of bliss and mental clarity as such, the person who attains it will be endowed with such qualities.

The truth of cessation is characterized by four attributes: cessation, peace, sublimity, and definite emergence. Realization of these opposes the four misconceptions Khedrup Jé explains below. ⸙

[168] The noble truth of cessation is: a separation that has abandoned any sort of seed of an object of abandonment through the noble truth of the path. As antidotes to the four superimpositions with respect to the truth of cessation [the four aspects are given below after the following classification of the four misconceptions]:

- holding that liberation is utterly non-existent
- holding some particular contaminated phenomena that haven't abandoned the afflictive emotions as liberation
- holding that there exists a liberation superior to the cessation of suffering

- holding that, while a temporary liberation exists, everlasting liberation is non-existent

⁊ *Holding that liberation is utterly non-existent* refers to the view that there is simply no such thing as liberation. It is thought to have been held predominantly by the Lokāyata school in ancient India. *Holding some particular contaminated phenomena that haven't abandoned the afflictive emotions as liberation* is a misconception that is exemplified by certain followers of the historical Nirgrantha, or Jain, school, which teaches that one goes beyond samsara and proceeds to liberation when one, having performed many practices of austerity to exhaust one's karma, ascends to a heavenly realm described as being shaped like an upward-pointing white umbrella located above the various ordinary worlds.[181] *Holding that there exists a liberation superior to the cessation of suffering* is a view that historically is attributed to the Sāṃkhya school, which involves holding that there is something over and above the cessation of suffering as described in the Buddhist texts. This school holds that by understanding the activity of a twenty-five-fold enumeration encapsulating all phenomena, one is liberated from samsara.[182] *Holding that, while a temporary liberation exists, everlasting liberation is non-existent* is a view of the Mīmāṃsaka sect of ancient India. According to Jamyang Shepa's *Great Exposition of Tenets*, this school holds that although the high status of beings such as Brahma are liberation, in the sense of being temporarily free of the sufferings of bad migrations and so forth, there exists no liberation that is above such a state. This school says that defilements abide in the nature of the consciousness of the person and can thus never be extricated from the mental continuum.[183] ⁊

The four aspects of the truth of cessation to be relied upon are:
- Because it has abandoned suffering, it is cessation.
- Because it has abandoned afflictive emotions, it is peace.
- Because there exists no other superior to it, it is sublime.
- Because once having achieved it, it is irreversible, it is definite emergence.

⁊ This first aspect of the truth of cessation, *cessation*, shows that the abandonment of the first noble truth, the truth of suffering, exists. Realizing this dispels the Lokāyata assertion that the cessation of suffering is nonexistent. The second aspect, *peace*, shows the abandonment of afflictions that are the truth of the origin. Realizing this aspect eliminates the Nirgrantha view that certain contaminated phenomena like their heavenly realm are actual liberation. A thorough understanding of *sublime* dispels grasping at certain afflictive phenomena as more superior than the cessations described by the Buddha. This aspect counteracts the superimposition of "holding that there exists a liberation superior to the cessation of suffering." The final aspect, *definite emergence*, emphasizes that the cessations of suffering are irreversible; once attained it is everlasting, which counteracts the Mīmāṃsaka sect's view.

The Truth of the Path

By analyzing the previous truth, one gains the understanding that cessation is possible and thus that there must exist antidotes to the afflictions. The truth of the path shows those antidotes, foremost among which is the yogic direct perception realizing selflessness, since it is the actual antidote to the mistaken conception that is the root cause of samsaric suffering. There are two categories of the truth of the path explicitly presented here: uninterrupted paths and paths of release. Uninterrupted paths are meditative equipoises that act as direct antidotes to the seeds of various levels of afflictions in a person's continuum. Paths of release are meditative states induced by the respective uninterrupted paths immediately preceding them in the same continuum. The paths of release are achieved at the same time as the objects of abandonment of the uninterrupted path are abandoned and the cessation of those objects actualized. Meditation on pairs of uninterrupted paths and paths of release is akin to a two-step process of evicting a thief from one's house. First, one physically drives him outside. Second, one locks the door tightly behind him. First, the uninterrupted path actually abandons its objects of abandonment. Second, the path of release generates stability in the state of having abandoned those objects of abandonment. This process of abandoning afflictions on the uninterrupted paths and paths of release, together with an explanation of the various aspects of the paths to liberation and enlightenment, is given in appendix 5. ⚡

[169] The truth of the path is: all exalted wisdoms of superior beings included in [either] (1) uninterrupted paths, the antidotes that directly abandon the seeds of the stains that are their corresponding objects of abandonment, and (2) paths of release, which have control over [in the sense of having irreversibly attained] the abandonments of those [objects of abandonment abandoned by uninterrupted paths].

⚡ In contemplating this fourth truth, one can use reasoning to establish that the wisdom realizing selflessness, being the ultimate antidote to the afflictions, can be enhanced so that it comes to act as an antidote to an individual's samsara in its totality. This wisdom has a stable basis both because it realizes truth as opposed to grasping as true something that is false, and because the innate pure clarity of awareness exists through all times. In addition, it is the nature of mental phenomena that through extended habituation they eventually will arise spontaneously and effortlessly, without renewed exertion. Tsongkhapa presents this reasoning in *Purifying Forgetfulness of Valid Cognition*:

> The subject, the wisdom realizing selflessness: if it is not separated from the limbs of meditation, it will eventually become clear [a direct realization] regarding the object of meditation, because the basis is stable, and it is a phenomenon of the mental continuum that, having become habituated to it, will not require further effort [to arise]; for example, attachment.[184]

"Stable basis" means that this wisdom has as its basis the mind of clear light. It is "stable" because it has no beginning and end. An example of how through habituation thoughts eventually become spontaneous is attachment. Attachment, through improper mental engagement, exaggerates the qualities of an object of attachment. Even though at times that object may not appear attractive, over time it appears more desirable, until merely seeing it will cause strong attachment to arise spontaneously. Attachment, being rooted in improper mental engagement, is not endowed with a stable basis. No matter how strong or habitual it becomes, attachment cannot fully overcome the pure nature of the mind because it is rooted in a misapprehension that is contrary to this very nature. Attachment overestimates its object's ability to give satisfaction and is blind to the flaws of its object. Because it is thereby not in accordance with reality, it gives rise to further disturbing mental states. On the other hand, the wisdom realizing selflessness is in accord with ultimate reality, can therefore become fully integrated, and can overcome all discordant mental states. This also explains the three points of the quote by His Holiness the Dalai Lama from *Illuminating the Path to Enlightenment* given above.

Dharmakīrti's *Exposition of Valid Cognition* also says:

> The nature of the mind is clear light because
> all stains are adventitious.[185]

In his commentary, *Clarifying the Path of Liberation,* Gyaltsab Darma Rinchen explains the meaning of these lines:

> The nature of the mind is clear light, because the darkness
> of self-grasping and so forth, however much it obscures that
> nature, cannot engage the nature of the mind, and because the
> mind is of the nature of disintegration and so forth.

And:

> The subject, all stains [such as] attachment and so forth, [they]
> are adventitious because they wrongly engage the mode of abid-
> ance of the mind.[186]

To elaborate slightly, ignorance misapprehending a concrete self of persons is a wrong consciousness. A correct consciousness, like the yogic direct perception realizing the non-existence or emptiness of such a concrete self, acts as the antidote to this wrong consciousness. Two consciousnesses observing the same object, the conventional mere person, but apprehending it in a contrary manner, one seeing the self as concrete and the other as lacking this concreteness, cannot abide simultaneously. Thus by habituation a correct consciousness of the truth of the path can eliminate ignorance.

The truth of the path is characterized by four attributes: path, knowledge, achievement, and deliverance. This truth is named after the first attribute "path," being the actual meaning of this truth. As Khedrup Jé explains below, there are four superimpositions that the realization of these four attributes serves to eliminate. ⁘

As antidotes to the four erroneous apprehensions [the four aspects are given below after the following classification of the four misconceptions]:
- holding the path to liberation as utterly non-existent
- holding that the wisdom realizing selflessness is not a path to liberation
- holding it [the wisdom realizing selflessness] as wrongly engaging the mode of existence of [its] object
- holding that it [the wisdom realizing selflessness] is not capable of permanently extinguishing suffering

⁘ The view of *holding the path to liberation as utterly non-existent* is historically attributed to the Lokāyata school in ancient India, who, due to not seeing liberation with direct perception, forthrightly rejected its existence along with the path thereto. *Holding that the wisdom realizing selflessness is not a path to liberation* and *holding it [the wisdom realizing selflessness] as wrongly engaging the mode of existence of [its] object* are prevalent views in the tenet systems of many non-Buddhist schools, particularly the Sāṃkhya and Nyāya sects, where a concrete self of persons was forcefully propounded. Holding these views precludes the arising of a wisdom realizing selflessness, let alone one that represents a path to liberation. *Holding that it [the wisdom realizing selflessness] is not capable of permanently extinguishing suffering* is a view accredited to the Mīmāṃsaka school, which holds the view that there is no meditative or religious practice above and beyond those that impel a temporary freedom from the sufferings of the bad migrations. ⸙

The four aspects of the truth of the path that are to be meditated upon are:
- Because of being a means of progressing [toward liberation], it is a path.
- Because of being a means of acting as an antidote to afflictions, it is [correct] knowledge.
- Because of being a means of achieving a non-mistaken [view of the nature of] the mind, it is achievement.
- Because of being a means of going, without any doubt, to the everlasting abode [of liberation], it is deliverance.

"The everlasting abode" means an irreversible abode. The path of no more learning is the result of the truth of the path, but it is not an actual truth of the path. If it were [a truth of the path], it would have to be a path and, in that case, it would have to be a means of progressing. In that case, it would [absurdly] follow that there is an object of progression beyond even the Buddha ground. The path of accumulation and the path of preparation are not the truth of the path because an uninterrupted path [that is] a path of accumulation or preparation, and that serves as the actual antidote to seeds of objects of abandonment, is impossible. Therefore the real truth of the path is only the path of seeing and the path of meditation.

⸙ Here, Khedrup Jé distinguishes between a truth of the path and an actual or real truth of the path. He says that because the path of no-more-learning is the result of the truth of the path, and more specifically of the paths of seeing and meditation, then it is not an *actual* truth of the path. However, he does not say it is not a truth of the path. Further, in Khedrup Jé's commentary, *Illumination of the Difficult Points*, he posits all uncontaminated paths as examples of the truth of the path and argues that the path of no-more-learning is a truth of the path because, if it were not, then it would absurdly follow that it is not the Dharma Jewel. To quote him: "Fourth, the truth of the path, an example of this is all uncontaminated exalted wisdoms; together with their associated paths there are five paths. If the path of no more learning is not a truth of the path, then because it is not a truth of cessation it would not be the Dharma Jewel..."[187] Therefore we must conclude that although he states the path of no-more-learning is not an actual truth of the path, he accepts that it is a truth of the path or a mere truth of the path.

The question then arises whether Khedrup Jé makes a similar distinction between path and actual path, and whether he posits the path of no-more-learning as a path. In *Clearing Mental Darkness* Khedrup Jé argues that the path of no-more-learning is not an actual path because if it were, then it would absurdly follow that it would have to be a path, and in that case it would be a means of progressing to a higher state. This would entail that there is a state higher than that of no-more-learner and thereby that a no-more-learner would absurdly have more to learn. However, in his commentary, *Illumination of the Difficult Points*, he says that there are five paths, from the path of accumulation to the path of no-more-learning. Other scholars, like Jetsun Chökyi Gyaltsen, accept that the path of no-more-learning is a path. One way to resolve this apparent contradiction in Khedrup Jé's statements is to say that above where he states the path of no-more-learning is not a path he means merely that it does not fulfil the etymology of the first aspect of the truth of the path. Another way to resolve the contradiction is to say that Khedrup Jé makes a distinction between paths and actual paths or real paths in the sense that *actual paths* are paths in the continuums of ārya beings that produce their resultant paths of no more learning, which arise simultaneously with liberation from samsara. When the path of no-more-learning is achieved, the complete cessation of afflictions together with their causes is achieved, and thus there is no need for any further *actual paths* to eliminate afflictions. Thereby, the path of no-more-learning is a path but not an actual path, just as it is a truth of the path but not an actual truth of the path.

The path of no-more-learning is a consciousness; therefore, it is impermanent and is a product of causes. For a person who has generated a path of no-more-learning in their mental continuum, all the instances of the truth of the path that they previously generated in their continuum are causes that contributed to producing that path of no-more-learning. Conversely, although the truth of cessation is said to be a result of the truth of the path, because it is not impermanent, it is not something produced from causes and so is not an actual result. In the section below Khedrup Jé proves in a similar way that the truth of cessation is a permanent phenomenon. ⚑

Someone says, "The definition of analytical cessation is that which is (1) a cessation and (2) an aspect of having abandoned an object of abandonment by a mind observing thusness."[188] Then again [they are] seen to accept that whatever is a truth of cessation is necessarily a compounded phenomenon. [We reply], "Well then, the subject, an aspect of having abandoned, by the path of seeing, the seeds of the objects of abandonment of the path of seeing: it follows that it is an analytical cessation because it is (1) a cessation and (2) an aspect of having abandoned an object of abandonment by a mind observing thusness. [170] If you accept this, then it follows that it is a compounded phenomenon because you accepted that [it is an analytical cessation]. You accepted the sign and the pervasion. If you accept, it absurdly follows that it is not a non-affirming negation." Therefore, as for those who say, "Because whatever is an analytical cessation is necessarily a non-affirming negation, whatever is an analytical cessation is necessarily a compounded phenomenon": they have merely demonstrated that they are not very learned.

As for the proponents of Buddhist tenets of the Ārya Land [i.e., India], they say: "there are no followers of the Vaibhāṣika who assert that the truth of cessation is not substantially established. Even they [followers of Vaibhāṣika] assert [analytical cessation] as a substantially established permanent [phenomenon]; they do not assert [it] as a substantially established impermanent [phenomenon]. As for followers of Sautrāntika: they assert that uncompounded space is, like the son of a barren woman [i.e., like a non-existing phenomenon and thus], not substantially established; analytical cessation and non-analytical cessation are also, similarly to that, not substantially established" because, as it is said:

> Space is similar to the son of a barren woman.
> Cessations are also like space.
> It is not like compositional factors and matter,
> like following the three times
> or non-obstructed form.

This is the thought of Sautrāntika followers.[189] Because you also have accepted this text as literal, your acceptance is also [internally] directly contradictory. As for saying that the truth of cessation is the effect of the [the truth of the] path: bear in mind that one must actualize cessation by depending on the path, and that one cannot actualize [cessation] without depending on the path. [The truths of the path and cessation] are not, like fire and smoke, causes and results that are the new arisings of previously non-existent natures. Because it is said that there is no permanent, self-arisen valid cognizer, nobody accepts the truth of cessation as a valid cognizer; there is no fault.

☙5.2 THE FOUR NOBLE TRUTHS ARE DEFINITE IN NUMBER

In the sūtras, the Buddha classified objects into two categories: *the side of thorough affliction* and *the side of thorough purification*. These two categories do not exhaustively encompass all phenomena but relate mainly to what a practitioner must abandon and adopt. Khedrup Jé explains the four noble truths from this point of view. ☙

[170] The second, definiteness in number.

If [you] ask, "Why are the four noble truths definite in number?" it is because (1) the side of thorough affliction is definite as two objects of

abandonment, cause and effect, and all phenomena of purification are definite as two objects to be adopted, cause and effect; and (2) all bases that
are [either] the objects to be adopted or discarded are definite in two, the
[sides of] thorough affliction and purification.

☙5.3 THE FOUR NOBLE TRUTHS ARE DEFINITE IN ORDER

From the point of view of their order of arising, causes always arise before
their effects, thus, the truth of the origin arises first, followed by the truth
of suffering. Likewise, the truth of the path comes first, followed by the
truth of cessation. However, the Buddha taught these two pairs of cause
and effect in reverse order, in accordance with how a practitioner trains in
understanding them. An analogy is a person with an illness. Although the
causes of the sickness arise first, the sick person first notices the illness itself
and then tries to find the causes of the sickness so that they can be eradi-
cated. Although she must take medicine to return to a state of health, she
must first ascertain the possibility of a return to health before she consents
to undergo a course of treatment. As Maitreya describes in the *Sublime
Continuum*:

> The illness is to be known, and its cause is to be abandoned;
> health is to be attained, and medicine is to be relied upon.
> Suffering, [its] cause, its cessation, and likewise the path
> are to be known, abandoned, reached, and relied upon.[190]

Khedrup Jé explains this in the following way. ☙

[170] As for the mode of definiteness of order: many modes of ascertaining order occur in the textual systems—order in terms of cause and effect,
order of difficulty and ease of ascertainment, order of explanation, order
of realization, order of inferiority and superiority or superiority and inferiority, order of the time of generation, and so on. Of these, [the four noble

truths] are taught here in accordance with the order of generation of the
object possessors clearly realizing [them].

⁖ To conclude his presentation of the four noble truths, Khedrup Jé gives a
brilliant step-by-step description of how to foster a mind yearning for freedom from samsara based on flawless and deeply compelling reasoning. ⁖

[171] It is as follows: In order to generate a mind seeking liberation, first
one must realize that cyclic existence is in the nature of suffering. Having
realized that, a mind wishing to be free from this will arise. When this
mind arises, before [engaging in action] one investigates and sees that an
effect can't be abandoned without abandoning its cause; and one analyzes
whether there is a cause of suffering or not. That suffering has a cause is
established by the reason that it is produced occasionally.[191] Having determined this, that cause is limited to being either permanent or impermanent; one analyzes which [of those two] it is by the reasons [given in
Dharmakīrti's *Exposition of Valid Cognition*]:

> Why? If the cause abided like that [permanently],
> the ceasing of the effect would not be seen,[192]

and so forth. By seeing the non-arising of the forward and reverse [perva-
sions] for a cause that is [incorrectly] permanent and so forth, one thereby
ascertains that the cause is impermanent.

Having searched, [the following question is asked]: "Furthermore,
what is that cause of suffering that is impermanent?" One sees that (1)
from grasping at the self of a person, craving that is attachment to the self
directly arises; (2) from that arises craving for happiness for oneself; (3)
from that arises craving for "mine," power and so forth, things that achieve
one's happiness, because one sees that the "I" can't achieve happiness by its
own power without depending on [things] other [than itself]; (4) then,
like a slave to those things that are "mine," power and so forth, achievers

of "my happiness," one accumulates karma of the three doors [physical, verbal, and mental] in order to achieve happiness; (5) for the purpose of happiness in this life, one accumulates non-meritorious karma, killing and so forth, and from that one attains aggregates of bad migrations; (6) out of attachment to the happiness of the attributes of the next life, one accumulates meritorious karma, and on that basis attains the aggregates of a good migration, a human or a god, in the desire realm; and (7) out of attachment to the happiness [or "bliss"] of meditative stabilization, one accumulates immovable karma, and on that basis achieves aggregates in the two higher realms.

That being the case, through the reasoning, [stated in Dharmakīrti's *Exposition of Valid Cognition*]:

Whoever sees the self, for that one,[193]

there comes the realization that the [truth of] origin, which is of the nature of karma and afflictions, is the cause of this [truth of] suffering, the appropriating aggregates. Therefore suffering is taught first and the origin is taught later. Also, when the desire to abandon the origin [of suffering] has arisen, one will analyze whether or not self-grasping, which is the root of all karma and afflictions, can be abandoned or not. [172] Having analyzed in this way, through the reasoning that [the self of persons] is not established as a nature [that is] either the same or different from the aggregates, and seeing the harm [logical reasoning does to] the existence of a self [of persons], one will realize that self-grasping can be abandoned. Having realized that, one realizes that one can be free from its [i.e., the origin's] effect, suffering. Then one will realize that one can actualize the cessation that has abandoned suffering. Therefore the truth of cessation is taught third. When one desires to actualize the truth of cessation, by seeing that one can't actualize that without making effort on the path, which is its [cessation's] cause, the desire to practice the path arises fourth. Thus the truth of the path is taught last.

⚡5.4 THE ASPECTS OF SELFLESSNESS

Above, Khedrup Jé established that the ignorance misapprehending a self of persons is the root cause of all suffering, and that the wisdom realizing selflessness is the antidote to this misapprehension. In order to understand the nature of these two opposing consciousnesses, it is essential to know how to generate the latter in one's own mind and gradually abandon the former. Khedrup Jé begins by identifying the kind of self that ignorance mistakenly grasps at as existing, and the reasons proving that no such self exists. Then he describes how to meditate on the wisdom realizing that this false self does not exist. He concludes by showing how meditation on this wisdom progresses in stages. Gradually ignorance and even the potential for such ignorance to arise again in the future are utterly eliminated. ⚡

[172] The second [part], settling in particular the aspect of selflessness, has four [parts]:
  • Identifying the two selves [of persons and phenomena] that are the objects of negation
  • Explaining the reasons that negate those [two selves of persons and phenomena]
  • The method of how to meditate on selflessness
  • The method of abandoning self-grasping through meditation [on that]

⚡Identifying the Selves of Persons and Phenomena

In the next section Khedrup Jé not only explains the difference between the apprehensions of the reified selves of persons and phenomena, but also between the realizations of selflessness of persons and selflessness of phenomena. It is important to know which self of the person is to be refuted. A self that appears to be self-sufficient, in the sense of being characteristically discordant with the aggregates, is the object of refutation here. To prevent people from falling into the extreme of nihilism, thinking that, by refuting the wrong self, nothing exists at all, he also explains how a conventional person that is imputed on the aggregates exists and the faults of negating this mere person. This presentation is made according to the Sautrāntika. For this school selflessness of person is the most profound object for meditation; they do not accept a selflessness of phenomena. The presentation of selflessness of phenomena given here is according to the Chittamātra. Proponents of Chittamātra assert that the apprehended and apprehender existing as substantially different is the self of phenomena, and the very negation of that is the selflessness of phenomena. This is asserted because they accept that the mind, the apprehender that knows its object, and the object that is apprehended are empty of being substantially different because they arise simultaneously by the power of a single imprint, as already elaborately explained above in the sections on the three conditions according to Chittamātra. ⸙

Identifying the two selves that are the objects of negation

First [identifying the two selves that are the objects of negation]: By dividing the self that is the object of negation into two, the selves of persons and of phenomena, the selflessness that is the negation of that also comes to be two, the selflessness of persons and the selflessness of phenomena.

If asked, "Among those, what is the person? What is the self of persons?": The mind, which has been with sentient beings from beginningless [time], observes the object of observation, "I." As an aspect, it does not merely impute a name on either the collection or the continuity [of the aggregates], but rather apprehends [that "I"] to be a substantial existent, in the sense of being self-sufficient, in the sense of being characteristically discordant with the aggregates. Because this mind observes the person and apprehends it as a self, it is called "apprehending a self of persons." Because it views the person, who is imputed in dependence upon the aggregates whose condition is transient and collective [rather than singular], as characteristically discordant with the transitory and so forth, it is called "the view of the transitory collection." Because it exists beginninglessly together with one's continuum, it is called "innate." The mere "I" that is the object of observation of this awareness is called the "person," and to it one also applies the label "being." It is also the basis of karmic cause and result. Therefore if the person, the being, the sentient being, and so forth did not exist, it would also [absurdly] follow that the accumulator of karma, the experiencer of fruition and so forth, would not exist.

[173] Because the object of the mode of apprehension of this aware-ness, the very person who is substantially existent in the sense of being self-sufficient and characteristically discordant with the aggregates, is the self of persons that valid cognizers negate, this object of the mode of apprehension does not exist, even conventionally. The very aspect that is a mere negation of that object is called "the selflessness of the person." Therefore, as for the object of observation of the innate view of the tran-sitory, it is the person, not the self of the person. As for the object of the mode of apprehension, it is the self of the person, not the person. If it was not like that—if there was no difference between the person and the self of the person—either the person would also come not to be established conventionally, in which case there would be no basis of karmic result, no accumulator of action, and no experiencer of fruition, or alternately, the self of the person would also come to be an established base [i.e., an existing phenomenon].

If [someone] says, "What is the fault if the self of persons is established conventionally? The negation of the self of persons doesn't negate conven-tional [existence]; it negates ultimate establishment. Therefore it negates conventionally the self of persons that is permanent, unitary, and indepen-dent; it doesn't negate the mere self of persons."

In that case, if [we respond], "The self of phenomena is established conventionally, and moreover, it is the factor of difference of the three— apprehended, apprehender, and knowing—of one mind. Because [reason] negates that [aspect of difference] being ultimately established, the mere self of phenomena is an established base. The self of phenomena that is substantially different from the three—apprehender, apprehended, and [self-] knowing [aspect of the apprehender]—of a single mind is negated even conventionally," what will you say?

If [you] accept that the self of phenomena is also an established base:

accepting that in our own system the self of persons and the self of phenomena are both definitely existent does not even have the mere trace of a Buddhist [tenet]. Furthermore, if the self [of persons] were established, the consequence that reason could not negate the self [of persons], the consequence of the mind realizing selflessness being a wrong consciousness, and the consequence that an antidote could not abandon self-grasping would follow.

If [somebody] replies, "We don't accept the establishment of the self of phenomena, but the self of persons is dissimilar: the three—apprehended, apprehender, and knowing—being substantially different is the meaning of 'self of phenomena' and 'mere difference' is not the meaning of *self of phenomena*."

[To this we reply], "The person who is substantially existent in the sense of being self-sufficient and who is characteristically discordant with the aggregates is the meaning of *self of persons*; 'the mere I' is not the meaning of 'self of persons.'" So [the description of self of phenomena and self of persons] is entirely similar. [174] Furthermore, if there were no difference between the mere person and the self of persons, then since mere phenomena and the self of phenomena would also be similar in having no difference, it would [absurdly] follow that whatever is an established base is pervaded by being the self of phenomena.

❧ Below Khedrup Jé makes it clear that the ignorance grasping at a reified self of the person, which falsely appears to be self-sufficient in the sense of being characteristically discordant with the aggregates, has the same object of observation as the yogic direct perception of wisdom realizing selflessness. The object of observation, the mere person, is the same for both these types of consciousness, but the two different ways they apprehend it are diametrically opposed. Ignorance grasping at a self of persons apprehends the mere person to have a self-sufficient self that is not merely imputed on the collection of or the continuum of the person's body and mind and is fundamentally different in character from the aggregates. An illustration is often made by Buddhist teachers that this self-sufficient self seems like it controls the aggregates as a king controls his entourage. The wisdom realizing selflessness of persons apprehends the mere person as being totally devoid of that very exaggerated self-sufficient self. In this way the wisdom of yogic direct perception becomes the antidote to ignorance. ⸙

Furthermore, the antidote, the wisdom realizing selflessness, and its corresponding object of abandonment, self-grasping, should be such that they observe a single object of observation but engage it in a contradictory manner. If there were no difference between the person and the self of the person, it would [absurdly] follow that the wisdom realizing the selflessness of persons would observe the self of persons like the grasping at the self of persons does. Therefore both the object of abandonment [self-grasping] and the antidote [the wisdom realizing selflessness] observe the object of observation, the mere person. As an aspect, the object of abandonment observes the self [of persons] while the antidote observes the selflessness [of persons]. Therefore this difference between the person and self of persons is similarly [presented as the difference] between phenomena and the selflessness of phenomena.

⸙ In the following section Khedrup Jé briefly touches on the presentation of the three turnings of the wheel, the three ways the Buddha taught the Dharma. According to the Chittamātra system, based on Buddha's own presentation in *Unraveling the Intention Sūtra*, the Buddha's three most important turnings of the wheel, which on the surface appear contradictory, were progressive levels of skillful means intended to guide disciples at different stages of development. During the first turning, beginning with the *Sūtra of Turning the Wheel of Dharma* delivered near Varanasi shortly after his enlightenment, the Buddha taught only the selflessness of persons according to the Sautrāntika view. In the second turning he explained selflessness according to the Madhyamaka view by teaching the *Perfection of Wisdom Sūtras* on Vultures Peak in Rajgir. In the third turning of the wheel he clarified the meaning of the second wheel for trainees who could not penetrate its profound intended meaning[194] in *Unraveling the Intention Sūtra*, taught in Vaishali. In this way the Buddha taught differently to various disciples, depending on and in accordance with their outlook, intelligence, and level of development. Based on these teachings, the four schools of Buddhist philosophy developed and different views regarding selflessness came about. Appendix 4 gives an overview of these differences. ⸙

However, as for the nature of the self of phenomena, generally, there are many ways to posit it based on the diversity of tenets. Here, in accordance with the above explanation, because it presents the paths for each of the three classes of trainees [śhrāvakas, pratyekabuddhas, and bodhisattvas], there are two presentations. One presentation, following the [Buddha's] first teachings, by way of presenting the path of śhrāvakas, accepts [the existence of] external objects in accordance with the followers of Sautrāntika. In accordance with the [Buddha's] last teachings, the [Buddha's] second teachings are determined to be interpretive, and, by way of teaching the Mahāyāna path, external objects are refuted in accordance with the Vijñānavāda. During the first sermon, apart from the mere selflessness of persons, since [the intended trainees] did not accept the selflessness of phenomena, it was not necessary to identify the self of phenomena. During the [teaching addressed to] Vijñānavāda, a single mind's factor of the three—apprehended, apprehender, and [self-]knowing [aspect of the apprehender]—existing as substantially different was [identified as] the self of phenomena; the very negation of that was [identified as] the selflessness of phenomena. These subjects are a major basis of analysis for scholars and are the main topic of [many] texts. If one desires to attain liberation and enlightenment, there is no method if one does not know them, and once known they are the main object of meditation. Thus they appear to be extremely important, but here I won't elaborate beyond just that, as it would become too verbose.

⸙ According to the Chittamātra system, meditation on the four noble truths need not involve meditation on the selflessness of phenomena;[195]

one can achieve liberation from cyclic existence merely by realizing the self-lessness of persons and thus eliminating ignorance and the other afflictive obscurations,[196] the root causes that bind us to cyclic existence. However, in order to abandon the more subtle cognitive obscurations,[197] which are rooted in the misapprehension of a self of phenomena and which obstruct the attainment of the omniscient consciousness of a buddha, one must also meditate on the selflessness of phenomena. Śhrāvaka and pratyekabuddha arhats have abandoned cyclic existence and are liberated, they will no longer take rebirth by the force of ignorance and craving into a suffering state, but they still lack the totality of realization that enables a buddha to work effortlessly exactly in accordance with the needs of suffering sentient beings. Therefore a practitioner aspiring to achieve the state of buddhahood must meditate on the selflessness of phenomena in conjunction with meditation on the four noble truths. Just as prolonged meditation on the selflessness of persons will lead to a yogic direct perceiver that acts as the direct antidote to afflictive obscurations, meditation on the selflessness of phenomena leads to a yogic direct perceiver that acts as the direct antidote to cognitive obscurations.

Negating the Selves of Persons and Phenomena

Next, after noting that the main reasoning refuting the self of phenomena has been explained above, Khedrup Jé presents the reasonings negating the existence of the self of persons. The self of persons that appears to be self-sufficient, in the sense of being characteristically discordant with the aggregates, is what is being negated, not the conventional mere self. While the mere self exists, the self of persons doesn't; and while the mind apprehending the self-sufficient self of persons, being ignorance, is the cause of suffering, the mind apprehending the mere self is not. In a similar way, according to the Chittamātra, while the mere conventional existence of phenomena is not refuted, the existence of substantially different apprehended and apprehender is negated. ❧

[175] Now, secondly, I will explain the reasonings that negates the selves of persons and phenomena. The reasons for negating the self of phenomena are reasons that negate an apprehended and apprehender existing as substantially other. From among those [reasons], the main one is the sign of definite simultaneous observation. I have already elaborately explained that above [in the sections on the presentation of the three conditions in the Chittamātra]. Now, the explanation of the reasoning negating the self of persons has [two parts]: (1) stating the sign and (2) establishing the mode.

In order to refute a concrete self of a person the reason of *being one with or different from the aggregates* is used. If this type of self exists, it should either be one with or different from the aggregates. This form of logic is an important tool to analyze reality, especially for coming to an understanding of the ultimate nature of reality through refuting what reality is not. Candrakīrti, one of the greatest masters of Madhyamaka philosophy, uses a similar type of reasoning to prove the lack of an inherently existing self with the example of a chariot. In his *Entering the Middle Way* he states:

> A chariot is neither asserted to be other than its parts, nor to be not other [or one with its parts].[198]

A simplified form of the reasoning used in the Middle Way philosophy to negate the self of a person is given in appendix 6. As explained here and below, whatever exists must always be either one with or different from any other existent phenomenon, there is no third possibility. This is what Khedrup Jé calls "a valid cognizer ascertaining one and different as a dichotomy." For example, whatever exists is either one with or different from table, there is no other possibility than this dichotomy. Table itself is one with table, but vase and everything else other than table is different from table.

Below Khedrup Jé uses the reasoning: if a self-sufficient person exists then it must be either one with or different from its aggregates. He uses the terms *inherently one with* and *inherently different from* because he is referring to persons and aggregates that are impermanent phenomena. According to the school under discussion here, the Chittamātra, all impermanent things exist inherently. This is because, from among the three natures or types of phenomena, other-powered and thoroughly established phenomena are held to exist inherently. Imputed phenomena, like uncompounded space, are not accepted to exist inherently. In the context of an impermanent phenomenon, to say that it does not inherently exist is equivalent to saying that it doesn't exist. If a self-sufficient person does exist, then of course it should be a person, and so, since all persons are impermanent, it should exist inherently. If it exists inherently, then it must be either inherently one with or different from the aggregates. In terms of generating the following proof in one's mind, first the dichotomy of one with and different from is ascertained, after which the pervasion that whatever is neither one with nor different from its aggregates is necessarily non-existent is ascertained. The sign, the self-sufficient self is neither one with nor different from its aggregates, establishes that the self-sufficient self cannot exist. The following proof is put forward: the subject, the self-sufficient self, does not inherently exist because it is neither inherently one with nor inherently different from the aggregates. ⚬

First [stating the sign]: Whatever is neither inherently one with nor inherently different from its aggregates is pervaded by not existing inherently; for example, the horns of a rabbit. The person who is substantially existent, in the sense of being self-sufficient, in the sense of being characteristically discordant from the aggregates and not a mere imputation on any collection or continuity, is also neither inherently one with nor inherently different from its aggregates [and thus does not exist inherently]. [This sign is a sign of] non-observation of nature.

[Second], establishing the mode has two parts: (1) establishing the pervasion and (2) establishing the property of the subject.

First [establishing the pervasion, that whatever is neither inherently one with nor inherently different from its aggregates is pervaded by not existing inherently]: From the combined function of the two, the valid cognizer ascertaining that inherently one and inherently different are directly contradictory, and the valid cognizer ascertaining the property of the subject, it is ascertained that (1) the sign does not exist in the discordant class [inherent existence], and (2) that it exists only in the concordant class [non-inherent existence]. In this sense the counter pervasion and the forward pervasion are established.

[Second], establishing the property of subject [that the self-sufficient person is neither inherently one with nor inherently different from the aggregates]: Those of sharp faculties establish that the aggregates and the self-sufficient person are not inherently different through direct perception. Those of dull faculties must ascertain this by relying on inference. [The following proof] establishes that they [i.e., the aggregates and self-sufficient person] are not established as inherently one: the subject, the aggregates of one's continuum, they and a self-sufficient person do not exist as inherently one because they [i.e., the aggregates] are impermanent and other-powered [phenomenon].

There is pervasion because if a person is a self-sufficient [entity] that is characteristically discordant with the aggregates, then it must be permanent and own-powered.

As for establishing the sign, the subject, [the aggregates of one's continuum], are other-powered [phenomena] because they are compounded [i.e., produced] by karma and afflictions. As for establishing that sign [that the aggregates are produced by karma and afflictions], it is ascertained by relying on the reasoning that was mentioned previously [by Dharmakīrti]: "Whoever sees the self, for that one..."[199] As for establishing the previous sign, the subject, the aggregates: they are impermanent because of being a product. The way to establish the modes of that [proof—i.e., that the aggregates are impermanent because of being a product] will be explained below. [176]

꙳In the next section a summary of the above is given by identifying the signs that establish the three modes of the proof as being three different types of correct signs: (1) a sign of nature, (2) a sign of result, and (3) a sign of non-observation. A sign of nature in the proof of something is a correct sign in the proof of that, and it is of one nature with the predicate of the probandum in that proof. For example, in the proof establishing that the subject, sound, is impermanent because of being a product, the sign, product, is in the same nature as the predicate, impermanent. A sign of result means that there is a cause-and-effect relationship between the sign and the predicate. For example, in the proof establishing that there is fire on a distant mountain because of smoke arising there, the sign, fire, is the cause of the predicate, smoke. Due to the presence of a specific result, one knows that its specific cause must exist. A sign of non-observation means that the predicate is a negative phenomenon. For example, in the proof that the self-sufficient person does not inherently exist because of being neither one with nor different from its aggregates, "does not inherently exist" is a negative phenomenon. In addition to summarizing the reasons used, Khedrup Jé also stresses the importance of using reasoning and relates the sixteen aspects of the four noble truths to the realization of selflessness. ⚘

Therefore, the root sign establishing the aggregates as selfless [i.e., the self-sufficient self doesn't exist because it is neither inherently one with nor inherently different from its aggregates], is a sign of the non-observation of nature.

⚘ Here the proof under discussion is: the subject, the self-sufficient self, does not inherently exist because it is neither inherently one with nor inherently different from the aggregates. In this proof, the sign, because of being neither inherently one with nor inherently different from the aggregates, is a sign of the non-observation of nature. It is a sign of non-observation because the explicit predicate of the probandum in that proof, does not inherently exist, is a negative phenomenon. It is a sign of the non-observation of nature because the sign, neither inherently one with nor inherently different from the aggregates, is one nature with the predicate of the probandum, not inherently existent. ⚘

The sign establishing the pervasion [that whatever is neither inherently one with nor inherently different from the aggregates is pervaded by not existing inherently] is a sign of the observation of a contradiction.

❧ Here the proof establishing the pervasion is: for the subject, object of knowledge, there is a pervasion that whatever is neither inherently one with nor inherently different from the aggregates is pervaded by not existing inherently, because the two, existing inherently and not existing as either inherently one with nor inherently different from something, are contradictory in the sense of mutual exclusion. Therefore if something is not included in inherently one with and inherently different from the aggregates, then it cannot possibly exist inherently. This sign, which is an observation of this contradiction in the sense of mutual exclusion, establishes the pervasion above. ❧

The first part of the property of the subject [the aggregates of one's continuum are impermanent] is ascertained by relying on a sign of nature; and the latter part [the aggregates of one's continuum are other-powered phenomenon] is ascertained by relying on a sign of result.

❧ Here the proof under discussion is: the subject, the aggregates of one's continuum, are not inherently one with the self-sufficient person because of being impermanent and other-powered phenomena. The proof establishing the first part of the property of the subject is: the subject, the aggregates in one's continuum, are impermanent because of being a product. Here the sign, product, is one nature with the predicate, impermanent, and so it is a sign of nature.

The proof establishing the second part of the property of the subject is: the subject, the aggregates in one's continuum, are other-powered phenomena having karma and afflictive emotions, that are their cause, because of being compounded by afflictive emotions. Here the sign, compounded by afflictive emotions, is the result of the explicit predicate of the probandum, karma and afflictions, that are their cause. Therefore the sign in the proof establishing the later part of the property of the subject is a sign of result. ⚡

Therefore, in order to abandon self-grasping, one must ascertain the aggregates as selfless. Ordinary people [non-ārya beings] cannot ascertain that directly [with direct perception], so they must rely on [inference using] signs to ascertain it. These signs also must be ascertained by the three signs of result, nature, and non-observation, through the means explained above. Hence, although those who have not turned their minds to reasoning may make effort in meditating on the meaning of selflessness, it amounts to mere hardship devoid of essence. Therefore the aggregates being karma's and afflictions' other-powered nature is the meaning-isolate of "compounded aggregate."

If one does not ascertain (1) that [i.e., the aggregates being other powered] and (2) the aggregates being impermanent, one will be unable to ascertain the aggregates being not of the same nature as the self of persons. For that reason, realizing the aggregates as impermanent and suffering is itself the supreme method for realizing the aggregates as selfless, and so [Dharmakīrti] said, "For that reason, from impermanence, suffering; from suffering, selflessness was taught."[200]

Therefore realizing the aggregates as empty of a self-sufficient person is itself the meaning of realizing selflessness of persons; realizing the aggregates as impermanent and as karma's and afflictions' other-powered nature is not in itself the meaning of realizing the selflessness of persons. If that were [the meaning], even meditation on the aggregates as impermanent and suffering would become meditation on the selflessness of person, and so it would [absurdly] follow that the mere reflection on the faults of cyclic existence would be a special insight meditation [on selflessness of a person]. Therefore, although if one realizes the selflessness of persons, one must realize the sixteen aspects [of the four noble truths], impermanence and so forth, saying that realization of the sixteen aspects, impermanence and so forth, is the meaning of realization of the selflessness of persons is a mistake.

⸖ How to Meditate on Selflessness

The realization of selflessness does not come about merely through intellectual speculation. It arises through an organic process involving many factors. It must be cultivated in a mindstream made fertile through reflection on the sufferings of samsara, moistened by the wish for self and others to be free, illuminated by an understanding of the sixteen aspects of the four noble truths, and then produced from the logic and reasonings described above. Even having realized selflessness in a conceptual manner using inference, a practitioner must continuously cultivate that realization, deepening and enhancing it over a long period of time until it becomes a yogic direct perceiver, an uncontaminated exalted wisdom. Even then, the practitioner must train in that direct realization, which is a liberating path, until it overcomes all afflictions. There is no qualitative difference in the direct realization one first achieves and the direct realization of an arhat or a buddha. The difference is in the length of time of cultivation and the collection of merit supporting this realization. In *The Golden Garland of Eloquence*, Tsongkhapa compares this to the difference of the morning sun on the horizon and the midday sun high in the sky. The sun's quality remains the same, but its ability to illuminate the world increases over time. Below Khedrup Jé explains the stages to prepare the mind for the realization of selflessness and how to meditate once that realization has arisen. ⸖

Third, the method of how to meditate on selflessness: all paths are numerically limited within the two, ripening paths and liberating paths. [177] As for *ripening paths*: they are those that make a [person's] continuum into a suitable vessel for the realization of an uncontaminated exalted wisdom. As for *liberating paths*: they are all uncontaminated exalted wisdoms that are included in the antidotes that liberate the continuum from the seed of any object of abandonment. If one does not first meditate on a ripening path, there is no method for generating a liberating path in one's continuum, like a disease arising when [someone] uses rice without letting it ripen. Therefore, first one must engage in meditation on ripening paths.

Furthermore, as for the order of putting the paths into practice: if one does not first become disgusted with samsara and generate a fully characterized mind wishing to be separated [from samsara], the wish to achieve liberation will not arise. If that doesn't arise, one will not come to train in the paths, so first one must make effort to generate an uncontrived revulsion of samsara. That too must be induced by a certainty in the suffering of samsara; revulsion won't come about by the mere words "samsara has no essence," because if you don't see the faults [of samsara], it will not bring about disgust [with cyclic existence].

There are three kinds of samsaric sufferings [as mentioned in the section on the truth of suffering above]. The sufferings of hell and the sufferings of hunger and thirst, for instance, upon merely arising can effortlessly be realized as suffering by all beings; [these are] the suffering of suffering. The suffering of change is, for instance, contaminated happiness; when it arises, it is not realized as suffering by some, but when it changes [to suffering], all [sentient beings] are able to effortlessly realize it as suffering. The other-powered and impermanent pervasive compounding suffering is interrelated with all samsaric beings without any distinction.

To generate a fully characterized disgust for samsara in general, one must realize pervasive compounding suffering. One need not meditate on the other two sufferings as suffering because most beings can realize them as in the nature of suffering through experience. However, that [realization of those two sufferings] alone cannot directly induce disgust for samsara in general. Otherwise there would be a pervasion that the mind of disgust for samsara in general would be effortlessly and directly produced in the continuum of hell beings and so forth. Therefore, by realizing the suffering of suffering and so forth, [one] cannot directly induce disgust that observes samsara in general; one will see the absence of the suffering of suffering in certain particular instances of samsara that are included in the upper realms, like Brahma's state, and again craving will arise. [178]

Therefore, to generate wholehearted disgust for samsara in general, since one must realize well the characteristics of pervasive compounding suffering, one must meditate on these very appropriating aggregates as in the nature of suffering. For that reason, intending pervasive compounding suffering, [Dharmakīrti] stated: "[The Buddha] said meditate on suffering."[201]

If, having realized these contaminated appropriating aggregates as suffering, one wishes to abandon them and to attain the liberation that is free from them, one will analyze whether or not one can abandon this suffering. Through [such analysis] one will see that, if [suffering's] causes are not abandoned, one will be unable to abandon [suffering] in the manner of not re-arising. Thus, one will ponder: "What is its cause?" Having thought in that way, one will come to see that [suffering] is rooted in self-grasping, whose mode [of grasping] is as explained above.[202] At that time, [impelled] by the wish to be free from the suffering of samsara, one will analyze whether or not one can abandon self-grasping.

Furthermore, whether or not the seed of that mind [of self-grasping] can be abandoned depends upon whether or not that mind's mode of apprehension [correctly] engages the nature of its object. If that mind's mode of apprehension accords with the object's nature, then, since it engages in accordance with the nature of the mind, one will be unable to abandon the seeds. If it engages and holds [its object] in a discordant [manner], then there exists [a correct consciousness, in accordance with reality, that] harms [that incorrect mind of self-grasping]. For this reason, one is able to stop completely [the mind of self-grasping] by means of an antidote. Therefore the means of analyzing whether or not self-grasping can be abandoned is to analyze whether or not self-grasping's mode of apprehension [correctly] engages the nature of its object.

Furthermore, whether or not self-grasping's mode of apprehension is concordant or discordant with actuality depends upon whether or not the self that it apprehends exists, so one must analyze that. If one analyzes in that way, then one will ascertain the non-existence of [such a] self by means of the aforementioned reasons negating the self. If one ascertains [selflessness], then one will ascertain that self-grasping can be abandoned and then ascertain that one is able to be free from the suffering of samsara; the suffering of samsara is the result of that [self-grasping]. [179] At that time, by depending on this reason one will also come to ascertain that there is a liberation that has abandoned all samsaric sufferings.

It is stated in this way: It pervades that, for whatever [phenomena for which] there is something having the power to harm its cause, there exists the extinction of the continuity of that [phenomenon] by an antidote's power. For example, one can see that the extinction of goose bumps, which are the result of cold, happens by being close to a powerful fire. The cause of the contaminated aggregates is also observed to have a powerful harmer. Also, it pervades that for whatever is seen to have a powerful harmer, there must exist the extinction of that by an antidote's power, because, just as, for example, we see that the sensation of cold is reversed by being close to a fire, the complete abandonment of the conception of a self of phenomena is established to exist by the sign that states, "The conception that apprehends the apprehended, apprehender, and [self-]knowing [aspect] of a single awareness as truly different is also observed to have a powerful harmer." If that is established, then it is established through reason of the power of the fact that that [realization] can be in one continuum along with the realization of the mode of abiding of the four noble truths. Thereby the existence of an all-knowing exalted wisdom will also be established by the power of the fact. This is so because that exalted wisdom realizes the nature of the four noble truths and is qualified by having abandoned the conception of a self of phenomena and is therefore called an "all-knowing exalted wisdom."

🌱 As explained above in the Chittamātra system, liberation from samsara can be achieved with the direct realization of the selflessness of persons in sustained meditative absorption that is motivated by an uncontrived wish for liberation. In order to achieve the state of full enlightenment of a buddha, one needs to abandon not only the afflictive obscurations that bind us to cyclic existence but also the more subtle cognitive obscurations that obstruct the attainment of the omniscient consciousness of a buddha. In order to attain this state, one must also meditate on the selflessness of phenomena to eliminate these cognitive obscurations. Based on the reason that the mind falsely apprehending a self of phenomena is seen to have an antidote with the power to harm it, Khedrup Jé establishes the possibility of abandoning the ignorance grasping at a self of phenomena. He describes this ignorance as a false conception that mistakenly grasps the aspect of the object apprehended, the apprehender, and the self-knowing aspect of a single consciousness to be truly different. Above in section 4.3 on self-knowing direct perceivers, Khedrup Jé described how for any consciousness or apprehender, the factor of clarity and knowing that experiences its own entity, which is the consciousness's self-knower, and the factor that is the appearance of the aspect of the consciousness's object, are aspects of that consciousness and thus not truly different from it.

In the following section Khedrup Jé first rejects the wrong view that self-grasping cannot totally be eliminated, which arises from the mistaken premise that wisdom realizing selflessness cannot be increased infinitely. He argues that this view is incorrect because, through the power of familiarization, the conceptual realization of selflessness becomes a direct perception with clear appearance of selflessness. When this direct perception has become further developed through habituation, it arises effortlessly and continuously ad infinitum. He compares this to the example of attachment: the more one becomes habituated to attachment, the more it arises without effort. ⨎

[179] Wrong conceptions [regarding the elimination of self-grasping] (like these) arise for some individuals, who develop doubts, thinking: "In order to eliminate all self-grasping without exception it is necessary to infinitely increase the wisdom realizing selflessness by way of familiarizing oneself with it over manifold rebirths. Heating water causes it to become a little hotter, but it will never turn it into fire, and a person's leap can be lengthened a little, but one will never, having increased it infinitely, be able to leap more than a krośha.[203] In the same way, the wisdom realizing selflessness can be increased slightly but not increased infinitely. Thus the wisdom realizing selflessness is unable to abandon all self-grasping without exception."

Such a wrong conception is to be eliminated by the reasoning establishing that the wisdom realizing selflessness can develop the most supreme [form] of clear appearance with respect to its object of familiarization. In accordance with this, moreover, the nature [correct] sign: As for the subject, the wisdom realizing selflessness, if one familiarizes oneself with it without being separated from the branches of familiarization, it will develop the most supreme [form] of clear appearance with respect to its object of familiarization because its basis is stable; it is a mental phenomenon that, having become familiar [with its object], does not depend upon renewed effort in the same way as attachment, for instance, does.

꙳ In general, there are instances of both conceptual and non-conceptual consciousnesses having clear appearance because both a meditative equipoise in single-pointed absorption on the emptiness of the path of preparation in the mind of an ordinary being and an uninterrupted path of the path of seeing have clear appearance. Most conceptual consciousnesses do not have clear appearance because their objects of the mode of apprehension appear as mixed together with their meaning generalities, and they have the dualistic appearance of object and subject as different. In the case of a meditative equipoise of the path of preparation realizing selflessness, through the force of meditation, and due to the subtlety of the object, the coarse dualistic appearance of object and subject has been eliminated, and so it is said to have clear appearance, although the object of the mode of apprehension still appears as mixed together with its meaning generality. The most supreme type of clear appearance is clear appearance to a non-conceptual mental consciousness realizing selflessness, such as is first achieved when one achieves the first moment of the uninterrupted path of the path of seeing. Such a consciousness has neither a dualistic appearance nor the appearance of its object as mixed with a meaning generality. Such a mind, which is best for abandoning the seeds and imprints of ignorance, is achieved through conscientiously focusing one's attention on an object of meditation again and again, supported by the accumulations of merit and wisdom and the purification of obscurations. Here it

is being argued that by such methods an ordinary conceptual consciousness apprehending selflessness can be gradually transformed into a direct
perceiver.

Having proven the possibility of direct perception of selflessness, Khedrup Jé now establishes the nature of the mind and its causes. The reasons
given get deepened further, and he concludes that a particular moment of
consciousness of a particular individual can only be produced by its previous moment; this leads to the establishment of reincarnation. The substantial cause of a particular consciousness at the time of conception can only
be a previous moment of that particular continuum of consciousness. ⚡

[180] The basis is the mere clear and knowing mind, and if [one asks] how
that is established as being stable, it is by way of establishing mere awareness as never reaching a beginning or end. Accordingly, were that awareness of a being just born not to have a cause, due to it being an occasional
phenomenon, there would be harm [to this assertion]. If it does have a
cause, is it permanent or impermanent? If it were a permanent thing, it
would be impossible to ascertain the forward and counter pervasions with
its effect, since it would be impossible for it to not pervade every last place
and time.[204]

In accordance with the latter [i.e., that the cause is impermanent], since
it is unacceptable that it be born from something other than either matter
or consciousness, it must be born from one of those. If matter acted as its
substantial cause, was it matter possessed of a sense power, or was it external matter that [did so]? In accordance with the first, is it necessary for all
of the sense powers to be assembled as the cause, or will a single particular
one suffice? According to the first, [it would absurdly follow that] mental
awareness would not be produced if the eye sense power were not complete, and according to the latter [i.e., that a single particular sense power
would suffice as the cause], thought consciousness would [absurdly] come
to clearly apprehend form just as the eye consciousness [does].

If external matter acts as the substantial cause, does a whole substance,
or atoms, do so? In accordance with the first from among the two—there

are whole substances having parts and those not having parts—regarding those having parts acting as the substantial cause, the question "Is it necessary to assemble all parts as the cause, or will a single particular one suffice?" is eliminated by the prior method of reasoning. If a partless whole, which is of a different substance to all of the parts, acts as the substantial cause, [it would absurdly follow that] when the face has been covered by clothing, so too the other parts will have been covered by clothing, and if the other [parts] are not covered, there will be two parts, covered and uncovered. If, furthermore, the two, covered and uncovered parts, do not exist in the whole despite existing within the parts, it [absurdly] follows that the face of the whole will be clearly seen at the time the face is concealed by clothing, and [this position] is harmed likewise by the reasonings applied to shaking and not shaking, changing and not changing direction, and so on.

Should atoms act as the substantial cause, if every single one independently produces [a consciousness that is] its [own effect], manifold mental conceptual consciousnesses would be simultaneously produced, and if the entirety must be assembled, it [i.e., consciousness] will not be produced if even a single atom is incomplete.

In dependence upon those reasonings, which negate the other possibilities, it is established that consciousness acts as the substantial cause [of the first moment of a being's consciousness]. [181] Regarding that, moreover, from among the two—[consciousness] conjoined with one's own continuum and that conjoined with the continuum of others—if the consciousness of another's continuum, such as that of one's father or mother, acts as the direct substantial cause, there would arise the fault of the consequence that the son of a father skilled at crafts and [the son of] a foolish one [father] would also be just like that [i.e., like their fathers, skilled or foolish at crafts, respectively]. Hence, only the previous awareness of one's own continuum acts as the substantial cause, and in accordance with that, awareness's never reaching a beginning or end, as well as past and future rebirths, are excellently established.

Therefore, the heat of water is a not a stable basis, since direct perception establishes that if [water] is boiled excessively it will dry up, and jumping, too, relies on each individual exertion assisting rather than having the capacity to be produced from its previous [cause] of similar type. Love, wisdom, and so forth are produced from their previous [causes] of similar type, and the sign that, as well as having become familiar with [their respective objects], they do not depend upon renewed exertion, is established by self-knowing direct perception.

༈ Above, an opponent argued that wisdom realizing selflessness cannot be cultivated over many lifetimes or increased to an infinite degree because it is limited due to being an unstable base, like boiled water, and due to requiring the same amount of effort to increase from the same starting level in each instance, like physically jumping up and down. Here, Khedrup Jé shows how virtuous minds like wisdom realizing selflessness, love, compassion, and so forth can be increased infinitely because they, in fact, are a stable basis for cultivation and because developing them to higher levels of maturity does not require making effort anew from the initial base level of development each time. While the opponent used the examples of boiling water and jumping to show how wisdom is similar to them, Khedrup Jé uses the same examples to show how the wisdom of selflessness is unlike them. In Khedrup Jé's analysis water is not a stable basis for heat because water only heats to the point of boiling and then quickly turns to steam and ceases to remain as a basis for more heat. There is a limit to which it can be heated, and then it dissipates as a result of further heat. Conversely, the mind is not an unstable basis for qualities of mind. As wisdom and compassion increase in a person's mind, there is not a limit beyond which these qualities cannot be increased or beyond which the basis for these qualities, the mind itself, breaks down and ceases to exist.

Each time one jumps from flat ground into the air, the same amount of effort must be made with each jump; the energy applied to make the previous jump does not carry over to subsequent jumps, and there is a physical limitation on how high a person can jump no matter how much they train. Conversely, when one develops a positive quality of mind like compassion, while it is the case that effort must be made again and again, if one puts energy into the work consistently and before the effects of previous efforts have declined, one does not need to begin from the same starting place each time. Rather, not only can we build on progress made earlier, but since the mind is a creature of habit, efforts made earlier support later efforts such that each time we try to generate compassion it becomes easier and easier. Finally, unlike jumping and other actions of the body, there is no limit to how much a positive quality of mind can be developed.

Having established the existence of reincarnation, the possibility of habituating ourselves with positive minds in general, and specifically the possibility of developing the conceptual realization of selflessness into a wisdom directly perceiving selflessness, Khedrup Jé now turns to the importance of generating genuine renunciation on the firm basis of understanding how we suffer in samsara and how liberation from this is possible. ❧

Through contemplating well and in the proper way, by way of manifold modes of reasoning like these, one understands that samsara is in the nature of suffering; thereafter one ascertains the cause of that, grasping at self, as an object of abandonment and as something that can be abandoned. The mind that strives for liberation is fully complete in defining characteristics when from the bottom of one's heart one has produced a mind ascertaining the existence of liberation and aspiring for the attainment of liberation. Furthermore, as long as they are not conjoined with the mind striving for liberation, even the entirety of whatever excellent deeds one might have accumulated are included in the enumeration of *partially concordant merits*, which issue forth results of samsaric happiness alone. From the time this mind has been well conjoined, even all of a beginner's excellent deeds—from giving away a mere morsel of food and upward—become the causes of liberation and of turning one's back on samsara, [and] hence they are counted in the enumeration of *virtues partially concordant with liberation*.

If one does not gain such a mind striving for liberation with deeply penetrating ascertainment induced by the path of reasoning, one will be relying merely on the words of others, and in dependence on others' mere words and counterfeit reasonings, [opponents] will be capable of over-turning, too, that counterfeit creation—one's renunciation that strongly wishes for liberation because of unendurably fierce suffering that descends upon oneself. When, having turned away from that fierce immediate suf-fering, one's mind is deceived by this life's happiness alone, one again turns away from such a renunciation; thereafter one will resort to a situation in which one is bereft of renunciation, in accordance with the statement: "If one turns away from that, to its very nature one will again resort."[205] [182]

⚜ *The Method of Abandoning Self-Grasping through Meditation on Selflessness*

Having explained the two objects of negation, the selves of persons and phenomena, the reasons that negate those two selves, and how to medi-tate on selflessness, Khedrup Jé now explains the method of abandoning self-grasping through these meditations according to the three vehicles: Śhrāvaka, Pratyekabuddha, and Mahāyāna. He first explains how people with different capacities and motivations enter the three different vehi-cles. After this, he gives an explanation of the objects of meditation of the three vehicles according to the two śhrāvaka schools, Vaibhāṣhika and Sautrāntika, as well as the Chittamātra. As explained in the section "Identifying the Selves of Persons and Phenomena," the different Bud-dhist tenet systems have different interpretations with regard to the main objects meditated upon while progressing on the five paths to liberation and enlightenment. ⚜

Fourth, as to the means by which self-grasping is abandoned through meditation: when the mind seeking liberation fully complete in defini-tion has been produced in one's mental continuum, seeing that without striving at the causes of that liberation one lacks the ability to attain it, one comes to train in the path of liberation. Moreover, among those who are training in the path in such a way there are, accordingly, three types of lineage-possessors:

- Those who are naturally of duller faculty actualize the śhrāvakas' path and achieve the state of an *arhat* [foe-destroyer] by aspiring for liberation from the suffering of samsara primarily for themselves alone.

- Those who are naturally of middling faculty actualize the self-liberators' path and achieve the state of a *pratyekabuddha* [solitary buddha] by primarily aspiring for solely their own liberation from the suffering of samsara.

- Those who are naturally of sharper faculty see that, just as samsara's suffering yields suffering for themselves, so too do all migrators suffer. Unable to bear this, and furthermore, after seeing that every sentient being has been none other than a kind person who was once their mother, they actualize the great compassion that thinks, "Sentient beings should be free from suffering." When they have produced the mind aspiring to liberate all sentient beings from suffering in dependence on great compassion such as this, they will perceive that they lack the ability to extricate all sentient beings from suffering. When they have searched well for one having this ability, they will come to ascertain that only a buddha possesses the ability to extricate all sentient beings from suffering. At that time, they come to produce the Mahāyāna mind-generation [i.e., bodhichitta] that thinks, "In order to liberate all sentient beings from suffering, I will attain the state of a buddha." Thereafter they actualize the state of a buddha through having trained in the path of the Mahāyāna.

[183] In addition to such paths having three different means of entry, the different features of the bodies of the three paths are, in accordance with the two śhrāvaka schools, asserted thus: Although all three lineage-possessors are similar in not meditating on a selflessness apart from the selflessness of persons, those possessing śhrāvaka lineage attain śhrāvaka arhatship by becoming familiarized [with that selflessness] over an extremely short period—three lifetimes and the like—and creating an extremely limited

accumulation of the collections [of merit and wisdom]. Those endowed with pratyekabuddha lineage attain pratyekabuddha arhatship through meditating on that very selflessness of persons in relation with the accumulation of the collections for as long as one hundred eons and so forth. Those possessing Mahāyāna lineage, by meditating on awareness realizing the selflessness of persons through many methods, supported by the collection of accumulations over three countless eons and so forth, abandon even non-afflicted ignorance [i.e., cognitive obscurations, obscurations to omniscience], attaining complete buddhahood possessing clarity of mind with respect to all objects of knowledge and the abandonment of all negative tendencies.

Therefore, in the context of indicating the method of attaining liberation and omniscience within the system of the Common Vehicle, in keeping with the assertions of the śrāvakas, in the second chapter [of *Compendium of Valid Cognition*] only the selflessness of persons is delineated, and the difference between the Greater and Lesser Vehicles is also taught to be distinguished solely through the extent of the method[206] and the length of the period of accumulating the collections. Hence, as it is said [in Dharmakīrti's *Exposition of Valid Cognition*]:

> Manifold means in various aspects—
> through habituation over a long period of time,
> all the demerits and merits with respect to that
> come to be completely clarified.
>
> Therefore, since the mind too is clarified,
> the imprints of the cause [of suffering] are eliminated.
> This is the distinction between the great Muni who engages in
>   the well-being of others
> and the rhinoceros [-like *pratyekabuddha*] and so forth.[207]

In this and other passages it [i.e., the difference between the Śrāvaka, Pratyekabuddha, and Mahāyāna Vehicles] has been extensively expounded.

In the context of the uncommon Greater Vehicle, the way that one trains in the path to attain liberation and omniscience in the system of the Vijñānavāda is as follows:

- Those possessing the śhrāvaka lineage will attain śhrāvakas' enlightenment by having abandoned the afflictive obscurations through familiarization with merely the selflessness of persons.

- Those endowed with solitary-realizer lineage attain a pratyekabuddha's enlightenment by having abandoned the afflictive obscurations, as well as just the cognitive obscurations of the conception of the apprehended, through familiarization with the selflessness of persons and the selflessness of phenomena, with respect to just the apprehended, for their own purposes over one hundred eons and so forth. [184]

- In conjunction with the method, great compassion, those possessing the Mahāyāna lineage delineate through reasoning the selflessnesses of persons and phenomena in their entirety. Then, in dependence on calm abiding, they become familiarized with the continuum of the ascertaining consciousness that has ascertained [those selflessnesses] with inferential valid cognition. Thereby, through thoroughly pacifying the waves of discursiveness by any means they generate the wisdom of the path of seeing, which realizes directly the aspects of the [four noble] truths qualified by the two selflessnesses, and come to eliminate without exception the objects of abandonment of the path of seeing subsumed within the afflictive and cognitive obscurations. By familiarizing for a long period with that very [direct realization of the two selflessnesses], they finally abandon the obscurations subsumed within the objects of abandonment of the path of meditation and come to manifest the wisdom of omniscience.

Therefore, the selflessness of phenomena is extensively delineated in chapter 3 [of *Compendium of Valid Cognition*] in the context of the uncommon Greater Vehicle. I have explained extensively the way in which the two obscurations that are the objects of abandonment of the antidote, the path realizing selflessness, are to be abandoned and so on in other places.[208] Hence, you should refer to those, and although there are a great many things to be explained with respect to these modes of traversing the path, fearing this will become overly verbose, I have not written about them here. This brief explanation of yogic direct perceivers along with points emanating [therefrom] is complete.

CHAPTER SIX

RESULTS OF VALID COGNIZERS

IN THIS CHAPTER, Khedrup Jé explains interrupted and uninterrupted results of valid cognizers. Interrupted results are particular
methods to attain different realizations and goals a Buddhist practitioner
strives for that lead to higher states of rebirth, liberation, and enlightenment.[209] These states can be attained through realizing the different
aspects of the four noble truths explained in the previous chapter. They
are called "interrupted results" because they are produced from the valid
cognizers that are their causes only indirectly and are separated from those
valid cognizers by other types of awareness that intervene. Uninterrupted
results of valid cognizers are realizations of the individual forms of valid
cognizers, other-knowers like sense and mental forms of valid cognizers,
and self-knowing valid cognizers. First interrupted and uninterrupted
results are explained in general, after which a debate about the results of
direct perceivers in the Chittamātra and Sautrāntika traditions follows.

6.1 INTERRUPTED AND UNINTERRUPTED RESULTS
OF VALID COGNIZERS

From the point of view of interrupted results, Khedrup Jé explains that in
order to progress on the path to liberation and enlightenment one must
abandon the first two noble truths, true suffering and true cause of suffering, and adopt the last two truths, true cessation and true paths. Through
direct valid perception of selflessness, which is a true path, one abandons
the ignorance apprehending a self and thereby eliminates the true cause of
suffering. The elimination of the true cause of suffering is true cessation.

In order to achieve these results, one needs to depend on valid cognizers, and thus they are results of valid cognizers. ⸙

[184] **Results of valid cognizers are of two types:**
  • interrupted results
  • uninterrupted results

Interrupted results
What are the interrupted results of valid cognizers? These [results] are mainly the purpose of beings: all that is included within higher states [of rebirth, like that of a human or god,] and excellence [of liberation and enlightenment], and realizing which of the four noble truths have to be adopted and which discarded and the methods to do so, and then engaging in [the last two truths] and turning away from [the first two truths]. This is the meaning because it is said [in Dharmakīrti's *Exposition of Valid Cognition*]:

> Because engaging in things to be adopted and discarded
> is the main [result.][210]

Since these results arise through the power of valid cognizers, thus they should be known as *produced results of valid cognizers*.

⸙ As just explained, interrupted results are indirectly caused by the valid cognizers that gave rise to them because their arising is separated from those valid cognizers by, or interrupted by, instances of awareness other than those that are a continuation of that valid cognizer. For example, a specific valid cognizer realizing that one's body is in the nature of suffering may be one cause for generating renunciation, but before this resultant renunciation arises, there may be many other kinds of awareness that intervene. Uninterrupted results don't have this kind of interruption. For example, an ascertaining or conceptual consciousness realizing the color blue, which is directly induced by a valid eye consciousness apprehending the color blue without any other consciousness interfering, is such an uninterrupted result. This type of uninterrupted result is below called a "valid cognizer that isn't its own nature" because its cause, a sense consciousness, is of a different type than itself, being a conceptual consciousness. The other subdivision of uninterrupted results Khedrup Jé gives, is *valid cognizers that are their own nature*. These are valid cognizers that arise in the aspect of the object and thus are also valid cognizers that are generated without any other consciousness interfering.

Uninterrupted results

There are two types of uninterrupted results:
- those valid cognizers that aren't their own nature
- those valid cognizers that are their own nature

Those valid cognizers that aren't their own nature

An illustration of this is an ascertaining consciousness directly induced by valid cognizers. Because it is a result that is directly produced by valid cognizers, it is called an "uninterrupted result."

Those valid cognizers that are their own nature

An illustration of this is the aspect of valid cognizers that realizes its object of comprehension.

If one asks, "Why are they called 'uninterrupted results of valid cognizers'?," [we answer,] "Because, by being an aspect that is of the nature of the valid cognizers itself, they are uninterrupted by other actors," and "because of being that which is posited by the very valid cognizers that arises in the aspect of the object." Therefore, [it is also said in Dharmakīrti's *Exposition of Valid Cognition*]:

> Because objects are of different aspects,
> the way mind conceives them is different.
> Because those [object aspects] exist, these [mental conceptions]
>   exist.[211]

⚜6.2 UNINTERRUPTED RESULTS OF DIRECT PERCEPTION

As explained previously in chapters 2 and 3, direct perception can be of two types: other-knowers and self-knowers. Uninterrupted results will now be explained according to this division, which is a common explanation of the Chittamātra and Sautrāntika, who both accept that the valid direct perceiver apprehending an object realizes that object through its aspect appearing. When it comes to how the objects cause a consciousness to arise, there is a big difference in the view of these two schools. The Sautrāntika accept that external objects are a cause for direct perception to arise; for them, the color blue is the observed object condition for the eye consciousness that is a direct perception apprehending blue—it exists before this eye consciousness and acts as a cause for it. The Chittamātra don't accept this. After a brief explanation of the uninterrupted results of direct perception, Khedrup Jé elucidates this difference between the two schools in the form of a debate. ⚜

Uninterrupted results of direct perception [194]
- results of other-knowing valid cognizers
- results of self-knowing valid cognizers

Results of other-knowing valid cognizers
Blue and so forth are called "objects of comprehension." The consciousness to which the aspect of this [object] appears and which is new and incontrovertible is called "a valid cognizer." Realizing blue and so forth is called "result." This presentation of results of valid cognizers is common to both the Sautrāntika and Chittamātra, because both the Sautrāntika and Chittamātra accept that the valid direct perceiver apprehending blue realizes blue through blue's aspect appearing. [Dignāga] says in the *Compendium of Valid Cognition:*

> Because [it] realizes in connection with an object,
> this is accepted as a result of valid cognizers.

The imputation of valid cognizers
is not there without its object.[212]

This quotation is explained [in Dharmakīrti's] *Exposition of Valid Cognition*, from:

[An agent] is that which accomplishes actions...

until:

Because of engaging through superimposition
upon things asserted to be [substantially] different.[213]

Results of self-knowing valid cognizers

The aspect of the apprehended is called "the object of comprehension." [195] The aspect that is an incontrovertible apprehender is called "a valid cognizer." The self-knower is called "the result." This result of self-knowing valid cognizers is a common assertion of both the Sautrāntika and Chittamātra, because both the Sautrāntika and Chittamātra accept that a particular awareness's aspect of the apprehender depends on that awareness's aspect of the apprehended [object], and therefore accept that [this aspect of the apprehender] is the self-knowing direct perceiver. This presentation is explained in [Dignāga's *Compendium of Valid Cognition*] as:

Moreover, the meaning of the result, self-knowing [valid
     cognizers],
is ascertained from its nature.[214]

[Dharmakīrti's] *Exposition of Valid Cognition* elaborates from:

[If one asks,] "What are [external] object knowers?," they are
the individual [objects' sense] knowers...

until:

Moreover, that [valid cognition to which] the desired or undesired
  [aspect appears]
does not become [a substantially different] object knower [of
  those aspects].²¹⁵

[197] The meaning of the quotation [from Dharmakīrti's *Exposition of
Valid Cognition*]: "Although external objects exist"²¹⁶ is as follows: [the
Chittamātra] refute the Sautrāntika's acceptance that the aspect that
appears to eye consciousness apprehending blue and so forth is an aspect
cast by the objects, blue and so forth.

❧ The Chittamātra reject the existence of external objects and say that
an object perceived and the consciousness that perceives it arise simultaneously by the power of a mental imprint, which is their common cause.
A mental imprint is a latency, a potential created in the past by a similar
kind of consciousness that became a potential, or imprint, at the time that
particular consciousness ceased to exist. This potential can, when meeting
the right conditions, ripen and produce an appearance of an object and
a consciousness perceiving this object. In this model, the object blue, for
example, arises simultaneously with the eye consciousness apprehending
blue and is therefore not a cause preceding that eye consciousness. In the
following, Khedrup Jé shows a similar debate that was mentioned in chapter 2 when explaining the three conditions. ❧

[The Chittamātra argue], "Sautrāntika, although the blue and so forth,
which you accept as an external object, exists, [198] as for that aspect of
blue, it comes through the power of a latency [or imprint], not from the
object itself. If it were such an aspect, you would have to accept that, when
a friend and an enemy looked at the body of single person, the pleasant
and unpleasant aspects appearing to their respective consciousnesses are
both aspects cast back from the side of the object, whereby it would follow that that single person's body is the nature of both pleasantness and

unpleasantness." As for [the passage in Dharmakīrti's *Exposition of Valid Cognition*]:

> If having asserted that, you still [say there is no fault]; [it would
>   follow that] two beings
> do not experience [two aspects] distinctly [when viewing
>   another being].
> If you say, "[both aspects] are not seen due to obscuration
>   [of past karma],"
> it follows that [that form] is not realized by means of the power
>   of the object.
> Within that multi-natured thing,
> only one [nature] is seen for oneself.
> Not seeing that [other nature],
> how would one come to [fully] see the object?
> In the event, [you say] desirable and undesirable appearances
> are [the objects of] conceptuality, not of [sense] object
>   awarenesses.
> To those [sense perceptions], too, [through] forebodings of
>   death and so forth,
> minds not relating [the formerly attractive to the pleasant but to
>   the unpleasant] are seen.[217]

[This] explains the way that faults arise by accepting that one person's body is of the nature of what is and is not desired.

꙳ The Chittamātra now goes a step further in debate by saying that the Sautrāntika cannot adequately posit results of valid cognizers as long as they accept external objects that are of a separate substance from the consciousness that apprehends them. ꙳

[In Dharmakīrti's *Exposition of Valid Cognition*], the meaning of

> Therefore, the external object of comprehension
> being experienced itself is the result.[218]

is: If the aspects of blue and so forth that appear to eye consciousnesses apprehending blue and so on were aspects cast from the side of the object, then the appearance to those minds of blue and so forth as distant and cut off from [those minds] would have to be established as it appears. Blue and so forth would become external objects. Those aspects are not aspects cast from the side of the object because, in terms of positing [them] as objects of comprehension, the blue and so forth that you accept as external objects are of one nature with consciousness; and the experience [of it] is the result. If you accept that blue and so forth are external objects [separate] from one's [consciousness], then putting forward a result of realization is incorrect.

In brief, where it says [in Dharmakīrti's *Exposition of Valid Cognition*], from:

> Although external objects do exist . . .

until:

> It is logical that [the object] is an effect of its own [essence, since]
> in accordance with the particular [imprint, an appearance factor]
>   of its nature
> is ascertained to [appear] as the object's [desired or undesired]
>   aspects.[219]

This explains the resultant knowledge of blue and so forth being in one nature with its own consciousness at the time that blue and so forth is the object of comprehension. This is proven through refuting external objects, like blue and so forth, being of a different substance than consciousness. This refutation is established through negating that aspects like blue and so forth are stable aspects of real objects, with signs [of reasoning] [that establish that if the above is correct then it follows that] the form [of the appearance] of one particular person, [if it were looked upon by an enemy and a close friend at a particular time], should appear with aspects of pleasant and unpleasant to the consciousnesses [of both enemy and friend at the same time].

CHAPTER SEVEN

INFERENTIAL CONSCIOUSNESS

THIS CHAPTER EXPLAINS inferential consciousness, a valid conceptual cognizer that is generated by a correct form of reasoning using logical thought. As explained in the first chapter, although an ordinary person can realize manifest phenomena by direct perception, in order to realize hidden phenomena, such a person needs to depend on inference. An inference that realizes slightly hidden phenomena, like sound being impermanent, is called "inference by the power of the fact." An inference that realizes very hidden phenomena, like the subtle workings of karmic cause and effect, is called "inference through belief." A third type of inference is an inferential cognizer through renown, which realizes its object by a common convention in the world, like the arbitrary fact that the formal residence of the United States president is called the "White House."

Generating an inference depends upon a correct sign that proves a probandum. A *probandum* is something to be proven, a quality or property of a particular object—for example, sound being impermanent, impermanent being a property of sound. In this case, a correct sign or reason to prove the probandum could be the sign, a product. This sign, a product, proves sound to be impermanent because (1) sound is a product, (2) whatever is a product is necessarily impermanent, and (3) it is possible to both realize that sound is a product and be in doubt about whether or not it is impermanent. The generation of a consciousness realizing a sign proving a probandum requires three modes of ascertainment. These three modes for the establishment of *sound being impermanent* by the sign *a product* are: (1) *property of the subject*—the sign, product, being established on or as a property of the subject, sound; (2) *the forward pervasion*—whatever is that sign, a product, is necessarily that predicate, impermanent; and (3) *the counter pervasion*—whatever is not that predicate, not impermanent, is necessarily not that sign, not a product.

Most textbooks on this subject, such as Purbu Chok's *Explanation of the Presentation of Objects and Object-Possessors*, define an inferential cognizer as a determinative knower that is new and incontrovertible, directly produced in dependence upon a correct sign that is its basis. Here "determinative knower" is synonymous with a conceptual consciousness, and "new" refers to a valid cognizer; a second moment of this cognizer is considered to be not a valid cognizer but a subsequent cognizer, according to Purbu Chok. "Incontrovertible" refers to a stable realization, able to withstand examination; the object and its particular quality that is realized can be examined, and one will not reverse one's assessment of it. For example, having realized the impermanent nature of sound, one will be totally convinced of this nature. When a protagonist argues that sound is permanent, due to the power of one's firm realization of sound's real nature, one will not be swayed. "Directly produced" refers to a consciousness that directly arises, without interruption, after the correct sign is established to prove the probandum. The "basis" for inference to arise is the "correct sign."

Khedrup Jé first defines inference from the point of view of a twofold division, inference for oneself and inference for another, after which he explains the three types of inference mentioned above. Purbu Chok maintains that inference for oneself and inferential cognizers are synonymous, while inference for another and correct proof statement are synonymous.[220] He holds that inference for another is not actual inference but rather a verbal expression that is the cause of inference in the listener's continuum. Such a proof statement helps another person to eliminate a wrong form of consciousness, such as thinking that sound is permanent.

[202] **Inferential consciousness, the second division of valid cognizer, is explained in two [sections]:**
- etymology
- divisions

Etymology

If one asks, why is it called "inference," it is because after seeing the sign and remembering the relation, one infers the probandum; we say "inference" [literally, "infer after"].

⚶ Here "relation" refers to the relation between the predicate and the sign. The "probandum" is that which is to be proven, the presence of the predicate on, or as a property of, the subject. Let's take the example of the proof: sound is impermanent because of being a product. Here, "sound" is the subject, "impermanent" is the predicate, and "product" is the sign. How does a person come to infer that sound is in fact impermanent in dependence on this proof? To put it simply, first they see the sign, product, and especially, they see that this sign is a property of the subject, sound. They see that sound is a product. Second, they remember the relation between the sign and the predicate—the relation between product and impermanent. Here, the relationship is such that whatever is a product must be impermanent. They remember this relation. Finally, on this basis, they infer the probandum that the predicate is a property of the subject, here meaning that sound is impermanent. Because the kind of valid cognizer described here is a realization of the probandum that is generated following upon the recognition of the relation, it is called "inference," which in Tibetan literally means to infer after, or to generate a subsequent understanding. This is the etymology of *inference*. ⚶

Division

[When divided], there are two:
- inference for oneself
- inference for another

Inference for oneself [203]
- etymology
- definition
- division

Etymology of inference for oneself
Because it performs the activity of eliminating a superimposition within the continuum of a person who possesses it, and because it is a mind that infers a probandum after seeing the sign and remembering the relation, we say "inference" [literally, "infer after"].

The definition of inference for oneself
An awareness that completely perceives its object of comprehension through a realization that is directly produced by the recollection that remembers the three modes [of ascertainment][221] of the sign that is its basis.

Division
When divided, [there are three types]:
- inferential valid cognizers by the power of the fact
- inferential valid cognizers through renown
- inferential valid cognizers through belief

The definition of an inferential valid cognizer by the power of the fact
An awareness that completely perceives its object of comprehension, some slightly hidden [phenomenon], through a realization that is directly produced by the recollection that remembers the three modes [of ascertainment] of the sign by the power of the fact that is its basis.

꘠ An illustration of an inferential valid cognizer by the power of the fact is: an inferential valid cognizer that realizes that sound is impermanent through the sign, "a product." With this inference one can realize a slightly hidden phenomenon, in this case the impermanence of sound. ꘠

The definition of inferential valid cognizer through renown

An awareness that completely perceives its object of comprehension, some [phenomenon] that is merely posited by a wish [i.e., the preference of the person naming it], through a realization that is directly produced by the recollection that remembers the three modes [of ascertainment] of the sign through the renown that is its basis.

༄ An illustration of an inferential valid cognizer through renown is an inferential valid cognizer realizing that it is suitable to name the formal residence of the US president the "White House," with the sign of its existing among objects of thought. The syllogism is stated like this: the subject, the formal residence of the American president, is suitable to be called "White House" because it exists among objects of thought. ༆

The definition of inferential valid cognizer through belief

[204] An awareness that completely perceives its object of comprehension, some very hidden [phenomena], through a realization that is directly produced by the recollection that remembers the three modes [of ascertainment] of the sign through the belief that is its basis.

༄ An illustration of an inferential valid cognizer through belief is an inferential valid cognizer realizing that the scripture "From generosity, resources, from ethics, happiness" is incontrovertible with respect to its meaning by the sign of "being a scripture free from the three contradictions." The sign *being a scripture free from the three contradictions* means that the quotation is not harmed by any of the three valid cognizers: valid direct perceiver, inferential cognizer by the power of the fact, and inference through belief. Not harmed by inference through belief here signifies that what is being written or quoted in other valid scriptures doesn't contradict the scriptures' explicit and implicit meanings and earlier and later explanations. Through inference of belief, an ordinary person can realize a very hidden phenomenon by depending on the scriptures—for instance, that a particular karma of practicing generosity created at a specific time and place caused particular instances of prosperity or resources to arise.

The above section explained the three types of inference for oneself. Inference for another will be explained below. This type of inference is used by a person who realized something by inference for themself, called a "defender," and then wishes to help another person, here called an "opponent," to realize the same. One uses a proof statement, a clear and correct proclamation, to help another person to eliminate a wrong consciousness, as for instance in the case above, the wrong conceptual consciousness apprehending sound to be permanent. As mentioned above, Purbu Chok says that inference for another is not actual inference but rather a verbal expression that is the cause of inference in the listener's continuum. Khedrup Jé gives a similar explanation. He says that inference for another and proof statement are synonymous; because it causes an inference to arise in the mind of the person who listens to the proof statement it is called "inference for another." The name of the result in the mind of the listener, *inference*, is applied to the cause, the *proof statement*. ⚜

Inference for another [205]
- enumeration [synonyms] of inference for another
- etymology
- definition
- illustration

Enumeration [synonyms] of inference for another
Inference for another, a word [that is a] correct sign, and correct proof statement are various names for the same thing.

Etymology
Because of performing the function of having a person other than the speaker himself realize the probandum, we say "others' purpose." We merely label it "inference" based on a reason and a need. The reason for imputation is: because it is the cause of the result, inference, we apply the

name of the result to the cause. The need for imputation is: in order to realize that the speech expressing the three modes [of ascertainment] has the power to generate inference.

Definition [208]
To say it is speech that, free from excess and omission, clarifies to another disputant in the appropriate circumstances the three modes of ascertainment that one disputant has seen is without error.

Illustration
This is divided into two:
  • presentation of the division
  • the analysis of the existence or non-existence of a correct proof statement having only one branch

⚡ Next, Khedrup Jé explains two types of correct proof statements, one using a similarity and one using a dissimilarity, that can cause a listener or opponent to eliminate a wrong view and generate an inference realizing the fact. The one using a similarity is, for example: to a person who thinks that sound is permanent, and who accepts and ascertains the pervasion that whatever is a product is necessarily impermanent, and who realizes sound to be a product and a vase to be impermanent, one can say, "Whatever is a product is impermanent—for example, a vase; sound is also a product." The one using dissimilarity is, for example: to a person who thinks that sound is permanent, and who accepts and ascertains the pervasion that whatever is permanent is necessarily a non-product, and who realizes sound to be a product and uncompounded space to be permanent, one can say, "Whatever is permanent is a non-product—for example, uncompounded space; as for sound, it is a product." Based on these proof statements the listener can generate the three modes of ascertainment and a correct sign that has the power to produce an inference that realizes sound to be impermanent. ⚡

Presentation of the division
There are two types of inference for another:

- **Definition of a correct proof statement using a qualitative similarity**
  The definition of a correct proof statement using a qualitative similarity is a correct [proof] statement, possessing the two branches [of being without addition or omission], that causes the direct understanding that the sign of a particular proof exists only in a concordant class of that proof statement. An illustration is: whatever is a product is impermanent—for example, a vase; sound is also a product.

- **Definition of a correct proof statement using a qualitative dissimilarity**
  The definition of a correct proof statement using a qualitative dissimilarity is a correct [proof] statement, possessing the two branches [of being without addition or omission], that causes the direct understanding that the sign of a particular proof does not at all exist in a discordant class of that proof statement. An illustration is: whatever is permanent is non-product—for example, [uncompounded] space; as for sound, it is a product.

⟡ A listener can be of various types; one may strongly believe in a wrong view, such as sound is permanent, another may merely wonder whether sound is permanent or impermanent and want to know the truth. For different types of listeners, different proof statements can be used as explained below. In either case the generation of a valid inference must be built up step by step. ⟡

The analysis of the existence of a correct proof statement having only one branch
[214] If one asks, "What is the time of formulating a proof statement? What is the need for formulating one? What is the way of formulating one?," we will respond and explain in accordance with the example of the syllogism proving sound to be impermanent with [the correct sign] being a product.

The time and need of the establishment of the proof statement

There are two kinds of defenders for whom sound must be established as impermanent:

- those for whom the superimposition holding sound as permanent is weaker and doubt [as to whether sound is permanent or impermanent] is stronger, and
- the main ones for whom the superimposition is stronger.

As for the first one:

[215] Those for whom the superimposition holding sound as permanent is weaker and doubt [as to whether sound is permanent or impermanent] is stronger.

[A person] who has not previously turned his mind toward [analyzing] whether sound is permanent or impermanent, or a person who, although having previously turned his mind toward [this question], by not having seen a proof of [sound] being either permanent or impermanent, has doubt, wondering, "Is sound permanent or impermanent?," and wishes to know for certain [one way or the other]. There are two kinds of opponents, one that doubts if sound is both permanent and impermanent, and one that does not doubt if it is both. If the person accepts the first [that sound should be both permanent and impermanent], one points out something that harms sound being permanent and subsequently one puts forward a proof statement that establishes sound to be impermanent. Regarding a person who does not doubt that sound should be the two, being either permanent or impermanent, but wants to know with certainty whether sound is permanent or impermanent and asks [for an answer], then it is sufficient to [merely] explain a proof statement establishing sound as impermanent; one does not need to explain something that harms sound being permanent.

The main ones for whom the superimposition is stronger

As for opponents for whom the superimposition is stronger, [there are two]: those who, through adherence to sound being truly permanent, hold single-mindedly [to this view], and those who think, "Probably sound is permanent." [The second] also has two: those who are certain that a third possibility [beyond] sound being permanent or impermanent is a direct contradiction, and those who are uncertain.

For those who are certain [that there is no third possibility beyond sound being permanent or impermanent], it is sufficient to point out something that harms sound being permanent or something that establishes sound as impermanent; both are not needed because through merely seeing that sound is not permanent, that opponent will be able to ascertain that [sound] is impermanent, and likewise through merely seeing it is impermanent he will be able to ascertain that it is not permanent.

As for those opponents who do not ascertain the direct mutual exclusivity that blocks there being a third possibility [other than] permanent and impermanent, one first points out something that harms sound being permanent, such as the consequence that [if sound were permanent], one would either always hear it or would not hear it even once, and so forth. Subsequently, a proof statement that establishes sound as impermanent is to be put forward.

❧ Khedrup Jé continues to explain the way to establish a correct proof statement for those of sharp and lesser faculties. The proof statement is given in order for the opponent to generate the three modes of ascertainment, first each individually in succession and then simultaneously. After the opponent can ascertain the three modes simultaneously, a correct sign can arise that has the power to produce an inference realizing sound to be impermanent. ❧

The way of formulating a proof statement

In the face of an opponent for whom it is timely to posit a proof of sound as impermanent, and for whom [this proof statement] of sound being impermanent becomes a correct [proof statement], one posits [such a proof] by way of stating, "As for whatever is a product, it is also necessarily impermanent—for example, a pot; sound is also a product," or "As for whatever is permanent, it is also necessarily a non-product—for example, space; as for sound, it is a product."

At the time of putting forward the proof statement, the opponent doesn't ascertain the three modes of the correct sign, product, establishing sound to be impermanent. Although product is posited as a correct sign to establish sound as impermanent, [for the opponent] it does not become [a correct sign because the three modes are not ascertained]. [216] Nevertheless, later the opponent serially establishes the property of the subject, the forward and counter pervasions, and having established them knows them individually [as these three modes were given one by one].

As for an opponent of sharp faculties, one need not again posit the proof statement, but through the force of recollecting the previously stated [proof statement, such an opponent] can know individually the three modes and can recollect them all at once. At that time, the previously posited proof statement itself becomes a correct proof statement. Thereby product, which was previously posited as a sign, becomes a correct sign [and thus the opponent will realize sound to be impermanent].

In the case of an opponent of dull faculties, after having established and understood the three modes individually, one needs to posit the proof statement again in order for him to recollect the three modes simultaneously. As for this [opponent], who has previously understood and not forgotten the three modes, he will recollect the three modes simultaneously in dependence on the proof statement, stating the three modes simultaneously, and the proof statement turns into a [correct] proof statement. [The product, which was previously posited as a sign, becomes a correct sign, and thus the opponent will realize sound to be impermanent].

In short, as for the function of a proof statement: given that it is to recollect the three modes of ascertainment that have already been known, and is not for coming to know [the three modes that have] not [previously] been known, therefore Dharmakīrti's *Exposition of Valid Cognition* says:

> That which abides on the three modes correctly
> and is recollected

abides correctly on the expression.
As for the power of the inner branches,
[they] abide correctly in the three modes.
As for generating the recollection of these,
[it abides] correctly in the expression itself.²²²

༈ Khedrup Jé concludes here by explaining how slightly hidden phenomena, like subtle impermanence and selflessness, can be realized for oneself through valid inference, and how one can help another person to realize the same by stating a proof. These are important aspects of understanding reality and developing the paths to liberation and enlightenment in one's own and others' minds. Inference is also used to understand the different types of samsaric suffering and their causes, and for generating the mind of renunciation, a mind that wishes to be liberated from samsara. Having seen that the root cause of samsara is ignorance, one generates a wish to eliminate this false apprehension of a self-sufficient self. By depending on inference realizing selflessness, one opposes ignorance. This inference then turns into a subsequent cognizer, and with more habituation it becomes a powerful mind realizing selflessness directly; at such time a yogic direct perceiver is generated. This wisdom mind directly realizing selflessness has the potential to uproot ignorance together with its imprints and thereby to establish nirvana, the state beyond all suffering. Thus by generating a mind that understands reality, the two truths, the four noble truths, the Three Jewels of Refuge, and the paths to enlightenment and liberation can be completely understood, and gradually one can not only achieve the ultimate happiness of nirvana but also lead all sentient beings to that sublime state. ༈

EPISTEMOLOGICAL ASPECTS OF
LOGIC AND REASONING

A CORRECT FORM of logical reasoning is essential in the study of
Buddhist philosophy. It enables one to eliminate wrong views and
come closer to a correct understanding of reality. There are different levels
of reality, conventional and ultimate truths, like the impermanent and
selflessness natures of a person, respectively. Those levels of conventional
reality that cannot be perceived by ordinary sense perception and ultimate
reality belong to the category of hidden phenomena. In order to know
these types of phenomena one needs to depend on reasoning and valid
inferences that are conceptual processes of the mental consciousness.

How a wrong view can be gradually weakened, eliminated, and replaced
with a realization of truth can be explained through the following example. A person first has a wrong conceptual consciousness, thinking that
sound is permanent, in the sense of not changing moment by moment.
When this person also accepts that sound is a product, one can put forward the consequence: "It follows that the subject, sound, is a non-product
because of being permanent." This will generate doubt regarding the initial
view of sound being permanent.

After hearing that sound is momentarily changing and thus impermanent because of being a product, the person starts to generate more
doubt about the initial view. Three types of doubt arise in the following
sequence: first there is doubt tending toward the non-factual, then doubt
that thinks sound is probably permanent, then doubt with qualms about
both sides equally—for example, doubt that wonders whether sound is
permanent or impermanent; after which doubt tending toward the factual

arises—for example, doubt that thinks sound is probably impermanent. After these types of doubt, a correctly assuming consciousness can arise. Although a correctly assuming consciousness doesn't have the unstable aspect of the two-pointed qualms to two extremes that doubt has, it is not an incontrovertible knower like a valid cognizer. When the person, having generated a correctly assuming consciousness apprehending that sound is impermanent, thinks more about the reasons for sound being impermanent, a correct valid sign will be generated and give rise to the generation of inference through which sound is realized to be impermanent. In order to generate inference, a correct sign has to be established as the basis, as explained in the definition of an inferential cognizer above. Most textbooks, such as Purbu Chok's *Explanation of the Presentation of Objects and Object-Possessors*, define an inferential cognizer as a determinative knower that is new and incontrovertible, directly produced in dependence upon a correct sign that is its basis.

The chart on page 239 shows the terminology of the syllogism stating a correct sign that establishes inference.

In order to become a correct sign that can generate inference, three modes of ascertainment should be realized:

- The sign being established on or as a property of the subject, which is sometimes translated as "the property of the subject": the subject, sound, being a product. This property of the subject can also be proved to the opponent, if not yet ascertained by her, with the reason: the subject, sound, is a product because of being produced. *Produced* is the definition of product. The definition and definiendum of a particular phenomenon are synonymous and mutually inclusive; whatever is the one is necessarily the other.
- The forward pervasion: whatever is the sign, a product, is necessarily the predicate of the probandum, impermanent. This pervasion can also be proved if not ascertained yet with the reason: whatever is a product is necessarily impermanent because whatever is a product is necessarily momentary. *Momentary* is the definition of impermanent.

Syllogism		
"The subject, sound, is impermanent because it is a product."		
Probandum		
Subject	Predicate of the probandum	Sign
Sound	**Impermanent**	**Product**
Three Modes of Ascertainment:		

The property of the subject:
The subject is related to the sign of a syllogism such that it possesses or is whatever the sign is. Here, sound is impermanent, and so impermanent is a property of sound.

The forward pervasion: Whatever is a given sign is necessarily that predicate. Here, whatever is a product is necessarily impermanent.

The counter pervasion: Whatever is the opposite of that given as the predicate is not that sign. Here, whatever is permanent is not a product, or is a non-product.

The shaded arrows in the chart above indicate how different parts of a correct syllogism should be related to each other in order that each of the three modes of ascertainment can be generated.

- The counter pervasion: By explicitly stating the forward pervasion, one implicitly states the counter pervasion, that whatever is permanent is necessarily a non-product. This refers to the absurd consequence used to induce doubt in the mind of a person who thinks that sound is permanent and accepts that sound is a product: "It follows that the subject, sound, is a non-product because of being permanent."

Correct proof statements explicitly expressing the three modes of ascertainment can be of two types: positive or negative, or, as Khedrup Jé explains them, those using a qualitative similarity and qualitative dissimilarity, respectively. The former establish a subject as *having* a particular property or *being* something else, while the latter establish a subject as *not having* a particular property or *not being* something else. For example:
- Positive correct proof statement/one using a qualitative similarity: "Whatever is a product is impermanent—for example, a vase; sound is also a product."
- Negative correct proof statement/one using a qualitative dissimilarity: "Whatever is permanent is a non-product—for example, [uncompounded] space; as for sound, it is a product."

In order to generate an inferential valid cognizer realizing that sound is impermanent by depending on a correct sign, a person must fulfill four criteria for the sign to be correct—that is, to have the power to generate the realization of sound being impermanent in his continuum:
- the person believes sound is permanent
- the person ascertains that whatever is a product is necessarily impermanent
- the person ascertains that sound is a product
- the person wishes to know whether or not sound is impermanent

Based on the above the person can realize the correct sign of "The subject, sound, is impermanent because it is a product"; the person can realize sound to be impermanent through inference. A similar process can be applied to realizing selflessness using the reason that there is no self-sufficient self that is inherently one with or different from the aggregates, as can be seen in the section "Negating the Selves of Persons and Phenomena" in chapter 5, and in appendix 6, Realizing Selflessness of Persons in the Madhyamaka.

MENTAL FACTORS

Mental factors are very important in the explanation of consciousness. On several occasions in *Clearing Mental Darkness*, Khedrup Jé refers to main minds and mental factors. Because Khedrup Jé's actual text doesn't list or explain mental factors, this appendix gives an overview of the relation between main minds and mental factors and lists the mental factors varyingly according to Vasubandhu and Asaṅga.

Mental factors are explained below in accordance with the Mūlasarvāstivādin Vaibhāṣhika tradition, which mainly depends on Vasubandhu's *Treasury of Knowledge*, and the Yogāchāra tradition, which mainly depends on Asaṅga's *Compendium of Knowledge*.[223] First, the relation between main mind and mental factor will be explained, after which the divisions of the mental factors will be given.

MAIN MIND AND ITS MENTAL FACTORS

In the Abhidharma, consciousness is divided into two types, main mind (*chitta*) and mental factors (*cetasikas*). Main minds, or primary consciousnesses, are of six types: eye, ear, nose, tongue, body, and mental primary consciousnesses.

Main mind and mental factors differ in the way they engage with their objects. Maitreya's *Distinguishing the Middle from the Extremes* (*Madhyāntavibhaga*)[224] says:

That which sees an object is primary consciousness.
That which sees its attributes is a mental factor.

This means, that which knows the mere entity of its object is a main mind. Although mental factors take as their basis the same objects as the main mind they accompany, they engage their objects by means of different attributes, such as function,[225] and examine the different aspects of their object. For example, apprehending one's body, the mental factor *discrimination* helps the main mind to focus on the impermanent aspect of the body. It is only through the action of mental factors that an object can be realized and that the main mind they accompany becomes virtuous, nonvirtuous, or neutral.

The way mental factors are related to the main mind they accompany can be understood as similar to the relationship between a prime minister and her retinue: a prime minister does not travel alone but is always accompanied by cabinet ministers and assistants who perform specific functions.[226] Similarly, every primary consciousness is accompanied by mental factors that perform specific functions for the main mind. They work together to engage objects in different ways.

In his *Treasury of Knowledge*, Vasubandhu explains five similarities between main mind and mental factors:

(1) Similar support: if a main mind is supported by a sense power (or sense organ), then the mental factors in its retinue are also supported by that sense power.

(2) Similar object of observation: a main mind and the mental factors in its retinue have the same object.

(3) Similar subjective aspect: when a main mind has the aspect of apprehending the color blue, then the mental factors in its retinue also have the aspect of apprehending the color blue.

(4) Similar time: a main mind and the mental factors in its retinue are simultaneous—they are produced, abide, and cease at the same time.

(5) Similar substance: one main mind can have only one mental factor of a similar type in its retinue. For example, one specific main mind can be accompanied by only one type of feeling—pleasant, unpleasant, or neutral—at any one time. It cannot have two or three different types of feeling or other mental factors accompanying it simultaneously.

Asaṅga also explains five similarities between main mind and mental factors in his *Compendium of Knowledge*: (1) similar substance, (2) similar object of observation and subjective aspect, (3) similar entity, (4) similar time, and (5) similar realm and level.[227] Of these five similarities: similar object of observation and similar time are the same as in the *Treasury of Knowledge*. There is a difference with regard to *subjective aspect*, *entity*, and *realm and level*. *Similar subjective aspect*, the third similarity mentioned in the *Treasury of Knowledge*, is the same as *similar entity* mentioned in the *Compendium of Knowledge*. *Similar realm and level* is uncommon to the *Compendium of Knowledge*. *Similar realm and level* means: if main mind belongs to the desire realm, then the mental factors in its retinue also belong to the desire realm.

The Division of Mental Factors

Vasubandhu's *Treasury of Knowledge* lists forty-six mental factors by dividing them into the following groups:

(1) Ten basis of mind grounds: common to all primary consciousnesses.

(2) Ten virtuous grounds: virtuous mental factors.

(3) Six great-afflicted grounds: non-virtuous mental factors.

(4) Two non-virtuous grounds: non-virtuous mental factors.

(5) Ten lesser-afflicted grounds: non-virtuous mental factors.

(6) Eight indirectly indicated mental factors: a miscellaneous group of mental factors that cannot be classified in any of the above groups.

In his *Compendium of Knowledge*, Asaṅga lists fifty-one mental factors classified into the following groups:

(1) Five omnipresent mental factors: common to all main minds.

(2) Five object-ascertaining mental factors: these mental factors hold an object through apprehending the individual features of the object; their function is to help the main mind they accompany to realize or ascertain its object.

(3) Eleven virtuous mental factors.

(4) Six root afflictions: these are non-virtuous mental factors.

(5) Twenty secondary afflictions: non-virtuous mental factors.

(6) Four changeable mental factors: can become virtuous, non-virtuous, or neutral, depending on the motivation or intention.

All the mental factors mentioned above are listed in the following tables.

FORTY-SIX MENTAL FACTORS IN VASUBANDHU'S *TREASURY OF KNOWLEDGE*

Ten basis of mind grounds:
1) Feeling
2) Intention
3) Discrimination
4) Aspiration
5) Contact
6) Intelligence/Wisdom
7) Mindfulness
8) Mental engagement
9) Belief
10) Stabilization

Ten virtuous grounds:
1) Faith
2) Conscientiousness
3) Pliancy
4) Equanimity
5) Shame
6) Embarrassment
7) Non-harmfulness
8) Effort
9) Non-attachment
10) Non-hatred

Six great-afflicted grounds:
1) Ignorance
2) Non-conscientiousness
3) Laziness
4) Non-faith
5) Lethargy
6) Excitement

Two non-virtuous grounds:
1) Non-embarrassment
2) Non-shame

Ten lesser-afflicted grounds:
1) Belligerence
2) Resentment
3) Deceit of hiding faults
4) Jealousy
5) Spite
6) Concealment
7) Miserliness
8) Deceit of pretending to have qualities
9) Harmfulness
10) Haughtiness

Eight indirectly indicated mental factors:
1) Investigation
2) Analysis
3) Contrition
4) Sleep
5) Anger
6) Attachment
7) Pride
8) Doubt

THE FIFTY-ONE MENTAL FACTORS IN ASAṄGA'S *COMPENDIUM OF KNOWLEDGE*

Five omnipresent mental factors:
1) Feeling
2) Discrimination
3) Intention
4) Contact
5) Attention

Five object-ascertaining mental factors:
1) Aspiration
2) Belief
3) Mindfulness
4) Meditative stabilization
5) Wisdom

Eleven virtuous mental factors:
1) Faith
2) Shame
3) Embarrassment
4) Non-attachment
5) Non-hatred
6) Non-ignorance
7) Effort
8) Pliancy
9) Conscientiousness
10) Equanimity
11) Non-harmfulness

Twenty secondary afflictions:
1) Belligerence
2) Resentment
3) Concealment
4) Spite
5) Jealousy
6) Miserliness
7) Deceit
8) Dissimulation
9) Haughtiness
10) Harmfulness
11) Non-shame
12) Non-embarrassment
13) Lethargy
14) Excitement
15) Non-faith
16) Laziness
17) Non-conscientiousness
18) Forgetfulness
19) Non-introspection
20) Distraction

Four changeable mental factors:
1) Sleep
2) Regret
3) Investigation
4) Analysis

Six root afflictions:
1) Attachment
2) Anger
3) Pride
4) Ignorance
5) Doubt
6) Afflicted views:
   • View of the transitory collection
   • View holding to an extreme
   • Conception of a bad view as supreme
   • Conception of bad ethics and modes of conduct as supreme
   • Wrong view

KARMA AND AFFLICTIONS

KARMA

KARMA is narrowly defined as the mental factor of intention but more broadly refers to physical, verbal, and mental intentional actions. These actions plant karmic seeds in the mind that can cause a result to come about in the future when the right conditions are met. These physical, verbal, and mental activities are preceded by an intention or motivation. This intention can be virtuous, non-virtuous, or neutral, and thus causes the activities and resultant karmic potentialities to be virtuous, non-virtuous, or neutral as well. The subsequent results experienced are therefore pleasant, unpleasant, or neutral, respectively.

The Buddhist treatises distinguish a threefold division of contaminated karma by way of its function:

- Impelling karma: a karmic action that issues forth a mere potential to impel a fruitional effect in the form of rebirth in one of the six realms of samsara.
- Establishing karma: having arisen at the time of death from the imprint left on the mental continuum by a previous impelling karma, it renders the fruitional effect certain to be established.
- Completing karma: gives rise to the various pleasant or miserable experiences one has on the basis of a specific birth.[228]

How to reflect on these three types of karma and how to relate this to the contaminated aggregates, which are created by karma and afflictions as explained in the chapter on the four noble truths, is well explained in Tsongkhapa's *Arranging the Path of Valid Cognition*. In that text, Lama

Tsongkhapa urges one to reflect on the following syllogisms to establish the aggregates as being under the power of karma and afflictive emotions: (1) This human body is preceded by good impelling karma . . . because of being a pleasant fruitional effect; (2) it is preceded by various other good and bad karmas because of possessing various desired and undesired effects. (3) This animal's body is preceded by bad impelling karma because of being an unpleasant fruitional effect . . . (4) Since accumulation of karma has to, moreover, be preceded by craving, these contaminated aggregates are preceded by craving that wishes to obtain its object because—without being impelled by Isvara and so forth—birth was taken within the unclean abode of the womb.[229]

Here, the first and third syllogisms relate to ways that virtuous and non-virtuous impelling and establishing karmas engender their respective results of pleasant and unpleasant rebirths. The second refers to the way completing karmas, upon meeting conditions for ripening, color people's lives with pleasant or unpleasant sensations. The final syllogism is associated with the way afflicted craving is a necessary precondition for the accumulation of contaminated karmas such as these.

The volitional physical, verbal, and mental activities that produce karmic imprints depend on the mind because every such activity is preceded by a particular intention, a motivation. Training the mind results in constructive behavior and prevents destructive actions of body, speech, and mind from arising, thereby preventing negative karma from being created and avoiding the suffering results of such karma. The causes of negative actions and suffering are the afflictions.

AFFLICTIONS

Afflictions not only cause negative results of in the context of karma, but they also disturb the peace of mind immediately when they arise. Therefore they are often also classified in psychology as destructive emotions. Asanga's *Compendium of Knowledge* defines an affliction as: "A phenomenon that has the characteristics of being very un-peaceful, and thus disturbs the mental continuum in which it arises, causes it to become un-peaceful."[230]

According to that same text, afflictions can be divided into six root and twenty secondary afflictions as illustrated in appendix 2. The secondary afflictions are rooted in the six root afflictions. When further condensed, there is a threefold division called the "three root poisons": attachment, anger, and ignorance.

- Attachment overestimates the appealing qualities of its object without seeing the faults; it is a mental factor that perceives a contaminated thing to be attractive and thereupon seeks and clings to it. Vasubandhu's *Treasury of Knowledge* gives as the definition, "a clinging of the three realms, its function is to produce suffering."

- Anger overestimates the faults and unappealing aspects of its object without seeing the positive qualities; it is a mental factor that has malice toward others, seeks to be separated from its object, and has the function of acting as a support for misconduct. *Treasury of Knowledge* defines it as "a malice toward sentient beings, suffering, and phenomena that are causes for suffering, its function is to act as a support for not abiding in contact and for misconduct."

- Ignorance can be of many types. The relevant ignorance here is that which is the root cause of samsara. It is explained in different ways according to the various schools of Buddhist philosophy. In the chapter on the four noble truths, following the Chittamātra school of thought, ignorance is posited as the apprehension of a self of a person that is self-sufficient, in the sense of being characteristically discordant with the aggregates.

Attachment and anger exaggerate the attractive qualities or faults of their objects, causing the mind to be disturbed and the person possessing them to experience suffering. Ignorance is a mind that, like attachment and anger, apprehends reality in a mistaken manner, being rooted in improper mental engagement. The wisdom realizing selflessness, on the other hand, is in accord with ultimate reality and can therefore become fully integrated. Because it directly stops the ignorance that is the root of all afflictive mental states, it can gradually eliminate even the seeds and subtle imprints of these afflictions. This aspect of the possibility of abandoning afflictions is elaborately explained in the chapter on the four noble truths and nicely summarized by Gyaltsab Jé in his *Clarifying the Path of Liberation*:

> Whatever mind wrongly engages the nature of things is pervaded by having a powerful harmer to its type. For example, the superimposition apprehending fire as non-existent on a smoky pass. The grasping at the self of person also wrongly engages the nature of things.
>
> Therefore there must exist a possibility of the misapprehension of a self of persons' continuity being extinguished, thereby preventing further accumulation of karma and cycling in existence.[231]

Thus with correct consciousness one can eliminate wrong forms of consciousness. Minds that accurately perceive their objects with detachment, lovingkindness, compassion, and wisdom knowing selflessness act as antidotes to destructive emotions like attachment, anger, and self-grasping, which apprehend their objects in a distorted way. Anger, for example, a mental factor belonging to the category of root afflictions, exaggerates the faults of its object without seeing any positive qualities. It has an aspect of wishing to harm, wants to be separated from its object, and causes the mind to be disturbed and the person possessing it to experience suffering. Conversely, lovingkindness has a balanced view of its object, seeing both positive qualities and faults, has an aspect of wanting to help, wants to be with its object, brings peace to the mind, and causes the person having it to experience happiness now and in the future. With more self-awareness, one recognizes and understands the nature of destructive emotions like anger, how they arise, how they abide and disturb the inner peace of mind, and how they disintegrate with time or in the face of an antidote. With this awareness one sees the negative aspects of the afflictions and sees that these emotions are not an innate part of the mind—like clouds not being an inherent part of the sky—and thus that they can be eliminated. By applying the antidotes, like lovingkindness to anger, one can both prevent destructive emotions from arising in one's mental continuum and also increase constructive states of mind. To do this one analyzes the negative aspects of individual destructive emotions and contemplates the positive aspects of their antidotes using many lines of reasoning. For example, lovingkindness, because of wishing beings to abide in happiness, apprehends the same object as anger but in a directly opposing way and is therefore the opposite from anger, which wishes to harm others. One particular consciousness cannot apprehend its object in two opposite ways in the same moment. For example, one mind wishing a particular person to experience both suffering and happiness at precisely the same time is impossible. When, through training the mind, lovingkindness becomes more prevalent in a person's mental continuum, instances of anger become less frequent, less powerful, and shorter in duration when they do arise; an inner happiness or well-being is achieved with an increased power and presence of virtuous states of mind like lovingkindness conjoined with the peace arising from the absence of the destructive emotion anger. Eventually these techniques are used in sustained contemplation. By drawing on explanations heard or read, past experiences, examples, scriptural citations, and logical reasoning, one will reach conclusions having fresh insight, seeing the faults of specific destructive emotions and the positive qualities of their antidotes. At such times one focuses single-pointedly on the conclusion in order to build up habituation with this wholesome state of knowing. When the mind becomes more and more interested in and familiar with the qualities of the antidote and positive states of mind, the destructive emotions lose their potential to become manifest. In a similar way, all mental afflictions can be eliminated, and thus the creation of new negative karma is also prevented. Familiarization through these mind trainings and meditation is very important. As Shāntideva says in his *Bodhisattvacharyāvatāra*, "There is nothing that will not become easier through familiarization." Through these techniques a stable mental health of inner well-being can be generated.

VIEW OF SELFLESSNESS IN THE SCHOOLS
OF BUDDHIST PHILOSOPHY

THE SŪTRAS that constitute Buddha's teachings are commonly arranged according to the three turnings of the wheel of Dharma. In each of the three wheels the Buddha gave different teachings to various disciples, depending on and in accordance with their interests, intelligence, and level of development. Based on these teachings the schools of Buddhist philosophy developed, with each holding different views regarding selflessness. In the teachings of the first turning, delivered in Deer Park near Varanasi, the Buddha taught only the coarse and subtle selflessness of persons as posited by the Great Exposition (Vaibhāṣhika), Sautrāntika, Chittamātra, and Madhyamaka Svātantrika schools. In the teaching of the second wheel, the *Perfection of Wisdom Sūtras*, taught on Vulture's Peak, he explained the subtle selflessness of both persons and phenomena according to the view now held by the two Madhyamaka schools. In the teachings of the third turning of the wheel at Vaishali, he taught the *Unraveling the Intention Sūtra*, which gives an alternate interpretation of the second wheel for trainees who cannot penetrate its profound meaning. The selflessness of phenomena explained in this teaching is held as foremost by the Chittamātra. The table below gives an overview of these differences as explained by Jetsun Chökyi Gyaltsen in his *Presentation of Tenets*. Phenomena in the phrase "selflessness of phenomena" means any existing phenomena other than a person.

School	Coarse selflessness of person
Vaibhāṣhika (Great Exposition)	Person's emptiness of being permanent, unitary, and independent
Sautrāntrika (Sūtra)	Person's emptiness of being permanent, unitary, and independent
Chittamātra (Mind-Only)	Person's emptiness of being permanent, unitary, and independent
Sautrāntrika-Svātantrika-Madhyamaka (Sūtra Middle Way Autonomy)	Person's emptiness of being permanent, unitary, and independent
Yogāchāra-Svātantrika-Madhyamaka (Yogic Middle Way Autonomy)	Person's emptiness of being permanent, unitary, and independent
Prāsaṅgika-Madhyamaka (Middle Way Consequence)	Person's emptiness of being self-sufficient, substantially existent

Subtle selflessness of person	Selflessness of phenomena		
Person's emptiness of being self-sufficient, substantially existent	Don't accept selflessness of phenomena		
Person's emptiness of being self-sufficient, substantially existent	Don't accept selflessness of phenomena		
Person's emptiness of being self-sufficient, substantially existent	Phenomena's emptiness of apprehended and apprehender existing as substantially different		
Person's emptiness of being self-sufficient, substantially existent	Phenomenon's emptiness of being truly established		
		Coarse selflessness of phenomena	Subtle selflessness of phenomena
Person's emptiness of being self-sufficient, substantially existent		Phenomena's emptiness of apprehended and apprehender existing as substantially different	Phenomena's emptiness of being truly established
Person's emptiness of being truly established in the sense of empty of inherent existence		The emptiness of gross objects composed of partless particles and their apprehenders existing as substantially different	Phenomena's emptiness of being truly established in the sense of inherently existent

APPENDIX 5

PATHS OF LIBERATION AND ENLIGHTENMENT

THIS APPENDIX explains the paths of liberation and enlightenment from a general perspective. The spiritual paths of Buddhism can be divided into three different vehicles:

- the Śhrāvaka Vehicle
- the Pratyekabuddha Vehicle
- the Bodhisattva Vehicle

Which vehicle a person enters depends primarily on the motivation of the practitioner as described below.

Motivations Marking the Entrance of the Paths

For the vehicles of śhrāvakas and pratyekabuddhas: *renunciation*, the uncontrived and spontaneously arising wish to attain liberation from samsara for oneself. This wish is generated through meditation on the various types of suffering of samsara until an uncontrived wish to be free of these sufferings effortlessly and naturally arises.

For the Bodhisattva Vehicle: an uncontrived realization of the mind of *bodhichitta*; the determination to become a buddha in order to liberate all sentient beings from suffering. This wish is generated through meditation not only on the various types of suffering of samsara but also on the wish to free all sentient beings from these sufferings and the incomparable benefits of becoming a buddha for this purpose. This meditation is also done until an effortless wish of bodhichitta—having the two aspirations to free all beings and, for that purpose, to attain the state of buddhahood—spontaneously and effortlessly arises.

The term "spontaneously arising" means that the practitioner habituates the mind through both analytical and placement meditation over a sustained period of time, producing an intention or insight that arises naturally or automatically without having to make an effort to generate it. At such point one has attained some degree of realization. Having generated either renunciation or bodhichitta, one enters the path. After having entered the path, one gradually progresses through five distinct paths that are stages of the path in general. These are the paths of (1) accumulation, (2) preparation, (3) seeing, (4) meditation, and (5) no-more-learning. The duration of the first four paths, the paths of learning, varies on the path of shrāvakas and pratyekabuddhas and the path of bodhisattvas because their results, called "the path of no-more-learning," are vastly different. A person on the path of no-more-learning of the former is a mere arhat, whereas the latter is a fully enlightened buddha. In order to become a buddha, having an omniscient mind, one needs to amass a greater accumulation of merit and wisdom than is achieved on the shrāvaka and pratyekabuddha path of no-more-learning; more causes have to be created. Also, according to the Chittamātra and Madhyamaka schools, to become a buddha one not only needs to abandon afflictive obscurations (obscurations to liberation), as is needed to achieve the mere state of arhat or liberation, one also needs to abandon the cognitive obscurations (obscurations to omniscience). Further, within the three different paths there are differences in duration depending on whether the practitioner is of higher or lower faculties.

Duration of the Paths
- For the shrāvaka path: depending on the type of person, the duration of the path varies between three and several lifetimes.
- For the pratyekabuddha path: depending on the type of person, the duration of the path is in most schools explained as one hundred eons.
- For the bodhisattva path: depending on the type of person, for the

one of sharpest faculties, the duration of the path is three countless great eons.

Result of the Paths

- For the śhrāvaka path: path of no-more-learning of the state of śhrāvaka arhat, liberated from samsara.
- For the pratyekabuddha path: path of no-more-learning of the state of pratyekabuddha arhat, liberated from samsara.
- For the bodhisattva path: path of no-more-learning of the state of buddhahood, liberated from samsara and attainment of full enlightenment.

Progression on the Paths

How a person actually progresses on the four paths of learning is given below. This chart gives a common overview and can be applied to the three vehicles: the vehicles of the śhrāvakas, pratyekabuddhas, and bodhisattvas. Depending on the different paths and schools of the Buddhist tenet systems, there will be a difference in the wisdom realizing selflessness, the main object of meditation, and the objects of abandonment. Here, just the general term "realization of selflessness" is used, although what this is in each case varies widely according to the different Buddhist tenet systems. For an overview of how the four schools of Buddhist philosophy describe selflessness, see appendix 4.

After having entered the path of accumulation, one habituates the mind to the conceptual realization of selflessness over three levels: small, medium, and great. When the realization of selflessness becomes a wisdom of meditation arisen from the union of calm abiding and special insight, one enters the path of preparation. This union of calm abiding and special insight is a wisdom realizing emptiness such that by the force of analysis the strength of single-pointed concentration is increased, and by this bliss and pliancy are induced.[232] On the path of preparation a meditator gradually prepares the conceptual mind realizing selflessness that they already possess to

Person:	Ordinary Being	
Paths:	Accumulation	Preparation
Realization of object of meditation:	Conceptual realization of selflessness based on calm abiding	Conceptual realization of selflessness based on the wisdom of meditation arisen from the union of calm abiding and special insight
Object of abandonment:	Incapability of the generation of the wisdom of meditation arisen from the union of calm abiding and special insight realizing selflessness	Duality of the object selflessness and the mind realizing selflessness

Paths:	Accumulation	Preparation
Divisions:	Great Medium Small	Supramundane qualities Forbearance Peak Heat

Ārya or Noble Being	
Seeing	Meditation
Direct realization of selflessness	Direct realization of selflessness
Intellectually acquired grasping at a self	Innate grasping at a self

Seeing	Meditation

Absorption that is neither
Subsequent attainment
Path of release
Uninterrupted path
	10th Uninterrupted path
	2nd–9th Uninterrupted paths, paths
	  of release and related subsequent
	  attainment
	Absorption that is neither
	Subsequent attainment
	1st Path of release
	1st Uninterrupted path

become a yogic direct perception. The appearance of duality for the mind conceptually realizing the object selflessness becomes weaker and more subtle over the four stages of this path. When a direct perception of self-lessness is generated, this dualistic appearance disappears and one enters the path of seeing.

On the path of seeing, the uninterrupted path of the direct perception of selflessness acts as the actual antidote to intellectually acquired grasp-ing at a self, the misapprehension of a self that is acquired through fol-lowing wrong philosophical tenets. When this object is abandoned one enters the path of release in the same session of meditative absorption as the uninterrupted path. After arising from this absorption one enters the state of subsequent attainment of the path of seeing. From this point until one attains the path of meditation, a practitioner repeatedly enters med-itative absorption focused on selflessness called "absorption that is nei-ther an uninterrupted path nor a path of release" in order to develop the strength of wisdom realizing selflessness until it has the power to abandon the grossest form of innate grasping at a self, the misapprehension of a self that has existed since beginningless lifetimes in the minds of all sentient beings. At the time one is able to generate an uninterrupted path that can eliminate the seeds of this grossest level of innate self-grasping, one enters the path of meditation and the first uninterrupted path of meditation simultaneously.

This first uninterrupted path of meditation is the actual antidote to the grossest forms of innate grasping at a self. When this object of aban-donment is abandoned, one enters the first path of release of the path of meditation in the same session of meditative absorption. After one arises from this meditation one enters the state of subsequent attainment.

There are nine levels of innate grasping at a self that are objects to be abandoned; they are divided into three groups—greatest, middle, and smallest—and each of these groups has three parts—great, middle, and small. There are uninterrupted paths of meditation that successively aban-don these obscurations from the most gross or coarse, the greatest great, which is most easily abandoned, to the most subtle, the smallest small, which is most difficult to abandon. The most subtle of these nine objects of abandonment of the path of meditation, the smallest small, is divided into two, gross and subtle, because it is more difficult to abandon. Thus the path of meditation has ten uninterrupted paths. The path of meditation has more stages and divisions than the path of seeing because it is more difficult to abandon innate grasping at a self than the intellectually acquired self-grasping. In general, the more a habituation is built up over a longer period of time, the stronger it becomes and the more difficult it is to eliminate this habituation. We have unwittingly taken the view of self-grasping to be true since beginningless time, so of course we are strongly habituated to it. Therefore to abandon it we have to strongly generate the opposite view, the wisdom realizing selflessness, supported by the whole-hearted aspirations for liberation and enlightenment in order to achieve the welfare of all sentient beings over a long time.

The tenth uninterrupted path of the path of meditation is the last moment of the paths of learning. It is the actual antidote to the smallest small innate grasping at a self. When this object of abandonment is abandoned, one enters the path of no-more-learning in the same session of meditative absorption.

Thus, based on the uncontrived realization of renunciation or bodhichitta, one enters the paths of the Śhrāvaka, Pratyekabuddha, or Bodhisattva Vehicles. After entering these paths, one eliminates the obstacles to be abandoned, the obscurations to liberation or the obscurations to omniscience, in stages. This elimination actually happens with the direct realization of selflessness on the uninterrupted paths of seeing and meditation. Finally, one reaches the last uninterrupted path, and during that very meditative absorption one reaches the result, the path of no-more-learning.

REALIZING SELFLESSNESS OF PERSONS
IN THE MADHYAMAKA

THIS APPENDIX presents a simplified form of the process of realizing selflessness of persons according to the Prāsaṅgika Madhyamaka. The root cause of afflictions and suffering is the mistaken apprehension, called "ignorance," of an inherently existing "I" and "mine." The Buddha said in the *Dhammapada* (18.243):

> Foremost among the taints is ignorance, which is the worst of all stains.

Before disturbing emotions like anger and attachment arise, there is a strong apprehension of a concrete inherent self that doesn't exist in the way it appears. Whatever appears to one's consciousness is not necessarily in accordance with reality. For example, when sitting in an unmoving train at a station awaiting departure and a train on one side moves, one can feel and think that one's own train is moving. One can totally believe this to be true until one looks at the platform on the other side and realizes that it is the other train that is moving. After this insight one will not generate the wrong consciousness that one's own train is moving. The inherently established self appears as existing separate from and independent of the body and mind, as if it exists totally from its own side without depending on imputation from the side of the mind. With the correct understanding of how the self actually exists—in a dependent way in relation with one's body and mind—one can eliminate this ignorance and thereby abandon the root cause of the afflictions. In this way the eradication of suffering

and the attainment of ultimate happiness are achieved. The four schools
of Buddhist philosophy—Vaibhāṣhika, Sautrāntrika, Chittamātra, and
Madhyamaka—describe the nature of ignorance and how it causes suffering to arise in different ways. Nāgārjuna, father of the Prāsaṅgika school,
says in his *Mūlamadhyamakakārikā* (18.5):

> Obstruction by ignorance continues [suffering] existence.

The same text also states:

> When [the views] of [an inherent] "I" and "mine" are extin-
> guished, karma and afflictions cease and liberation [is obtained].

Dharmakīrti says in his *Pramāṇavārttikakārikā* (2.221):

> If there is self [grasping], one discerns another,
> grasping at the part of self and opposing that of others.
> From thorough association with these,
> all faults come to arise.

Based on a strong apprehension of a concrete "I" and "mine," one becomes
more selfish, which is not only a cause of suffering for oneself but also leads
to more problems with people around one. Seeing oneself as more important than others can lead to many conflicts. Elimination of this perception
of the self leads to a strong generation of lovingkindness and compassion
toward those around us, bringing more happiness for self and others. Total
elimination of this misapprehension of a self, in the minds of self and
others, gradually brings ultimate happiness for everyone.

In order to eliminate ignorance, the root cause of the afflictions, we
engage in analysis and mental training, utilizing our fundamental human
intelligence to investigate the difference between how the self ordinarily
appears and how it actually exists. Whereas the self ordinarily appears as
inherently or independently existing, and we grasp at this appearance as

real and accurate, under analysis it is found that this is just a distorted superimposition. The following analysis is based on the first two reasons of Candrakīrti's sevenfold reasoning, using the example of a chariot. In *Entering the Middle Way* (6.151) he states:

> A chariot is asserted to be neither [inherently] other than its parts nor [inherently] non-other.

The first step is recognizing how the self appears to one's consciousness, recognizing the object of negation. It appears in an independent manner, as being separate from body and mind, existing from its own side. This appearance of a concrete self is especially evident at times when destructive emotions like anger and attachment arise. At these times there is a strong apprehension of a concrete "I" and "mine."

The second step analyzes the necessity that if a concrete self exists as it appears, it must be either one with or different from body and mind; there is no other possibility.

The third step establishes that this mistakenly appearing self cannot be one with body and mind. If it were one with the body and mind, then the self should be multiple since the body and mind are multiple. *Entering the Middle Way* (6.127) says:

> If the aggregates [of body and mind] were the self, then since there are many aggregates, the self would also be many.

The fourth step establishes that the concretely appearing self cannot be inherently different from body and mind. If it were inherently different from body and mind, how could an interdependent relationship exist between the conventional self and body and mind? *Entering the Middle Way* (6.122) says:

> There is no [inherent] self other than the aggregates because without the aggregates it is not apprehended.

Based on the previous reasons, the fifth step concludes that an inherently established or concrete "I" cannot exist. One focuses upon this conclusion for some time and familiarizes one's mind with this understanding of the ultimate reality of the self. Following this insight, one concludes that the self is a mere imputation upon the aggregates of body and mind in a nature of dependent origination. Through this one finds the view of the Middle Way. Nāgārjuna says in his *Mūlamadhyamakakārikā* (24.18):

> Whatever is dependently originated,
> that is explained to be emptiness.
> That [emptiness] being a dependent designation,
> this indeed is the Middle Way.

The above method for the meditation on selflessness can be applied to the meditation on selflessness presented in other Buddhist schools as well. When describing how to recognize the object of negation, one should focus on how this object is described in a particular school. After this, one can use a similar form of the logical reasoning described above by analyzing that if that particular self exists, it should be one or different from the aggregates, and so forth. Thereby one can realize the various gross and subtle views of selflessness asserted by the different Buddhist schools.

GLOSSARY

IN ENGLISH a word's definition should ideally make the meaning clear for non-specialist readers, but in Buddhist philosophy this is not necessarily so. In Buddhist philosophy the purpose of a definition is largely twofold. On the one hand, a definition must describe the object it defines, the definiendum, in such a way that whatever fulfills the characteristics described by that definition is necessarily that definiendum, and whatever is that definiendum necessarily possesses all the characteristics described by its definition. For example, a phenomenon that is not momentarily disintegrating is the definition of *permanent*. It is the case that whatever possesses the characteristics of both being a phenomenon, meaning that it exists, and being not momentarily disintegrating or not changing from moment to moment is in fact permanent. Whatever is permanent also fulfills the two characteristics of being a phenomenon and not momentarily disintegrating—for example, the mere absence of wings on a pig. Conversely, "anything that is not momentarily disintegrating" would not be a suitable definition of *permanent* because things that do not exist, like cats on the moon, do fulfill the characteristic of being not momentarily disintegrating, but they are not permanent.

A second function of definitions in Buddhist philosophy is to show how the object defined relates to other objects and larger categories in both positive and negative ways. For example, the definition of Chittamātra (*sems tsam pa*) is "a Buddhist school or tenet holder propounding Mahāyāna tenets who does not accept external objects but does assert truly existent self-cognizers." This definition possesses both positive and negative aspects. It positively shows that Chittamātra is a Mahāyāna tenet system or tenet holder, and one that does accept truly existent self-cognizers.

However, this definition negates that this school accepts external objects in the sense of objects that are not one entity with the mind realizing them. You can see that to understand these kinds of definitions requires further learning. Their meaning is not clear at first sight because each term in the definitions refers to other types of objects and broader concepts that must also be understood in order to grasp the meaning of the definition.

In traditional Buddhist institutions for philosophical studies students first memorize the definitions without fully understanding the meaning. Then they receive explanations from teachers, debate extensively about these definitions with their peers, and read multiple commentaries on issues surrounding the terms defined, thereby gradually gaining a full understanding of their import. Having gone through this process of learning, the pithy definitions memorized earlier now serve to succinctly refer to a larger array of concepts and precisely locate the object defined within that landscape.

In this glossary most definitions have two entries. The first is a standard definition as found in mainstream Tibetan works on Buddhist philosophy. Since this is a translation of Khedrup Jé's *Clearing Mental Darkness*, we have given the definitions he uses in this text when possible. These will be useful for serious students to refer back to as they come across the terms defined in various contexts and to perhaps memorize. The second entry is a more idiomatic gloss of the term and its definition to help readers get a general idea of what it means without necessarily being a definition that could be defended in debate. In many cases we have also pointed out terms that are synonymous and those that are contradictory in an illuminating way. Most of the terms listed here are explained more extensively in the text itself and we encourage readers to refer back to those explanations.

appearing object (*snang yul*; *pratibhāsaviṣaya*). An object that is experienced by an awareness through having appeared to it.

The object that primarily appears to a consciousness, thereby enabling it to engage its main object. All appearing objects of direct perceivers are impermanent, while all appearing objects of conceptual consciousnesses are permanent.

aspect of the apprehended (*gzung rnam*; *grāhyākāra*). An other-knowing consciousness that is directed outward and is generated in the aspect of the objects it apprehends.

Synonymous with *other-knower*. A consciousness that is directed to objects other than itself or to objects other than an aspect of mind with which it is concomitant and one entity. It has the appearance of the aspect of an object that is not an apprehender, meaning not a consciousness. For example, an eye consciousness apprehending blue is generated as possessing an appearance of the blue it engages and thereby both has and is the aspect of blue. Contrast with *aspect of the apprehender* and *self-knower*.

aspect of the apprehender (*'dzin rnam*; *grāhakākāra*). A knower that is exclusively directed inward and is generated in the aspect of the consciousness that is its object.

This type of mind accompanies all other-knowing consciousnesses and functions merely to experience the consciousness that it accompanies. From within the two, remembering an object we have known and remembering the experience of having known that object, the aspect of the apprehender is what enables us to remember the latter, the experience of knowing an object. See also *self-knower*. Contrast with *aspect of the apprehended*.

awareness (*blo*; *buddhi*). That which is generated as experience. Synonymous with *consciousness*.

awareness to which the object appears but is not ascertained/inattentive awareness (*snang la ma nges pa'i blo*). A knower that is a common locus of having clear appearance of the specifically characterized phenomenon that is its object of engagement and being unable to induce ascertainment with regard to that specifically characterized phenomenon.

Often we are intently focused on one object, say an engaging conversation, and simultaneously other objects, like the sensations in our feet or things we pass by, appear to one of our consciousnesses, such as our body or eye sense consciousness. These unnoticed objects are not realized by the consciousnesses they appear to. Therefore, although such objects did appear to our mind, we cannot generate memories of them. Minds that experience their objects in this inattentive way are called *awareness to which the object appears but is not ascertained*.

bodhisattva (*byang chub sems dpa'*). A sentient being who has generated bodhichitta, the mind aspiring to achieve complete enlightenment in order to accomplish the welfare of all sentient beings.

cause (*rgyu*; *hetu, kāraṇa*). That which produces.

Any phenomenon that produces effects. Synonymous with impermanent, functioning thing, and specifically characterized phenomenon. See also *effect*.

Chittamātra (*sems tsam pa*). A Buddhist school or tenet holder propounding Mahāyāna tenets who does not accept external objects but does assert truly existent self-cognizers.

A Buddhist tenet system or tenet holder that embraces the ideal of striving for full enlightenment in order to serve other sentient beings and does accept that some phenomenon such as self-cognizers and other forms of consciousness truly exist. This school uniquely does not accept the existence of external objects in the sense of objects that are not one entity with the mind realizing them. They hold that all phenomena are one entity with the mind observing them in a similar way that objects appearing to a dream consciousness are one entity with the dreaming mind.

conceptual consciousness (*rtog pa, rtog pa'i shes pa*; *kalpanā, kalpanā-jñāna*). A determinative knower that apprehends sound generality and meaning generality as suitable to be mixed.

All consciousness can be divided into conceptual and non-conceptual consciousness. Conceptual consciousness is distinct in that it engages its main object by means of a generic mental image of that object, called a "meaning generality," appearing to it due to the activation of imprints planted in the person's mind through previous experiences. The generic mental image and the actual object, although they are two separate things, appear mixed together as one single object. Hence, conceptual consciousness is mistaken with regard to its appearing object because it has the false impression that the generic mental image of its main object is that object, whereas it is not. All our minds remembering something are examples of conceptual consciousness.

conceptual consciousness that does not realize its object (*ma rtogs pa'i rtog pa*). An awareness whose mode of conception can be directly negated by a valid cognizer.

All conceptual consciousness can be divided into those that correctly apprehend their object and those that incorrectly apprehend. If a consciousness incorrectly apprehends its object, then the way it conceives of or apprehends its object is false, because something conceived of in that way does not exist. This false "mode of conception" can be identified as false and can thereby be negated by a valid cognizer. For example, a consciousness apprehending that Earth is at the center of the solar system does not realize its object, Earth at the center of the solar system, and can be conclusively known as false by a valid cognizer in dependence on the realization that Earth orbits the Sun.

concordant isolate type (*ldog pa rigs mthun*). For all positive phenomena it is said that two phenomena are the same type if when a person, be they trained in terminology or not, sees those two phenomena and, through just seeing them in an attentive manner, an awareness apprehending them to be similar is spontaneously generated. For all nonfunctioning negative phenomena they are posited through their object of negation being of the same type, because the different divisions of negative phenomena are not made by way of the entity of the negative phenomena but are divided according to their objects of negation.

Two or more positive things, like banana and plantain, are of a concordant isolate type if an ordinary attentive person finds they are similar. Negative phenomena, like not poodle and not Pekingese, are of concordant isolate type if the objects they negate, poodle and Pekingese, respectively, are of similar type, in this case dog.

concordant substantial type (*rdzas rigs mthun*). Different things that are generated from the same substantial cause.

The substantial cause of something is the cause that primarily determines the structure or entity of the thing. There can be two different things that are effects produced from one substantial cause. In that case the two are of a concordant substantial type. The petals of a single flower are examples of things that are of a concordant substantial type.

consciousness (*shes pa*; *jñāna*). That which is clear and knowing.

Anything that can experience an object and is not embodied, as for instance human beings and animal are, is a consciousness. Something that is a consciousness does not have any constituent parts that are matter. In this definition "clear" is generally held to mean that any existent object can appear to an awareness, and no one aspect of an object is fixed in the face of an awareness. "Knowing" means that it experiences objects by virtue of its own entity. That all consciousnesses are "knowing" does not mean that they all realize their objects, because even wrong consciousnesses that do not realize any object are clear and knowing.

conventional truth (*kun rdzob bden pa*; *saṃvṛtisatya*). A phenomenon that is established as merely imputed by conceptual consciousness, or a phenomenon that is not ultimately able to perform a function. This definition is according to the Sautrāntika.

Synonymous with *permanent phenomenon* and *generally characterized phenomenon*. For the Sautrāntika, phenomena that do not have the ability to produce effects, and especially do not have the ability to cast their appearance to a consciousness in the way that, for instance, a scent of lavender does, are in a way not as real as objects of the senses.

correct proof statement using a qualitative similarity (*chos mthun sbyor gyi sgrub ngag yang dag*). A correct proof statement that causes the direct understanding that the sign of a particular proof exists only in a concordant class of that proof statement. An illustration is whatever is a product is impermanent—for example, a vase; sound is also a product.

To prove something, we can use either examples showing similarity or counter examples showing dissimilarity. In the first case, what is mainly being established is that whatever is the phenomenon that is posited as the sign in a proof statement must necessarily be the phenomenon that is posited as the predicate in that proof. In a given correct proof, if A is posited as the sign and B is posited as the predicate, then whatever is A must be B. For example, in the proof "Socrates is mortal because he is a man," "man" is the sign and "mortal" is the predicate. It must be established that whatever is a man is necessarily mortal. To establish this we can give a similar example of a man, like Heraclitus. This kind of proof statement uses an example having similar qualities to the subject to establish the forward pervasion that whatever is that posited as the sign in a proof must be that posited as the predicate.

correct proof statement using a qualitative dissimilarity (*chos mthun sbyor gyi sgrub ngag yang dag*). A correct proof statement that causes the direct understanding that the sign of a particular proof does not at all exist in a discordant class of that proof statement. An illustration is whatever is permanent is a non-product—for example, uncompounded space; as for sound, it is a product.

This kind of proof uses an example of something that has qualities that are diametrically dissimilar to the subject to establish that whatever belongs to the class of things that are not the predicate is necessarily not the specific sign in a proof. To put this another way, it is established that whatever is the specific sign in a proof necessarily does not belong to the class of things that are not the predicate in that proof, the discordant class. For example, in the syllogism "Sophia is mortal because she is a woman," the sign is "woman" and the discordant class is "not mortal." To give a related proof statement using qualitative dissimilarity we could state: Whatever is not mortal is not a woman, like stone; as for Sophia, she is a woman and so she is mortal. Compare with *correct proof statement using a qualitative similarity.*

correct sign (*rtags yang dag*; *samyaklinga*). That which fulfills the three modes. A reason given in a syllogism that unmistakably establishes the probandum by being the three modes of the syllogism—the property of the subject, the forward pervasion, and the counter pervasion. See *three modes of the sign.*

To be a correct sign in a proof something must fulfill three criteria. First, the sign must be a property or characteristic that is true of the subject. Take the example of the proof "Socrates is mortal because he is a man." The correct sign in this proof is "man." It is true that Socrates is a man. The sign, "man," is a property of the subject, "Socrates." Second, it must the case that whatever is a given sign is the relevant predicate, meaning that there is a forward pervasion. Whatever is a man is indeed mortal. Finally, it must be such that whatever is not the predicate is necessarily not that sign. Whatever is not mortal is not a man. This is the counter pervasion. Therefore, man is all three modes of the sign in this syllogism and is thus a correct sign.

correctly assuming consciousness (*yid dpyod*; *manaḥparīkṣā*). A factually concordant determinative knower that is controvertible with regard to determining its object.

Determinative knower is synonymous with *conceptual consciousness*. A conceptual consciousness that realizes its object does so in dependence on a correct sign. It is thereby incontrovertible with regard to that object, meaning that it will never transform into doubt about whether what has been realized is true. However, a correctly apprehending conceptual consciousness that has not realized its object in dependence on a sound reason just assumes what it thinks to be true without any sound logical basis. Such a consciousness, although it is correct in what it apprehends, is *controvertible*, meaning that it can fall into doubt about what has been correctly apprehended when faced with information or arguments counter to what it assumed.

counter pervasion (*ldog khyab*; *vyatirekavyāpti*). The set of phenomena associated with the sign in a syllogism exclusively not existing in the dissimilar class of that syllogism.

A correct sign in a proof must be the counter pervasion in that proof, meaning that it must be the case that whatever belongs to the discordant class of the proof's predicate must not belong to the class of things that are that sign. For example, in the proof "Sophia is mortal because she is a woman," the predicate is "mortal" and the sign is "woman." The discordant class of this predicate is "not mortal." The counter pervasion is that "whatever is not mortal is not a woman." It follows that whatever is a woman necessarily does not belong to the class of phenomena that are not mortal.

This being true is one reason that "woman" is a correct sign in this syllo-gism. In any syllogism, if the forward pervasion is established, then the counter pervasion is also established. See also *correct sign*.

determinative knower (*zhen rig*). Synonymous with *conceptual conscious-ness*.

When a non-conceptual consciousness, like an eye or an ear sense con-sciousness, is merely directed toward or is in the range of things suitable to be its object, like visual forms or sounds, those objects appear to it with-out any effort from the side of the consciousness. Conversely, a concep-tual consciousness must make effort to apprehend its objects by thinking, "This is this," or "That is that." This effort put forth in apprehending an object is called "determining" or "conceiving" (*zhen pa*).

determined object (*zhen yul*). That which is the object of the mode of determination of the conceptual consciousness that apprehends it. Syn-onymous with *object of engagement* and *object of the mode of apprehension*.

Only conceptual consciousnesses have *determined objects* because only conceptual consciousnesses think about things and thereby *determine* this is this or that is that. Whatever is the determined object of a conceptual consciousness is also the object of engagement of that consciousness. Since all things that exist are objects of a conceptual consciousness that appre-hends them, all existent phenomena are determined objects.

direct perceiver (*mngon sum*; *pratyakṣa*). A knower that is free from con-ceptuality and non-mistaken.

That a direct perceiver is "free from conceptuality" means that for any con-sciousness that is a direct perceiver, it does not have any instances that are conceptual consciousness. For example, eye consciousness is a direct per-ceiver and there are no instances of eye consciousness that are a conceptual consciousness. There is no overlap between the two. *Valid cognizer* is not a conceptual consciousness, but because some instances of it are conceptual consciousness, like inferential cognizer, it is not a direct perceiver. That direct perceivers are non-mistaken means that their appearing objects exist in the way that they appear to direct perceivers. Blue exists in the way it appears to an eye consciousness apprehending blue. This is not the case for conceptual consciousness. See also *conceptual consciousness*.

discordant substantial type (*rdzas rigs mi mthun*). Different things that are generated from different substantial causes. For example, two children born of different sets of parents, or a rose and an orchid. Contrast with *concordant substantial type*.

doubt (*the tshom; vicikitsā*). An awareness whose mode of apprehension has the aspect of qualms to two extremes. For example, the mind wondering whether or not past and future lives exist.

There are three kinds of doubt: doubt tending away from the fact, balanced doubt, and doubt tending toward the fact. They are similar in that, with regard to two possible answers to a question, like does rebirth exist, instead of decisively realizing or believing in one answer or the other, they waver between the two possibilities in indecision. There are both afflicted and useful forms of doubt.

effect (*'bras bu; phala*). That which is produced. For example, an apple.

All impermanent phenomena are effects of their causes. All impermanent phenomena are also causes of the things they produce. In essence, everything that is produced from some things that precede it necessarily produces other things that arise subsequent to it. For example, apple is an effect of the tree that bore it, and yet apple is also a cause of the eye sense consciousness that sees it. Therefore, cause and effect, though having different meanings, are coextensive; whatever is one is necessarily the other. However, with regard to one object, like apple, its cause and effect are mutually exclusive; whatever is the cause of apple is not its effect and vice versa.

empowering condition (*bdag rkyen*; *adhipatipratyaya*). That which mainly and directly produces an effect under its own power.

For example, an eye sense power is the empowering condition of an eye consciousness apprehending blue. Under its own power the eye sense power that is the cause of seeing blue mainly and directly produces an eye consciousness apprehending blue. In general all causes are empowering conditions of some effect.

existent (*yod pa*; *sat*). That observed by a valid cognizer.

In Buddhist philosophy the mark of existing is being known, realized, or experienced by an awareness that correctly engages its object in a way that is vivid and infallible.

explicit realization (*dngos su rtogs*). Certain knowing that is induced by the power of a valid cognizer turning its attention toward an object and that object appearing to such a knower without having relied on other, later awarenesses. Also commonly translated as "directly realize."

Minds realize things both explicitly and implicitly in a similar way that words and phrases express meanings both explicitly and implicitly. The main characteristic of a mind explicitly realizing an object is that the object realized appears to that mind. For example, if we hear an animal crunching the leaves outside our window and, looking to see what it is, we discover a deer, the deer appears to our eye consciousness and to our subsequent conceptual consciousness thinking, "It is a deer." Contrast with *implicit realization*.

explicit realization for a valid direct perceiver (*mngon sum tshad ma'i dngos su rtogs*). A valid direct perceiver's eliminating superimposition in relation to its object of comprehension through that object's aspect explicitly appearing.

When a mind realizes an object, it removes superimpositions with regard to that object. Superimpositions are fallacies projected onto an object, such as thinking that a reflection of our face in the mirror is a real face. When we touch the hard glass of the mirror, this superimposition is removed. When a valid direct perceiver realizes an object by means of that object directly appearing to it, this is *explicit realization* for that mind.

explicit realization for an inferential cognizer (*rjes dpag tshad ma'i dngos su rtogs*). An inferential cognizer's eliminating superimposition with regard to its object of comprehension by means of that object's meaning generality explicitly appearing.

Because the main appearing object of an inferential cognizer or any other conceptual consciousness is a meaning generality of the object that is primarily realized, explicit realization in this case is distinguished not by the main object realized appearing, as with direct perceivers, but by the meaning generality of that mind's main object appearing.

forward pervasion (*rjes khyab*; *anvayavyāpti*). The sign in a syllogism existing only in the similar class of that syllogism in accordance with the manner posited.

For example, in the syllogism "sound is impermanent because of being a product," the sign, "product," is the forward pervasion of that syllogism because it exists only in the similar class of that syllogism, "impermanent," in accordance with the manner posited, "being." In essence, because sound is asserted as being impermanent on the basis of it being a product, and whatever is a product is indeed only impermanent and not in any case permanent, therefore the forward pervasion is established.

functioning thing/thing (*dngos po*; *vastu, bhāva*). That which is able to perform a function.

The main function generally implied is that of producing its various effects, such as subsequent moments in the continuum of the same object and awarenesses perceiving the object.

generality (*spyi*; *sāmānya*). A phenomenon that encompasses its manifestations.

Any phenomenon that has multiple instances of things that are it, and can exist even in the absence of each of those instances, is a generality. For example, impermanent is a generality of vase, flower, and dog because those three are all instances of impermanent, and impermanent can exist in the absence of any one of those. Impermanent is not a generality of cause or functioning thing because it cannot exist in the absence of either of those. This is because whatever is cause is impermanent. The definition of impermanent is not a generality because there are not multiple instances of it. There is only one definition of impermanent.

generally characterized phenomenon (*spyi mtshan*; *sāmānyalakṣaṇa*). A phenomenon that is merely imputed by a term or conceptual consciousness and is not established by way of its own character. Synonymous with *permanent phenomenon*. Contrast with *specifically characterized phenomenon*.

Another way to describe permanent phenomena is those that do not have specific attributes through being produced as they are by their causes and conditions, but instead exist through being determined by conceptual consciousness in accordance with fact. Compare the way leaves on a tree and 1+1=2 exist. The former are produced each with a host of uniquely distinguishing features by their individual causes. The fact that 1+1=2 is not produced by causes and instead is known and thus exists by force of conceptual consciousness correctly conceiving it to be so.

hidden phenomenon (*lkog gyur; parokṣa*). That which is explicitly realized by an inferential valid cognizer. Synonymous with *existent*. See chapter 1 for some debate about how to define this term.

Hidden phenomena are delineated as those phenomena that an ordinary being needs to initially realize in dependence on conceptual consciousness using reasoning. For example, the fact that sound is impermanent, meaning that it continually changes through even the shortest units of time, is a hidden phenomenon. It is something that ordinary people cannot experience with their ear consciousness but can come to know through reason. An ordinary person first generates an inferential consciousness realizing that sound is impermanent in dependence on the reason that sound is a product.

immediately preceding condition (*de ma thag rkyen; samanantara-pratyaya*). A knower that primarily and directly produces the consciousness that is its result as a clear and knowing experiencer. Synonymous with *consciousness*.

Any moment of an awareness is produced as a knower by another instant of awareness that existed in the immediately prior moment and gave rise to it. This fact (which materialists of any flavor would highly contend) is the logical basis for Buddhists to assert the existence of a person's previous rebirths and the lack of a beginning to their mental continuum.

impermanent (*mi rtag pa; anitya*). A momentarily disintegrating phenomenon. Synonymous with *cause*, *effect*, and *functioning thing*.

All phenomena that are produced from causes continually change without the slightest pause. As such, they are never entirely the same for two consecutive moments and are said to disintegrate in that the way they were in the previous moment is no more in subsequent moments.

implicit realization (*shugs la rtogs*). Certain knowing by a consciousness that removes superimpositions with regard to an object that does not appear to it by explicitly realizing a different object.

When a consciousness realizes an object indirectly in the course of explicitly realizing a different object. For example, when searching for a lost passport one might look in an empty desk drawer and, explicitly seeing the bottom and sides of the drawer devoid of a passport, implicitly realizes the passport is not there. Whereas the surface of the inside of the drawer devoid of a passport directly appears to this eye consciousness, the absence of a passport does not appear and yet it is realized. Compare with *explicit realization*.

implicit realization for a valid direct perceiver (*mngon sum tshad ma'i shugs la rtogs*). Eliminating superimposition in relation to an object that does not appear to it by the force of having eliminated superimposition with regard to its object of comprehension through the aspect of the object of comprehension directly appearing.

See the example given for *implicit realization*. The inside of a drawer devoid of a passport is the object of comprehension for a person's eye consciousness that is looking for a lost passport there. That directly appears. By eliminating superimposition or dispelling not knowing with regard to what is inside the drawer, although mere lack of a passport does not appear to that eye consciousness, yet lack of a passport is known indirectly and so superimposition is also cleared away with regard to it. Contrast with *explicit realization for a valid direct perceiver*.

implicit realization for an inferential cognizer (*rjes dpag tshad ma'i shugs la rtogs*). Eliminating superimposition with regard to another object whose meaning generality does not appear to it through the force of eliminating superimposition by the meaning generality of its object of comprehension explicitly appearing.

The explanation is similar to that of implicit realization, except that here there is emphasis on the appearance or non-appearance of an object's *meaning generality*, or generic mental image (see *conceptual consciousness* for a fuller explanation of this). When an inferential cognizer realizes its main object through that object's meaning generality appearing to it, it can also indirectly realize another object whose meaning generality does not appear. For example, to the inferential cognizer realizing that tree is impermanent, the meaning generality of "tree is impermanent" appears, and it thinks, "Tree is impermanent." The meaning generality of "tree is not permanent" does not appear, and that mind does not think, "Tree is not permanent," yet tree is not permanent is implicitly realized. Contrast with *explicit realization for an inferential cognizer.*

incontrovertible knower/non-deceptive cognition (*mi bslu ba'i rig pa*). A knower that attains its object of analysis in the sense of eliminating superimpositions with regard to its object.

All valid cognizers and subsequent cognizers are incontrovertible. Correctly assuming consciousness, doubt, and wrong consciousness are not. For a consciousness to be incontrovertible means that it knows its object with such a degree of certainty that no matter what experiences the person possessing that mind may have in the future, they will not generate doubt about whether what that mind has realized is true or not.

inference for another (*gzhan don rjes dpag; parārthānumāna*). Speech that, free from excess and omission, clarifies to another disputant in the appropriate circumstances the three modes of ascertainment that one disputant has seen.

A syllogism that is verbally stated by someone who has realized what is to be proven by that proof, the probandum, in dependence on the three modes of ascertainment of it. They state the syllogism in order to induce ascertainment of the probandum for someone who has not already realized it, who has doubt and a desire to know with regard to it, and who under the circumstances has the potential to realize that probandum. One of the main prohibiting circumstances to being able to realize something in dependence on a syllogism would be that a person has strong wrong views that prevent them from realizing one of the three modes of ascertainment of the syllogism. See *three modes of ascertainment* for an explanation of those.

inference for oneself (*rang don rjes dpag; svārthānumāna*). An awareness that completely perceives its object of comprehension through a realization that is directly produced by the force of the recollection that remembers the three modes of ascertainment of the sign that is its basis. Synonymous with *inferential consciousness*.

For example, imagine a person who is (1) certain that vase is impermanent, (2) certain that whatever is a product, having been produced by causes and conditions, is impermanent, and (3) certain that sound is such a product, but (4) has doubt about whether or not sound is impermanent. To such a person a syllogism might be stated by another person or arrived at through internal reflection that sound is impermanent because of being a product. Once this person has realized that (1) sound is a product, (2) whatever is a product is necessarily impermanent, and (3) whatever is not a product is necessarily not impermanent, in light of recalling these three ascertainments the person firmly concludes that indeed sound is without a doubt impermanent. This final realization is an inference for oneself. See also *inferential consciousness*.

inferential consciousness (*rjes dpag; anumāna*). A new and incontrovertible determinative knower that is directly produced by the recollection that remembers the three modes of ascertainment of the correct sign that is its basis.

Whatever is both a conceptual consciousness and a valid cognizer is an inferential consciousness, also commonly called an "inferential valid cognizer." Such a consciousness is generated in dependence on a correct sign in a valid proof. See *correct sign* and *three modes of the sign* for further explanation. There are three kinds of inferential valid cognizer that correlate to three kinds of sign that are their bases—inference by the power of fact, inference through belief, and inference through renown.

inferential valid cognizer by the power of the fact (*dngos stobs rjes dpag*; *vastubalānumāna*). An awareness that completely perceives its object of comprehension, a slightly hidden phenomenon, through a realization that is directly produced by force of the recollection that remembers the three modes of ascertainment of the sign by the power of the fact that is its basis.

An inferential valid cognizer generated in dependence on a sign by the power of fact. An example of a sign by the power of fact is sound is impermanent because of being a product. An inferential cognizer that realizes that sound is impermanent in dependence on the sign "product" in this proof is an inferential valid cognizer by the power of fact.

inferential valid cognizer through belief (*yid ches rjes dpags*; *āptānumāna*). An awareness that completely perceives its object of comprehension, a very hidden phenomenon, through a realization that is directly produced by force of the recollection that remembers the three modes of ascertainment of the sign through the belief that is its basis.

An illustration of an *inferential valid cognizer through belief* is an inferential valid cognizer realizing that the scripture "From generosity, resources, from ethics, happiness" is incontrovertible with respect to its meaning, by the sign of being a scripture free from the three contradictions. "Being a scripture free from the three contradictions" means that the scriptural statement is not harmed by any of the three valid cognizers: valid direct perceiver, inferential cognizer by the power of the fact, and inference through belief.

inferential valid cognizer through renown (*grags pa'i rjes dpag; prasiddhānumāna*). An awareness that completely perceives its object of comprehension, some phenomenon that is merely posited by a wish (i.e., the preference of the person naming it), through a realization that is directly produced by the force of the recollection that remembers the three modes of ascertainment of the sign through the renown that is its basis.

An illustration of an inferential valid cognizer through renown is an inferential valid cognizer realizing that it is suitable to name the formal residence of the US president the "White House," with the sign of its existing among objects of thought. The syllogism is stated like this: the subject, the formal residence of the President of the United States, is suitable to be called "White House" because it exists among objects of thought.

Madhyamaka (*dbu ma pa*). A Buddhist tenet holder or school propounding Mahāyāna tenets that does not assert true existence even conventionally.

This Buddhist tenet school is unique from the others in asserting that there are no truly existent phenomena. The other schools all hold that if there is no true existence, then there is no way to posit the functioning of cause and effect and direct perception. A Mahāyāna tenet holder accepts the Sanskrit canon of sūtras as the word of Buddha and embraces the aim of achieving full enlightenment in order to work for the welfare of all sentient beings until they are free from suffering.

main mind (*gtso sems; pradhānacitta*). A main knower that is posited by way of apprehending the entity of its object.

There are six main minds: the eye, ear, nose, tongue, and body sense consciousnesses, and the mental consciousness. They all merely apprehend the entity of their objects without performing further functions such as experiencing feelings of pleasure or pain, generating intentions to act, or labeling their objects. They are accompanied by mental factors that perform such functions. See also *mental factor* and appendix 2.

manifest phenomenon (*mngon gyur*; *abhimukhī*). That which is explicitly realized by a valid direct perceiver.

Manifest phenomena, like the color blue, are delineated as those that can be initially realized by a valid direct perceiver of an ordinary being, like a sense consciousness—for example, the eye consciousness apprehending the color blue. Blue is a manifest phenomenon. Conversely, hidden phenomena are delineated as those phenomena that an ordinary being needs to initially realize in dependence on conceptual consciousness using reasoning.

meaning generality (*don spyi*; *arthasāmānya*). An appearing object of conceptual consciousness, it is a generic image of that phenomenon that is the determined object of the consciousness for which it is the appearing object.

A meaning generality of an object is an appearance of the elimination of all that is not that object. For example, the meaning generality of house is the appearing object of the conceptual consciousness determining "house." The meaning generality of house is the appearance of the elimination of all that is not house. Although the meaning generality of house is not house, it appears to the conceptual consciousness apprehending house as if it is house. A meaning generality is a permanent phenomenon. See also *conceptual consciousness*.

mental direct perceiver (*yid kyi mngon sum*; *mānasapratyakṣa*). A nonmistaken, other-knowing mental consciousness that is directly produced from the mental sense power that is its own uncommon empowering condition.

A non-conceptual mental consciousness such as the clairvoyance able to read another person's mind.

mental factor (*sems byung*; *caitta, caitasika*). A knower that apprehends any of the features of its object and accompanies whatever main mind is concomitant with it. See appendix 2 for further explanation.

mistaken consciousnesses (*'khrul shes*; *bhrāntajñāna*). A consciousness that is mistaken with regard to its appearing object.

A consciousness is mistaken when its appearing object appears in a way that is different from how the appearing object actually exists. For example, a dream consciousness to which the people and sounds in a dream appear to be real people and sounds, when in fact they are not, is mistaken. All direct perceivers are non-mistaken. All conceptual consciousnesses are mistaken because their appearing object is a meaning generality that appears to be the object it is a meaning generality of when in fact it is not. For example, the conceptual consciousness apprehending vase is mistaken with regard to its appearing object, the meaning generality of vase, because that meaning generality appears to that consciousness as if it were a vase while in fact it is not. All wrong consciousnesses are also mistaken.

non-conceptual wrong consciousness (*rtog med log shes*). An other-knowing consciousness that has a clear appearance of its object through a corrupted sense power that is its empowering condition.

When our sense faculties are corrupted, they give rise to false appearances. An eye consciousness that sees snow mountains as blue is a wrong non-conceptual sense consciousness. It has a clear appearance of its object, blue snow mountains, meaning that the object appears independent of a meaning generality appearing. The white snow mountains falsely appear as blue due to a fault in the eye sense power.

non-valid awareness (*tshad min gyi blo*; *apramāṇabuddhi*). A knower that is not new and incontrovertible. Compare with *valid cognizer*.

object (*yul*; *viṣaya*). That which is known by an awareness. Synonymous with *existent*.

object of engagement (*'jug yul*; *pravṛttiviṣaya*). Whichever object the activity of a valid cognizer engages for the purpose of thoroughly realizing that object. Also known as the "object of engagement of a valid cognizer."

The objects that consciousness comprehends, actually gets at, or engages in. Synonymous with *object of the mode of apprehension*. *Object of engagement, determined object,* and *object of the mode of apprehension* are synonymous.

object of the mode of apprehension (*'dzin stangs kyi yul*). A phenomenon that exists in just the way an awareness in accordance with fact apprehends it. Synonymous with *existent*. See *determined object*.

object of the mode of determination (*zhen stangs kyi yul*). A phenomenon that exists in just the way a conceptual consciousness in accordance with fact determines it. Synonymous with *determined object* and *existent*.

object possessor (*yul can*; *viṣhayin*). A functioning thing that possesses its respective object. All consciousnesses, persons, and expressive sounds are object possessors.

observed object condition (*dmigs rkyen*; *ālambanapratyaya*). That which mainly and directly produces an awareness as having the aspect of the main object observed and apprehended by that awareness.

For example, the observed object condition of a direct perceiver apprehending blue is blue, because blue is that which mainly and directly produces this consciousness as having the aspect of blue. The observed object condition of a conceptual consciousness apprehending blue is the imprint planted by a former consciousness that caused the conceptual conscious-ness to be generated having the aspect of blue.

other-knower (*gzhan rig*). A consciousness that is directed outward and engages external objects. See also *aspect of the apprehended*. Contrast with *self-knowing valid direct perceiver*.

permanent phenomenon (*rtag pa*; *nitya*). A phenomenon that is not momentarily disintegrating.

For example, the number one. It has not arisen from causes, does not pro-duce effects, and does not change from moment to moment. Yet it exists and can be known. Permanent phenomena do not necessarily endure for all of time. They can also come into and pass out of existence.

pervasive compounding suffering (*khyab pa 'du byed kyi sdug bsngal*; *saṃskāraduḥkhatā*). A neutral contaminated feeling that possesses poten-tialities such that it will definitely give rise to painful feelings when condi-tions for that are met. The main minds and mental factors that accompany such a neutral feeling, and the contaminated objects that when observed act as conditions giving rise to it, are also pervasive compounding suffer-ing. It is called "pervasive" because all beings in all realms of samsara pos-sess this kind of suffering. This kind of suffering is only identified by those who correctly determine the fundamental causes of samsara, karma, and afflictive emotions together with the ignorance that is their root cause.

pratyekabuddha (*rang sangs rgyas*). A person who is a no-more-learner of the vehicle seeking to attain liberation from samsara for themselves only, has accumulated a greater collection of merit than a śrāvaka, generally prefers to study and practice alone, in their final rebirth does not rely on listening to teachings, has achieved liberation at a time and place when there are no buddhas appearing as a supreme emanation body, and after becoming an arhat teaches others non-verbally.

predicate of the probandum (*sgrub bya'i chos*; *sādhyadharma*). That which the subject in a syllogism is asserted to be, in accordance with the manner of positing it, by reason of that syllogism's sign. For example, in the syllogism "the subject sound is impermanent because of being a product," "impermanent" is the predicate of the probandum. "Sound is impermanent" is the probandum. In the proof "Socrates is mortal because of being a man," mortal is the predicate. Mortal is being predicated or asserted to be true of Socrates by virtue of the reason that he is a man.

probandum (*sgrub bya*; *sādhya*). In a syllogism the aggregate meaning composed of both the subject and the predicate that is being established in dependence on the sign.

A probandum is something to be proven, a quality or property of a particular object—for example, sound being impermanent, impermanent being a property of sound.

property of the subject (*phyogs chos*; *pakṣadharma*). That which is ascertained by valid cognition as existing only in accordance with the manner posited, as a property of the faultless subject sought to be known in a particular syllogism.

samsara (*'khor ba*). The continuum of uncontrollably taking rebirths repeatedly in aggregates that perpetuate defilements by the power of karma and afflictive emotions.

Sautrāntika (*mdo sde pa*). A Buddhist tenet holder or school propounding Hīnayāna tenets that accepts both self-cognizers and external objects.

self-knower (*rang rig*; *svasaṃvedana*). A consciousness that has the aspect of an apprehender.

A knower that is only directed inward at the consciousness it accompanies, which is its object and with which it simultaneously arises, abides, and ceases. It is unmistaken, free from conceptuality, and is generated in the aspect of the consciousness that is its object. Synonymous with *aspect of the apprehender*.

self-knowing valid direct perceiver (*rang rig mngon sum gyi tshad ma*). A knower that is new and incontrovertible, free from conceptuality, directed inward only, and has the aspect of an apprehender.

A self-knower that is a valid cognizer.

sense direct perceiver (*dbang po mngon sum*; *indriyapratyakṣa*). A knower that is unmistaken, free from conceptuality, and arises in dependence on a physical sense power that is its uncommon empowering condition.

For example, a sense direct perceiver apprehending form that has a flower as its object. It is unmistaken because the flower appears to it as the flower actually exists. It is free from conceptuality because there are no conceptual consciousnesses that are it. It arises in dependence on a physical sense power that is its uncommon empowering condition because it is produced from the eye sense power that is its cause. This eye sense power enables the sense direct perceiver apprehending form to see and experience visible forms like shapes and colors but does not enable it to experience sounds, scents, flavors, and so forth. It gives the sense direct perceiver apprehending form its uncommon ability to experience a specific range of phenomena. The same is true for the other four sense direct perceivers, those apprehending sounds, odors, flavors, and tangible objects.

śhrāvaka (*nyan thos*). A person on the path of the vehicle seeking to attain liberation from samsara for themself only, who is intent on achieving individual liberation as quickly as possible, generally prefers to study and practice with others, relies on listening to teachings until final rebirth, and after becoming an arhat teaches others verbally.

sign of definite simultaneous observation (*lhan cig dmigs nges kyi rtags*). Logic used by the Chittamātra to establish that sense consciousnesses and the objects they apprehend are empty of existing as substantially different from each other because such consciousnesses and their objects are observed at all times and places to definitely arise simultaneously. This is a primary reason the Chittamātra refutes the existence of external objects.

specifically characterized phenomenon (*rang mtshan*; *svalakṣaṇa*). A phenomenon that is established by way of its own character without being merely imputed by a term or a conceptual consciousness.

Such phenomena have the ability to cast their appearance to a direct perceiver and to produce effects. They do not rely on conceptual consciousness in order to appear to a person's mind. Synonymous with *impermanent phenomena*, *functioning thing*, *cause*, and *effect*. Contrast with *generally characterized phenomenon*.

subject (*chos can*; *dharmin*). A basis possessing both the sign and the predicate in a syllogism. For example, within the syllogism "the subject 'sound' is impermanent because of being a product," "sound" is the subject. It possesses both the sign, "product," and the predicate, "impermanent," in the sense that it is both a product and impermanent, and thus both of those are properties or characteristics of the subject "sound."

subsequent cognizer (*bcad shes*; *chedajñā*). A knower that realizes what has already been realized by the valid cognizer that induces it.

In the very first moment of newly experiencing or realizing something, we generate a valid cognizer knowing that object. If we continue observing the same object, the second moment of knowing that object onward are consciousnesses that are induced by the valid cognizer of the first moment. These subsequent cognizers know the same object by force of the valid cognizer of the first moment that induced them. Subsequent cognizers do not realize their object with the same force and vividness as valid cognizers.

suffering of change (*'gyur ba'i sdug bsngal*; *vipariṇāmaduḥkhatā*). A contaminated feeling of pleasure that over time gives rise to painful feelings. The main minds and mental factors that accompany such a feeling of pleasure, and the contaminated objects that when observed act as conditions giving rise to it, are also the suffering of change.

suffering of suffering (*sdug bsngal kyi sdug bsngal*; *duḥkhaduḥkhatā*). A contaminated, painful feeling of suffering. The main minds and mental factors that accompany it, and the contaminated objects that when observed act as conditions giving rise to it, are also the suffering of suffering.

superimposition (*sgro 'dogs*; *āropa*). An untruth projected onto an object. For example, when grasping at a mirage to be real water, water is superimposed on something that is in fact not water. To clear away superimpositions with regard to an object means to know the entity of an object as it is. This does not entail knowing accurately everything about the object. To clear away superimpositions with regard to a mirage would be to know that it is a mirage without mistaking it for water.

three modes of ascertainment (*tshul gsum*; *trirūpa*). See *three modes of the sign*.

three modes of the sign (*rtags kyi tshul gsum*). The property of the subject, the forward pervasion, and the counter pervasion in a proof or syllogism. Whatever is all three modes of a particular syllogism is a correct sign in that syllogism. See *correct sign* and appendix 1 for explanations of each mode.

truth of suffering (*sdug bsngal bden pa*; *duḥkhasatya*). A truth on the side of the thoroughly afflicted that is distinguished by being impermanent, suffering, empty, and selfless.

Each of the four noble truths are defined in terms of having four distinguishing characteristics or aspects. Together these are known as the sixteen aspects of the four noble truths. They are central objects of meditation in Buddhist practice because realizing them refutes sixteen misconceptions regarding the four noble truths. These misconceptions are obstacles to liberation from samsara.

The first two of the four noble truths—the truths of suffering and the origin of suffering—are on the side of the afflicted, meaning that they both arise from and serve to further produce afflictive emotions and their associated karma. Meditation on the four aspects of the truth of suffering, impermanent and so forth, in relation to one's own aggregates, for example, respectively refutes falsely grasping at them as pure, pleasurable, permanent, and self. See chapter 5 for further elaboration.

truth of the origin (*kun 'byung bden pa*; *samudayasatya*). A truth on the side of the thoroughly afflicted that is distinguished by being a cause, an origin, an intense producer, and a condition.

Whatever is a truth of the origin is also a truth of suffering. Whereas truth of suffering describes phenomena that are produced from afflictive emotions and their associated karma, truth of origin describes those afflictive emotions such as anger, attachment, and ignorance, and their associated karmas, that repeatedly give rise to rebirth in samsara and all the ensuing dissatisfying and painful experiences. Meditation on the four aspects described here, being a cause and so forth, counteract holding suffering as arising in ways or from causes that do not in fact produce it.

truth of cessation (*'gogs pa'i bden pa*; *nirodhasatya*). A truth on the side of the completely purified that is distinguished by being a cessation, peaceful, sublime, and definitely emancipated.

The last two of the four noble truths, the truth of cessation and the truth of the path, are also a paired cause and effect, the truth of the path being a cause that gives rise to the attainment of the truth of cessation. They are on the side of the purified meaning that they purify the truths of suffering and origin, as does the path, or are the resultant purity of having completely eliminated these, as is the truth of cessation.

Realization of the four aspects of the truth of cessation acts as an antidote to wrong concepts with regard to it, such as holding that the cessation that is liberation from samsara is impossible to attain, that deluded states that are not liberation from samsara are liberation, that there is a liberation superior to the cessation of suffering, or that cessation of suffering can be lost once attained. These are views historically held by non-Buddhist schools in India.

truth of the path (*lam gyi bden pa*; *margasatya*). A truth on the side of the completely purified that is distinguished by being a path, a knower, an accomplishment, and a definite emancipator.

Meditation on the four aspects of the truth of the path refutes the wrong views holding that the path to liberation is utterly non-existent, that the wisdom realizing selflessness is not a path to liberation, that the wisdom realizing selflessness wrongly engages its object, or that the wisdom realizing selflessness is not capable of permanently extinguishing suffering. See chapter 5 for a more detailed explanation.

ultimate truth (*don dam bden pa*; *paramārthasatya*). A phenomenon that is not merely imputed by conceptual consciousness but is established from its own side, or a phenomenon that is ultimately able to perform a function. Synonymous with *impermanent* and *functioning thing*. This definition is according to the Sautrāntika. Compare with *conventional truth*.

Vaibhāṣhika (*bye brag smra ba*). A Buddhist tenet holder or school propounding Hīnayāna tenets that does not assert self-cognizers but does assert truly existent external objects.

valid cognizer (*tshad ma*; *pramāṇa*). A knower that is new and incontrovertible.

A valid cognizer is new in that it is an initial realization of an object and knows its object solely by force of its own action, as opposed to being induced by a preceding consciousness that has just realized the same object. It is incontrovertible in that once a valid cognizer has realized something, for the person possessing that understanding, no doubt will arise regarding what they have come to unshakably know. Even if some try to convince them otherwise, they will not fall into doubt regarding what has been realized by a valid cognizer. A valid cognizer cannot transform into doubt about what it has realized.

valid direct perceiver (*mngon sum gyi tshad ma*; *pratyakṣapramāṇa*). A new and incontrovertible knower that is free from conceptuality.

A valid cognizer that is non-conceptual. See also *direct perceiver*.

wrong conceptual consciousness (*rtog pa log shes*; *kalpanābhrāntijñāna*). A conceptual consciousness whose object of the mode of determination is not established even conventionally. Synonomous with *conceptual consciousness that does not realize its object*.

A consciousness that thinks, apprehends, or determines something that is not true—for example, that sound is permanent, or that Socrates is immortal. Since the thing determined by such a consciousness does not in fact exist (a Socrates that is immortal does not exist), this kind of mind is described as one whose object of determination is not established. "To be established" is synonymous with *existing*.

wrong consciousness (*log shes*; *viparyayajñāna*). An awareness that engages its object erroneously.

There are both conceptual and non-conceptual wrong consciousnesses. Since the objects they apprehend do not exist and yet they engage them as if they do, they are characterized as engaging their objects erroneously.

yogic direct perceiver (*rnal 'byor mngon sum*). An other-knowing exalted wisdom in the continuum of an Ārya that is free from conceptuality and non-mistaken and that directly realizes its object, an aspect of truth, in dependence on its own uncommon empowering condition, a meditative stabilization that is a union of calm abiding and special insight.

See *direct perceiver* for an explanation of "free from conceptuality and non-mistaken." See *explicit realization* for an explanation of "directly realize." Yogic direct perceivers are only attained by a person on the path of seeing or higher. They realize primarily objects of meditation, like the four noble truths, subtle impermanence, and selflessness, that are central for abandoning delusions, especially the ignorance that is the root of samsara. They are generated as having the uncommon ability to directly and non-conceptually realize these objects in dependence on achieving a meditative absorption that is a union of calm abiding and special insight. This empowering condition is achieved on the path of preparation. See appendix 5 for further details.

NOTES

1. *Ocean of Reasonings*, 356.
2. Adapted from the *Collections of Biographies of Renowned Beings of the Land of Snows*, compiled by Dondor and Tenzin Chosdrak.
3. Throughout this text the corresponding page numbers of the Tibetan-language print version of Khedrup Jé's *Clearing Mental Darkness* are given in brackets.
4. As translated by Napper, *Explanation of the Presentation of Objects*, 16.
5. Napper, *Explanation of the Presentation of Objects*, 13.
6. Napper, *Explanation of the Presentation of Objects*, 13.
7. Dharmakīrti, *Pramāṇavārttika*, 3.63, 121a1.
8. Dharmakīrti, *Pramāṇavārttika*, 1.17, 94a6.
9. Devendrabuddhi, *Pramāṇavārttikapañjikā*, 3, 146b2. Devendrabuddhi (Lha dbang blo) was a direct disciple of Dharmakīrti. Dharmakīrti asked Devendrabuddhi to write a companion to his commentary, *Exposition of Valid Cognition*. Dharmakīrti found Devendrabuddhi's first attempt so dissatisfying that he threw it into a river. The second attempt he tossed into a fire. The third attempt he let stand.
10. Śhākyabuddhi, *Pramāṇavārttikaṭīkā*, 162b4. Śhākyabuddhi (Shakya Lö) was a disciple of Devendrabuddhi.
11. Here, a superimposition (*sgros dogs*) is a wrong idea conceptualized with regard to (or imputed to) an object. For example, the thoughts that table is not matter or that a distant tree that has a shape similar to a human is a human are superimpositions with regard to table and that tree, respectively. In order to realize the fact that table is matter or that the distant tree is a tree, one must remove these wrong superimpositions.
12. The meaning of "meaning generality" will be explained in the section below.
13. The pervasion is that if something is an object of that phenomenon, it must be either the appearing object, object of apprehension, determined object, or object of engagement of that phenomenon. The sign that has been accepted is that if something is an object, it is necessarily one of these four objects.
14. Napper, *Explanation of the Presentation of Objects*, 9.
15. Dharmakīrti, *Pramāṇavārttika*, 3.01, 118b3.
16. Dharmakīrti, *Pramāṇavārttika*, 3.54, 120b3.
17. Dharmakīrti, *Pramāṇavārttika*, 3.01, 118b3.
18. Dharmakīrti, *Pramāṇavārttika*, 3.54, 120b3.
19. Dharmakīrti, *Pramāṇavārttika*, 3.01, 118b3.
20. Dharmakīrti, *Pramāṇavārttika*, 3.54, 120b3.
21. Gyaltsab Darma Rinchen, *Clarifying the Path of Liberation*, 54.

22. Here the terms "thing" and "non-thing" are not used in their ordinary sense to refer to inanimate and animate objects but to refer to things that are able to perform functions, such as producing effects and those that aren't able to produce effects.

23. Napper, *Explanation of the Presentation of Objects*, 15.

24. The Madhyamaka Prāsaṅgika (Middle Way Consequence) school is one of the two main sub-schools of the Madhyamaka school, the other being Svātantrika (Autonomy).

25. "Proponents of true existence" refers mainly to the first three of the four main tenet schools in Buddhist philosophy, the Vaibhāṣhika (Great Exposition), the Sautrāntrika (Sūtra), and the Chittamātra (Mind-Only).

26. This type of phenomenon is characterized in three ways: being unmixed with regard to being an object, with regard to time, and with regard to nature. The meaning of each of these three characteristics will be discussed below. This type of phenomenon is also discussed in Gyaltsab Darma Rinchen, *Clarifying the Path of Liberation*.

27. Napper, *Explanation of the Presentation of Objects*, 46.

28. This means Dignāga and Dharmakīrti.

29. "The seven treatises" is a phrase commonly used to refer to a single group of seven separate commentaries by Dharmakīrti; it is not one text.

30. Dharmakīrti, *Pramāṇavārttika*, 1.80, 97b5.

31. Dharmakīrti, *Pramāṇavārttika*, 3.01, 118b3. This line was also cited by Khedrup Jé above in the section explaining how the delineation of valid cognizers into two is related to the division of phenomena into specifically and generally characterized phenomena.

32. Dharmakīrti, *Pramāṇavārttika*, 1.171, 101a4.

33. Dharmakīrti, *Pramāṇavārttika*, 2.14, 108a3.

34. Dharmakīrti, *Pramāṇavārttika*, 3.01, 118b3.

35. Dharmakīrti, *Pramāṇavārttika*, 3.03, 118b4.

36. These two, ultimate and conventional existents, also known as ultimate and conventional truths, will be extensively explained in the section "Conventional and Ultimate Truths" below.

37. The Sāṃkhya school is a non-Buddhist school whose views have often been refuted by the Buddhist schools. The Sāṃkhya school, for example, also asserts that sound is permanent.

38. Dharmakīrti, *Pramāṇavārttika*, 1.167, 101a2.

39. Napper, *Explanation of the Presentation of Objects*, 15.

40. Substantial cause and cooperative condition are two important phenomena that produce a particular result. For example, a seed of a particular plant is the substantial cause, and heat, moisture, fertilization, and so forth are the cooperative conditions for the plant to grow.

41. Dharmakīrti, *Pramāṇavārttika*, 1.42, 96a5.

42. Superimposed phenomena are synonymous with imputed phenomena, permanent phenomena, and generally characterized phenomena.

43. Dharmakīrti, *Pramāṇavārttika*, 3.03, 125a7.

44. Dharmakīrti, *Pramāṇavārttika*, 3.03, 125a6.

45. Dharmakīrti, *Pramāṇavārttika*, 3.184, 125a2.

46. Here the Tibetan term *rjes su 'gro*, translated as "pervade," literally means to follow after. In the case of a generality being said to "follow after" its instances, this term indicates that wherever and whenever those instances exist, that generality also exists. It does not indicate its former and later times.

47. Dharmakīrti, *Pramāṇavārttika*, 1.162, 100b6.

48. Here innate awareness is an awareness not affected by or fabricated through having studied philosophical tenets.

49. Here, "and so forth" refers to further features of oxen that distinguish them from other animals, such as having hooves, curved horns, loose skin hanging down below the neck, etc.

50. This is an epithet honoring Jé Tsongkhapa as singular among the scholars of Tibet (land among snow mountains) for clearly distinguishing the way of dividing objects into generally and specifically characterized phenomena.

51. Dharmakīrti, *Pramāṇavārttika*, 1.70, 96a7.

52. Dharmakīrti, *Pramāṇavārttika*, 1.70, 97a7.

53. Anything that is concealing in the sense meant here is necessarily false.

54. Śhrāvaka teachings are in the Sautrāntika and Vaibhāṣhika schools, since those on the śhrāvaka paths follow one of these two tenet schools.

55. The Sautrāntika (Sūtra) has a twofold subdivision: the Sautrāntika following scripture and the Sautrāntika following reasoning.

56. Jetsun Chökyi Gyaltsen is the author of most textbooks followed by Sera Jey Monastery.

57. Jetsun Chökyi Gyaltsen, *Presentation of Tenets*, 7–8.

58. Here, "although wishing to show the selflessness of phenomena" does not mean that the Buddha meant to teach one thing but accidentally taught something else. It means rather, seeing that it would be counterproductive to directly explain the most profound truth to this specific group of trainees, the Buddha taught them a coarser level of truth as a means of leading them to an understanding of the most subtle level of truth.

59. Here "father and son" is in the sense of a spiritual relationship rather than a biological one and refers to Dignāga and Dharmakīrti, who were teacher and disciple, respectively.

60. A consciousness free of the two extremes is one that realizes the meaning of such-ness or emptiness and thus is free of the extremes of permanence and nihilism. Such a mind is free of the extreme of permanence because it directly refutes grasping at the existence of a self of phenomena. It is free of the extreme of nihilism because a person possessing such a mind does not hold that the emptiness of a self of phenomena does not exist. Since here some views of the Chittamātra school are being presented, self of phenomena is delineated as external existence or the existence of subject and object as substantially other, and suchness is considered to be the mere negation of that.

61. Whatever is substantially established is a specifically characterized phenomenon, a functioning thing and impermanent, while whatever is a superimposition by awareness is a generally characterized phenomenon, a permanent and a non-functioning thing. Here sense consciousness observing forms, sounds, and so forth is the main basis for distinguishing these two kinds of Chittamātra proponents. The object of apprehension of an eye sense consciousness apprehending ball is ball. An aspect of this object of apprehension, or an aspect of ball, appears to such an eye consciousness. For True

Aspectarians this aspect of the object of apprehension is substantially existent; it exists not merely through the force of superimposition by awareness but through the force of its own characteristics. For False Aspectarians, this aspect is merely superimposed by awareness and does not have any substantial existence.

62. Dharmakīrti, *Pramāṇavārttika*, 3.214, 126b4. In the main body of the text we have made a literal translation of these three verses. What follows is an interpretation of the same verses with the meaning filled out according to Khedrup Jé's commentary.

This separate abiding of things is
dependent on [the conceptual consciousness to which] they
    [i.e., apprehended objects and apprehending subjects] appear as separate.
Since that [conceptual consciousness] is polluted,
their separateness is also polluted.

Other than the aspects of apprehended and apprehender,
there isn't any other character.
Thus, because empty of character,
lack of inherent existence was thoroughly explained.

Through the instances [of all definiendum such as form] aggregate and so forth,
all definitions [such as suitable to be called form] are agents.
These [definitions that are] possessors of attributes do not exist [as possessors
    of attributes ultimately or] in suchness.
For that reason too, these [definitions, and by extension all phenomena,] are
    devoid of characteristics [and thus not inherently existent].

63. Vijñānavāda (*rnam rig pa*), or "Proponents of Cognition," is another name for the Chittamātra, or Mind Only, school.

64. Here non-thing is synonymous with permanent phenomenon.

65. Āryas, or noble beings, who perceive slightly hidden phenomena like subtle impermanence and selflessness, directly with yogic direct perceivers, can be divided into two: those who are learners and those who are no-more-learners. The first group are those who abide on the paths of seeing and meditation, and the last group are those who abide on the paths of no-more-learning.

66. A non-affirming negation is a type of phenomenon whose terminological designation necessarily eliminates directly its object of negation and doesn't imply any other positive phenomenon like affirming negatives do. An example is selflessness, whose designation merely asserts the lack of the self as a self-sufficient substantial entity without asserting any other positive phenomenon in its place.

67. Here the author presumably means that obscurations to omniscience obstruct knowing or directly perceiving all objects of knowledge rather than meaning that they somehow impinge upon these objects themselves.

68. This is impossible because a buddha's consciousnesses are all direct perceivers. They do not have conceptual consciousnesses.

69. Napper, *Explanation of the Presentation of Objects*, 8.

70. Dharmakīrti, *Pramāṇavārttika*, 3.09, 118b6.

71. Dharmakīrti, *Pramāṇavārttika*, 3.402, 134a2.

72. Dharmakīrti, *Pramāṇavārttika*, 3.66, 121a2.

73. It looks like Khedrup Jé is holding that "sound is impermanent" is not the object of apprehension or appearing object of this or any inferential consciousness because he holds that sound is impermanent is itself a functioning thing, while whatever is the appearing object of a conceptual consciousness must be a permanent phenomenon.

74. Compositional factors are impermanent phenomena that are not matter and not consciousness—for example, a person and impermanence by itself.

75. Napper, *Explanation of the Presentation of Objects*, 11.

76. Jinpa, *Science and Philosophy in the Indian Buddhist Classics*, vol. 2, 41.

77. Chapa Chökyi Sengé was a Tibetan scholar of the twelfth century who composed the first Tibetan text on valid cognition called *The Collected Topics [of Valid Cognition]* (*Bsdus sgra*). Shortly after this text was composed, the great scholar from the Sakya tradition Sakya Paṇḍita Kunga Gyaltsen (Sa pan Kun dga' Rgyal mtshan, 1182–1251) composed his famous text on valid cognition called *The Treasury of Reasoning (Tsad ma rigs gter)*.

78. Napper, *Explanation of the Presentation of Objects*, 13.

79. These will be explained in chapters 3 and 7.

80. Napper, *Explanation of the Presentation of Objects*, 43.

81. Dharmakīrti, *Pramāṇavārttika*, 1.206, 102b1.

82. Dharmakīrti, *Pramāṇaviniśhcaya*, 1, 154b1.

83. Napper, *Explanation of the Presentation of Objects*, 33.

84. Napper, *Explanation of the Presentation of Objects*, 33.

85. An ārya's wisdom of meditative equipoise realizing the aggregates as selfless as a yogic direct perceiver is a non-conceptual consciousness and therefore not an inferential cognizer. It is the very hallmark of having attained the state of ārya.

86. Dharmakīrti, *Pramāṇavārttika*, 2.03, 107b4.

87. Sakya Paṇḍita, *Treasury of Reasoning*, <volume #?>: 2.12, 4b1.

88. Napper, *Explanation of the Presentation of Objects*, 47.

89. Napper, *Explanation of the Presentation of Objects*, 35.

90. Jamyang Shepa, *Presentation of Awarenesses and Knowers*.

91. Sakya Paṇḍita, *Treasury of Reasoning*, 3:2–3.

92. Napper, *Explanation of the Presentation of Objects*, 38–39.

93. Śhāntarakṣita, *Tattvasaṃgraha*, 26.3343 and 3587.

94. Dharmottara, *Pramāṇaviniśhcayaṭīkā*, 104:779.

95. Dharmakīrti, *Pramāṇaviniśhcaya*, 7b5.

96. Dharmakīrti, *Pramāṇaviniśhcaya*, 107b.

97. Dharmakīrti, *Pramāṇaviniśhcaya*, 107b.

98. Dharmakīrti, *Pramāṇaviniśhcaya*, 107b.

99. Dharmakīrti, *Pramāṇavārttika*, 3.53, 120b3.

100. Dharmakīrti, *Pramāṇavārttika*, 1.179, 101b1.

101. Dharmakīrti, *Pramāṇavārttika*, 1.211, 102b4.

102. A negation, a negative phenomenon, negates a particular aspect of a phenomenon and can be of two types: (1) an affirming negation and (2) a non-affirming negation.

A non-affirming negation is a type of phenomenon whose terminological designation necessarily eliminates directly its object of negation and doesn't imply any other positive phenomenon. An example is selflessness, whose designation merely asserts the lack of the self as a self-sufficient substantial entity without asserting any other positive phenomenon in its place. An example of an affirming negation is "the rotund person doesn't eat during the day." This statement negates eating during the day but implies that the person eats at night, which is a positive phenomenon and thus is an affirming negative.

103. More explanation regarding this statement can be found in commentaries on Lama Tsongkhapa's *Essence of Eloquence* and Candrakīrti's *Entering the Middle Way*.

104. Dharmakīrti, *Pramāṇavārttika*, 2.04, 107b5.

105. Dharmakīrti, *Pramāṇavārttika*, 2.05, 107b5.

106. Dharmakīrti, *Pramāṇavārttika*, 2.06, 107b5.

107. Prajñākaragupta, *Pramāṇavārttikabhāshyam*, 3.02, 206a1.

108. Napper, *Explanation of the Presentation of Objects*, 14.

109. Dignāga, *Pramāṇasamucchaya*, 1.03, 124.

110. Dharmakīrti, *Pramāṇaviniśhcaya*, 3.01, 154b1.

111. Napper, *Explanation of the Presentation of Objects*, 14.

112. Dignāga, *Pramāṇasamucchaya*, 1.04, 124.

113. Napper, *Explanation of the Presentation of Objects*, 14.

114. Dharmakīrti, *Pramāṇavārttika*, 3.461, 136a2.

115. Remember that here the presentation of empowering conditions is being made according to the Sautrāntika (Sūtra) tradition. To posit that the Sautrāntika hold a tenet that is unique to the Vaibhāṣhika would be a contradiction.

116. One might think there is a fault because the particular object being apprehended has ceased to exist at the time of the sense consciousness apprehending it. This is because that object deteriorates each moment (or said another way, does not remain during even the very next moment following the time it was established), and the sense consciousness apprehending it arises only in the moments subsequent to it.

117. Napper, *Explanation of the Presentation of Objects*, 8–11.

118. Dharmakīrti, *Pramāṇavārttika*, 3.341, 131b2.

119. An overview of these paths is given in appendix 5, Paths of Liberation and Enlightenment.

120. "Mind-basis-of-all" and "afflicted mind" are two types of main mind posited by the Chittamātra True Aspectarians. They assert the existence of eight types of main mind: the five sense consciousnesses, mental consciousness, mind-basis-of-all, and afflicted mind. Mind-basis-of-all is held to be a continuum of consciousness upon which all the imprints of one's karma and perceptions are laid. Unlike other types of consciousness, its continuum is unbroken from life to life and during deep sleep, fainting, and meditative absorption on cessation. Afflicted mind is a type of deluded mind that observes solely the mind-basis-of-all and grasps that as being an independent, substantially established self of persons. It is an innate grasping at the self of persons.

121. The term "consciousnesses of the five doors" is a synonym for the five sense consciousnesses. The five doors are the doors of the eyes, ears, nose, tongue, and body.

122. Persons of the desire realm and the form realm are composed of the five aggregates of form, feeling, discrimination, compositional factors, and consciousness. Persons of the formless realm consist of only four aggregates because they do not possess the aggregate of form.

123. Meaning if it is not either mental consciousness, the material body, or the collection of the mental and physical aggregates.

124. The five omnipresent mental factors are the mental factors of feeling, discrimination, intention, contact, and mental engagement. "Basis-of-all" (*kun gzhi*) is short for "mind-basis-of-all" (*kun gzhi rnam shes*).

125. The five aspects of similarities according to Purbu Chok are similar support, object of observation, aspect, time, and similar entity. A mental factor depends on a sense/mental power upon which the main mind is supported. Their supports are similar: a mental factor observes that object that the main mind observes. Their objects of observation are similar: a main mind is generated having an aspect, for instance, blue; its mental factor is also generated in that aspect, blue. Their aspects are similar: a main mind and its mental factor are simultaneous in regard to production, abiding, and cessation. Their times are similar: main minds of a similar type are distinct entities; likewise, mental factors, such as feelings, of a similar type are also distinct entities, and therefore their entities are similar.

126. Being one essence with something and being a cause of that thing are mutually exclusive because whatever is one essence with A necessarily is produced and destroyed at the same time as A, whereas whatever is a cause of A is necessarily produced before it.

127. The reason being that both the observed object condition and the empowering condition are imprints on the previous consciousness, so if one is the previous consciousness, the other would also have to be so.

128. Dignāga, *Ālambanaparīkṣā*, 6, 86a3.

129. Dignāga, *Ālambanaparīkṣā*, 6, 86a4.

130. Dignāga, *Ālambanaparīkṣā*, 7, 86a3.

131. Khedrup Jé's *Opening the Eyes of the Fortunate*, quoted in Jeffrey Hopkins, *Reflections on Reality*, 221.

132. Dignāga, Ālambanaparīkṣāvṛtti, 87b1.

133. Dignāga, *Ālambanaparīkṣāvṛtti*, 87b1.

134. Khedrup Jé is referring to several debates in his text that have not been translated here. In those debates, opponents of the Chittamātra's assertions set out many faults of accepting visible objects, sounds, and so forth to be consciousness. They say, for example, that blue would be not blue but would be an omniscient mind, all direct perceivers would be self-knowing direct perceivers, all persons with bodies would have eye consciousness, and so forth.

135. Dharmakīrti, *Pramāṇavārttika*, 3.381, 133a6.

136. For clarification of the three modes of a syllogism, please refer to appendix 1, Epistemological Aspects of Logic and Reasoning.

137. Dharmakīrti, *Pramāṇavārttika*, 3.388, 133a5.

138. Dignāga, *Ālambanaparīkṣā*, 7, 86a4.

139. Napper, *Explanation of the Presentation of Objects*, 15.

140. Sakya Paṇḍita, *Treasury of Reasoning*, 9:109.b5.

141. Vasubandhu, *Treasury of Knowledge*, 1.17, 2b3. The eighteen consisting of the six objects, the six sense powers, and the six consciousnesses.

142. Vasubandhu, *Abhidharmakośha*, 1.17, 2b3. This is an alternate translation in Tibetan of the foregoing line cited from the *Treasury of Knowledge*. Above, this line was rendered in English as "that is the immediately preceding of [any of] the six…"

143. Napper, *Explanation of the Presentation of Objects*, 16.

144. Sakya Paṇḍita, *Treasury of Reasoning*, 109.a5.

145. Dharmakīrti, *Pramāṇavārttika*, 3.371, 132b3.

146. Bhāvaviveka, *Madhyamakahṛdayavṛttitarkajvālā*, 5, 211a1.

147. Napper, *Explanation of the Presentation of Objects*, 17.

148. As cited by Jetsun Chökyi Gyaltsen in *General Meaning of Chapter One*, 215.

149. As cited by Jetsun Chökyi Gyaltsen, *General Meaning of Chapter One*, 216.

150. Śhāntideva, *Bodhisattvacharyāvatāra*, 1.28.

151. Tsongkhapa, *Songs of Spiritual Experience*, 185–86.

152. The Buddha's first turning of the wheel of Dharma refers to his explicit teaching on the four noble truths given primarily to disciples seeking mere liberation from samsara. It was most famously taught to the five disciples at Deer Park, Sarnath, forty-nine days after the Buddha first manifested enlightenment in Bodhgaya. The second turning of the wheel of Dharma refers to the explicit teaching of all phenomena as being empty of true existence, which was primarily taught to disciples seeking full enlightenment. It is commonly associated historically with the Perfection of Wisdom Sūtras taught at Vultures Peak, Rajgir, in the months following the Buddha's initial teaching at Sarnath. The third turning of the wheel of Dharma refers to the explicit teaching on the three natures (the thoroughly imputed, the other-powered, and the thoroughly established) as asserted by followers of the Chittamātra tenet system. It was renowned as being taught later in the Buddha's life, most famously in the Indian city of Vaishali.

153. Here the Tibetan term translated as "taking birth" (*nying mtshams sbyar ba*) is a technical term that literally has the connotation of "bridging the gap between lives." At the time of taking rebirth one is emerging from an intermediate state called the "bardo" and entering a particular kind of body, thus bridging such a gap between rebirths. Inasmuch as the meaning is the same, the term has been rendered as "taking birth" here in the interest of simplicity.

154. Tsongkhapa, *Arranging the Path of Valid Cognition*, 15–16.

155. Here "the subject" refers to the Buddha inasmuch as he forms the subject within the following syllogism: "The subject, The Bhagavan Shakyamuni. It follows he is a valid being with respect to the pursuit of liberation. Because he is, in relation to the pursuit of liberation, a being endowed with both incontrovertibleness and clarity regarding a meaning previously unknown [which in this case refers to the four truths]." Tsongkhapa, *Arranging the Path of Valid Cognition*, 10–11.

156. Dharmakīrti, *Pramāṇavārttika*, 2.272. The Tibetan in the first line of this verse appears in several prints as *bden pa bzhi la brten pa dang*, while in others as *bden pa bzhi la rtags pa dang*. Inasmuch as the latter makes more contextual sense and is in keeping with the relevant word commentaries in both Khedrup Jé's and Gyaltsab Jé's *Clarifying the Path of Liberation*, the translation follows this version.

157. The twelve links of dependent origination are ignorance, karmic formations, consciousness, name and form, six sense bases, contact, sensation, craving, grasping, becoming, birth, and old age and death.

158. *Nandagarbhāvakrāntinirdeśha-sūtra.* 760, 109.3.3–6. The three sufferings presentation is, likewise, expounded in these three types of suffering illustrated in the *Abhidharma Sūtra* [*Chos mngon pa'i mdo,* quoted in Gendun Tenpa Dargye, *Illuminating the Ornament of the Essence,* chap. 1]: "The four—birth, aging, sickness, and death—as well as the fear of meeting with hateful enemies, are the suffering of suffering. Hope of meeting with loving friends, and searching for but not finding objects of attachment, are the suffering of change. In short, as for the five appropriating aggregates: they are suffering."

159. Āryadeva, *Catuḥshataka,* 2, 12. This translation is taken from Tsongkhapa, *Great Treatise,* vol. I, 291–92.

160. Tsongkhapa, *Great Treatise,* vol. I, 290–91.

161. The aggregates of body and mind can be subdivided into the following five: form, feeling, discrimination, compositional factors, and consciousness.

162. As found in Gyaltsab Darma Rinchen, *Explanation of the Compendium of Abhidharma [by Asaṅga],* 294.

163. Dharmakīrti, *Pramāṇavārttika,* 2.147, 113a3.

164. Dharmakīrti, *Pramāṇavārttika,* 2.177–78.

165. To this effect, for example, it is taught in Panchen Losang Chökyi Gyaltsen's *Lamrim Prayer,* a subsection of his *Lama Chöpa:* "Having abandoned the mind which sees this intolerable, prison-like cyclic existence as akin to a pleasure grove, bless me to uphold the three trainings, treasury of the āryas' jewels, and grasp the victory-banner of liberation!" [verse 88]. A similar prisoner example is discussed in Pabongkha Dechen Nyingpo, *Liberation in the Palm of Your Hand,* 428–29.

166. Khedrup Jé, *Illumination of the Difficult Points,* chap. 1.

167. The interpretation of "empty" here is based on Lama Tsongkhapa's *Purifying Forgetfulness of Valid Cognition* and on Gyalwa Gedun Drup's [the first Dalai Lama] *Ornament of Reasoning on Valid Cognition.* There is an ostensibly alternate presentation of the meaning of "empty" as presented in Asaṅga's *Compendium of Knowledge.* Gyaltsab Jé's commentary thereon explains: "With respect to 'empty': It is the selflessness of persons such that whoever directly realizes it is able to abandon the afflictive obscurations" (*An Explanation of the Compendium of Abhidharma,* 273).

168. The interpretation of "selfless" here is based on Lama Tsongkhapa's *Purifying Forgetfulness of Valid Cognition* and on Gyalwa Gedun Drup's *Ornament of Reasoning on Valid Cognition.* With regard to "empty" and "selfless," there are also other interpretations by various scholars in the monastic institutions. Some assert the emptiness of a self that is "permanent, unitary, and independent" for the aspect "empty," and the emptiness of a self that is a "self-sufficient substantial existing self" for the aspect "selfless."

169. Dharmakīrti, *Pramāṇavārttika,* 2.221.

170. The twelve links of dependent origination are ignorance, karmic formations, consciousness, name and form, six sense bases, contact, sensation, craving, grasping, becoming, birth, and old age and death. For an elaborate explanation see Lama Tsongkhapa, *Great Treatise,* vol. I, 315–19.

171. Dharmakīrti, *Pramāṇavārttika,* 2.190, 114b6.

172. Just as people have no desire to eat grass even when they are hungry, without craving people have no desire for contaminated or samsaric objects of enjoyment.

173. Dharmakīrti, *Pramāṇavārttika*, 2.221, 116a1.

174. Dharmakīrti, *Pramāṇavārttika*, 2.258, 117a7.

175. Some commentators, such as Sera Jey Monastery's textbook author Jetsun Chökyi Gyaltsen, assert that which is form is necessarily not an instance of the truth of the origin, thus emphasizing the truth of origin as something that gives rise to suffering from within the context of the mental continuum alone. Sera Mey Monastery's textbook author, Gendun Tenpa Dargye, posits some instances of form (e.g., the form that is an instance of the link of "name-and-form" from among the twelve links of dependent arising), included within the scope of the truth of suffering, as also being the second noble truth. Drepung Loseling's Panchen Sönam Drakpa, taking this a step further, posits the first two noble truths as mutually inclusive (meaning what is one is necessarily the other), while Tsongkhapa's *Golden Garland of Eloquence* conversely explains: "The Origin is pervaded by [being the Truth of] Suffering, but Suffering is not pervaded by that [Origin]: for example, the mind-basis-of-all, the [contaminated] worldly environment, the five [contaminated] sense powers, and all contaminated things that are not obscurations and are not indicated in scripture [as either virtuous or non-virtuous, are Suffering but not the Origin]."

176. Gungthang Lodrö Gyatso, *Clearing the Darkness of Those Desiring Liberation*, 1.

177. Changkya Rölpai Dorje, *Beautiful Adornment of Mount Meru*, 1.

178. Gyaltsab Darma Rinchen, *A Guide on the Path of Valid Cognition*, 93.

179. Dalai Lama Tenzin Gyatso, *Illuminating the Path to Enlightenment*, 21.

180. A non-affirming negation is a type of phenomenon whose terminological designation necessarily eliminates directly its object of negation and doesn't imply any other positive phenomenon. Another example is selflessness, whose designation merely asserts the lack of the self as a self-sufficient substantial entity without asserting any other positive phenomenon in its place. From among the four major Buddhist tenets, all but the Vaibhāṣhika school accept the truth of cessation as a non-affirming negation.

181. Gungthang Tenpai Drönme, *A Festival of the Wise*.

182. Khedrup Jé, *Ocean of Reasonings*, chap. 1.

183. Jamyang Shepa, *Great Exposition of Tenets*, 5.

184. Tsongkhapa, *Purifying Forgetfulness of Valid Cognition*, 38.

185. Dharmakīrti, *Pramāṇavārttika*, 2.210.

186. Gyaltsab Darma Rinchen, *Clarifying the Path of Liberation*, 519–20.

187. Khedrup Gelek Palsang, *Illumination of the Difficult Points*, 43.

188. "Thusness" is the translation of the Tibetan term *de bzhin nyid*, referring to the meaning of selflessness or emptiness.

189. The source for this verse is unclear, but there is a verse similar to it with a slightly different translation in Jitāri, *Distinguishing the Scriptures of the Sugata*, 7a7.

190. Maitreya, *The Sublime Continuum*, 4.55.

191. Whatever is produced when the causes and conditions suitable to produce it are present, and does not arise when these are not present, is said to be "produced occasionally." Thus whatever is produced occasionally must have a cause.

192. Dharmakīrti, *Pramāṇavārttika*, 2.134, 112b3.

193. Dharmakīrti, *Pramāṇavārttika*, 2.219, 115b7.

194. For an extensive presentation, see Hopkins, *Emptiness in the Mind-Only School*; and Cabezon, *A Dose of Emptiness*.

195. According to the Prāsaṅgika, one also needs to realize the selflessness of phenomena in order to achieve liberation from samsara.

196. Afflictive obscurations are sometimes translated as "obscurations to liberation" because they, the afflictive emotions together with their seeds, obscure or prevent the achievement of liberation.

197. Cognitive obscurations are sometimes translated as "obscurations to omniscience" because they, the imprints or latencies of the afflictions, obscure or prevent the achievement of an all-knowing mind of a buddha. The difference between "seed," mentioned in note 195, and "imprint," mentioned here, is that a seed is a something posited by a previous afflictive mind that has the potential to produce a latter afflictive mind, whereas an imprint doesn't have this potential. Rather, an imprint is something posited by a previous afflictive mind that has the potential to produce a latter distorted appearance to a mind.

198. Candrakīrti, *Madhyamakāvatāra*, 6.151.

199. Dharmakīrti, *Pramāṇavārttika*, 2.219, 115b7.

200. Dharmakīrti, *Pramāṇavārttika*, 2.255, 117a6.

201. Dharmakīrti, *Pramāṇavārttika*, 2.254, 117a5.

202. This was explained in section 5.1 in regards to the truth of the origin and in section 5.4 under identifying the two selves of persons and phenomena.

203. The Sanskrit term *krośha* (Tib. *rgyang grags*) refers to a distance of several kilometers and is sometimes translated as "ear-shot." It is technically defined as a length of 500 "arm-spans" (approx. 1.81 km) in the system of Abhidharma and 2,000 (approx. 3.62 km) in that of Kālachakra.

204. In Dharmakīrti's system, a cause-and-effect relationship is only complete when there is pervasion that the effect will exist if the cause does, and that if the cause does not exist, the effect will not. In this case, since a cause being permanent implies that it is not necessarily disintegrating momentarily, it would absurdly follow that it has unlimited capacity to produce its effect over and over again, at all manner of times and places. A similar reasoning is also illustrated in the context of the four aspects of the noble truth of the origin above.

205. Dharmakīrti, *Pramāṇavārttika*, 2.252, 117a5.

206. Here "method" refers to the method side of the path, and within that primarily refers to the difference in scope of the motivations.

207. Dharmakīrti, *Pramāṇavārttika*, 2.137, 112b5.

208. Khedrup Jé, *Presentation of the Grounds and Paths*; and *Illumination of the Difficult Points*, chapters 1 and 2.

209. As Lama Tsongkhapa explains in his *Great Treatise*, vol. 1, aiming for higher states of rebirth like that of a human and god, aiming for liberation, and aiming for enlightenment are the three scopes of the three kinds of spiritual practitioners.

210. Dharmakīrti, *Pramāṇavārttika*, 2.3, 107b4.

211. Dharmakīrti, *Pramāṇavārttika*, 2.5, 107b5.

212. Dignāga, *Pramāṇasamucchaya*, 1.9, 2a2.

213. Dharmakīrti, *Pramāṇavārttika*, 3.301–319, 130a2. This section, which spans verses 301–320 of the "Direct Perception" chapter, explains briefly the Sautrāntika school's own position on valid cognition and its effects, refutes the views of several outsider schools, and then goes on to cut off a number of doubts about how such presentations might be coherent.

214. Dignāga, *Pramāṇasamucchaya*, 1, 2a3.

215. Dharmakīrti, *Pramāṇavārttika*, 3.320–339, 130b5. This section, which covers verses 320–341 of the "Direct Perception" chapter, lays out the Chittamātra's own position regarding the conception of valid cognition and its effects for self-knowers, refuting at the outset the reasons establishing object-knowers put forth by the Sautrāntrika school. It goes on to refute the Sautrāntika presentation of sense perceptions arising from their apprehended objects to suggest that sense perceptions and their respective objects are of the same substantial entity (chap. 3, verses 320.3–341.3, *thar lam gsal byed smad cha*, pp. 247–61, *mkhas grub tIk chen smad cha*, pp. 288–309).

216. Dharmakīrti, *Pramāṇavārttika*, 3.341, 131b2.

217. Dharmakīrti, *Pramāṇavārttika*, 3.345, 131b4.

218. Dharmakīrti, *Pramāṇavārttika*, 3.346, 131b4.

219. Dharmakīrti, *Pramāṇavārttika*, 3.341–346, 131b2. The second line, translated in the text body ("in accordance...") here, is not quoted in Khedrup Jé's commentary but has been included as it actually falls between the first ("It is logical...") and third lines ("is ascertained..."). The section glossed by Khedrup Jé here spans verses 341 to 346 of the "Direct Perception" chapter and primarily seeks to cast doubt over and ultimately refute the Sautrāntrika position that although all forms exist as external objects, still to individual beings' sense consciousnesses they appear with desirable or undesirable aspects. Refuting this view, the Chittamātra position to be established is that sense consciousnesses and their objects are of one substantial entity.

220. Napper, *Explanation of the Presentation of Objects*, 21.

221. The three modes of ascertainment are the subject being established in the sign and the forward pervasion and counter pervasion.

222. Dharmakīrti, *Pramāṇavārttika*, 4.20, 140a3.

223. Vasubandu's *Treasury of Knowledge*, explaining the Mūlasarvāstivādin tradition, and Asaṅga's *Compendium of Knowledge*, explaining the Yogāchāra tradition, are the two basic texts in the study of the Abhidharma of the Nālandā Sanskrit traditions followed by Tibetan monastic institutions.

224. Maitreya, *Madhyāntavibhāga*, 40a, Pd 70:103. This text is followed by Asaṅga, the author of *Compendium of Knowledge*.

225. This is explained by Gyaltsab Darma Rinchen in *An Explanation of the Compendium of Abhidharma*, his commentary on Asaṅga's *Compendium of Knowledge*.

226. Bhikkhu Bodhi, *A Comprehensive Manual of Abhidhamma*.

227. See also Yongzin Yeshe Gyaltsen, *A Necklace for Those of Clear Awareness*.

228. These definitions are taken from Jetsun Chökyi Gyaltsen, *An Ocean of Play for the Naga Lords*, 346.

229. Tsongkhapa, *Arranging the Path of Valid Cognition*, 26.
230. As cited in Yongzin Yeshe Gyaltsen, *A Necklace for Those of Clear Awareness*, 52.
231. Gyaltsab Darma Rinchen, *Clarifying the Path of Liberation*, 501.
232. Tsongkhapa, *Great Treatise*, vol. 3, 357–59.

Bibliography

Kangyur

Dhammapada. Dhammapada. Chos kyi tshigs su bcad pa. Pali canon. See Ācārya Buddha-rakkhita below.

The Teaching to Nanda on Entering the Womb. Nandagarbhāvakrāntinirdeśa-sūtra. Dga' bo mngal du 'jug pa bstan pa'i mdo. Toh 57, Ratnakūṭa, ga, 205–36.

Unraveling the Intention Sūtra. Saṃdhinirmocana-sūtra. Dgongs pa nges par 'grel pa'i mdo. Toh 106, Sūtra, ca.

Sūtra of Turning the Wheel of Dharma. Dharmachakra-sūtra. Chos kyi 'khor lo'i mdo. Toh 337, Sūtra, sa.

Tengyur

Āryadeva. *Four Hundred Stanzas. Catuḥshataka. Bstan bcos bzhi brgya pa.* Toh 3846, Madhyamaka, tsha.

Asaṅga. *Compendium of Ascertainments. Viniśhcayasaṃgraha. Rnam par gtan la dbab pa bsdu ba.* Toh 4038, Chittamātra, zhi, zi.

———. *Compendium of Knowledge. Abhidharmasamucchaya. Chos mngon pa kun las btus pa.* Toh 4049, Chittamātra, ri.

———. *Śrāvaka Levels. Śrāvakabhūmi. Nyan thos kyi sa.* Toh 4036, Chittamātra, dzi.

Bhāvaviveka. *Blaze of Reasoning: Commentary on the Heart of the Middle. Madhyamakahṛdayavṛttitarkajvālā. Dbu ma'i snying po'i grel pa rtog ge 'bar ba.* Toh 3856, TBRC W1PD95844.

Candrakīrti. *Clear Words. Prasannapadā. Tshig gsal ba.* Toh 3860, Madhyamaka, 'a.

———. *Entering the Middle Way. Madhyamakāvatāra. Dbu ma la 'jug pa.* Toh 3861, Madhyamaka, 'a.

———. *Entering the Middle Way Autocommentary. Madhyamakāvatārabhāṣya. Dbu ma la 'jug pa'i bshad pa.* Toh 3862, Madhyamaka, 'a.

Devendrabuddhi (Lha dbang blo). *Commentary on Difficult Points in the Exposition of Valid Cognition. Pramāṇavārttikapañjikā. Tshad ma rnam 'grel gyi dka' 'grel.* Toh 4217, Pramāṇa, che.

Dharmakīrti. *Ascertainment of Valid Cognition. Pramāṇaviniśhcaya. Tshad ma rnam nges.* Toh 4211, Pramāṇa, ce.

———. *Drop of Reasoning. Nyāyabindu. Rigs pa'i thigs pa.* Toh 4212, Pramāṇa, ce.

———. *Drop of Reasons. Hetubindu. Gtan tshigs thigs pa.* Toh 4213, Pramāṇa, ce.

———. *Exposition of Valid Cognition. Pramāṇavārttika. Tshad ma rnam 'grel.* Toh 4210, Pramāṇa, ce.

———. *Exposition of Valid Cognition Autocommentary. Pramāṇavārttikasvopajñavṛtti. Tshad ma rnam 'grel gyi 'grel ba.* Toh 4216, Pramāṇa, ce.

Dharmottara. *Explanatory Commentary on the Ascertainment of Valid Cognition. Pramāṇa-viniśhcayaṭīkā. Tshad ma rnam par nges pa'i 'grel bshad.* Toh 4229, Pramāṇa, dze.

Dignāga. *Compendium of Valid Cognition. Pramāṇasamucchaya. Tshad ma kun las btus pa.* Toh 4203, Pramāṇa, ce.

———. *Investigation of the Object. Ālambanaparīkṣā. Dmigs brtag.* Toh 4205, Pramāṇa, ce.

———. *Investigation of the Object Autocommentary. Ālambanaparīkṣāvṛtti. Dmigs brtag rang 'grel.* Toh 4206, Pramāṇa, ce.

Jitāri. *Distinguishing the Scriptures of the Sugata. Sugatamatavibhaṅga. Bde bar gshegs pa'i gzhung rnam par 'byed pa.* Toh 3899, Madhyamaka, a.

Maitreya. *Distinguishing the Middle from the Extremes. Madhyāntavibhāga. Dbus dang mtha' rnam par 'byed pa.* Toh 4021, Chittamātra, phi.

———. *Ornament of Clear Realization. Abhisamayālaṃkāra. Mngon par rtogs pa'i rgyan.* Toh 3786, Prajñāpāramitā, ka.

———. *The Sublime Continuum. Uttaratantra. Rgyud bla ma.* Toh 4025, Cittamātra, phi.

Nāgārjuna. *Fundamental Treatise on the Middle Way. Mūlamadhyamakakārikā. Dbu ma rtsa ba'i tshig le'ur byas pa.* Toh 3824, Madhyamaka, tsa.

Prajñākaragupta. *Ornament for Valid Cognition. Pramāṇavārttikabhāshyam. Tshad ma rnam 'grel kyi rgyan.* Patna: Kashi Prasad Jayaswal Research Instititute.

Shākyabuddhi. *Presentation of the Commentary on (Dignāga's) Compendium of Valid Cognition. Pramāṇavārttikaṭīkā. Tshad ma rnam 'grel kyi 'grel bshad.* Translated by Subhutiśrī and Dge ba'i blo gros. Bstan-'gyur, Sde dge edition 4220. Tshad ma, vols. je and nye, 1–282a. Reproduced in Barber 1991, vol. 47.

Shāntarakṣita. *Compendium of Reality. Tattvasaṃgraha. De kho na nyid bsdus pa.* Toh 4266, Pramāṇa, ze.

———. *Ornament of the Middle Way. Madhyamakālaṃkāra. Dbus ma rgyan.* Toh 3884, Madhyamaka, sa.

Shāntideva. *Entering the Bodhisattva Way. Bodhisattvacharyāvatāra. Byang chub sems dpa'i spyod la' jug pa.* Toh 3871, Madhyamaka, la.

Vasubandhu. *Treasury of Knowledge. Abhidharmakośha. Chos mngon pa' i mdzod.* Toh 4089, Abhidharma, ku.

———. *Treasury of Knowledge Autocommentary. Abhidharmakośhabhāṣya. Chos mngon pa'i mdzod kyi bshad pa.* Toh 4090, Abhidharma, ku, khu.

TIBETAN WORKS

Barber, A. W., ed. 1991. *The Tibetan Tripitaka: Taipei Edition.* Taipei: SMC Publishing.

Changkya Rölpai Dorje (Lcang skya Rol pa'i rdo rje, 1717–86). 2012. *Beautiful Adornment of Mount Meru: A Presentation of Tenets. Grub pa'i mtha' rnam par bzhag pa thub bstan lhun po'i mdzes rgyan.* Bod kyi gstug lag gces btus 24. New Delhi: Institute of Tibetan Classics.

Chapa Chökyi Sengé (Phywa pa Chos kyi seng ge, 1109–69). 2006. *Valid Cognition Eliminating the Darkness of the Mind (Tshad ma sde bdun yid kyi mun sel)*. Collected Works *(Gsungs 'bums) of the Kadampas*, vol. 9. Chengdu: Si khron mi rigs dpe skrun khang.

Dondor, with Tenzin Chosdrak (Don rdor, with Bstan 'dzin Chos grags). 1993. *Collections of Biographies of Renowned Beings of the Land of Snows. Gangs ljongs lo rgyus thog gi grags can mi sna*. Tibet: Bodjong Mimang Publications *(Bod ljongs mi dmangs dpe skrun khang)*.

Dpal dge ldan pa'i tshad ma rig pa'i gzhung (Geluk Epistemology). New Delhi: Institute of Tibetan Classics. For the forthcoming Library of Tibetan Classics English translation, see "Samuels, Jonathan" below.

Gendun Tenpa Dargye (Dge 'dun Bstan pa dar rgyas, 1493–1568). *Illuminating the Ornament of the Essence: An Explanation of the General Meaning of the Root Text and Commentary of (Maitreya's) "The Ornament of Clear Realization Treatise"*. *Shes rab kyi pha rol tu phyin pa'i man ngag gi bstan bcos mngon par rtogs pa'i rgyan rtsa 'grel gyi spyi don rnam bshad nying po rgyan gyi snang ba*. Bylakuppe, Karnataka: Se ra dpe mdzod khang. TBRC W1KG8580.

Gungthang Lodrö Gyatso (Gung thang Blo gros rgya mtsho). 2016. *Clearing the Darkness of Those Desiring Liberation, Sun of the Field of Thorough Goodness: An Annotated Commentary on Haribhadra's Commentary on the Abhisamayālaṃkāra*. *'Grel ba don gsal gyi mchan 'grel kun bzang zhing gi nyi ma thar 'dod mun sel*. Lhasa: Ser gtsug nang bstan dpe rnying 'tshol bsdu phyogs sgrig khang. TBRC W1KG25324.

Gungthang Tenpai Drönme (Gung thang Bstan pa'i sgron me, 1762–1823). 2003. *A Festival of the Wise, Port of Entry for Those Desiring Liberation: A Presentation of the Four Truths. Bden bzhi'i rnam bzhag thar 'dod 'jug ngogs mkhas pa'i dga' ston*. In *Gsung 'bum/ Dkon mchog bstan pa'i sgron me* 2: 577–608. Pe cin: Mi rigs dpe skrun khang. TBRC W2DB4591.

Gyaltsab Darma Rinchen (Rgyal tsab Darma rinchen, 1364–1432). 2008. *Clarifying the Path of Liberation: Complete Explanation of the Stanzas of the Commentary on Valid Cognition, the Faultless Revealer of the Path to Liberation. Tshad ma rnam 'grel gyi tshig le'ur byas pa'i rnam bshad thar lam phyin ci ma log par gsal bar byed pa*. Sarnath, India: Gelugpa Students' Welfare Committee.

———. 2017. *An Explanation of the Compendium of Abhidharma [by Asaṅga]. Legs par bshad pa chos mngon rgya mtsho'i snying po*. Bylakuppe, Karnataka: Sera IMI House.

———. 2010. *A Guide on the Path of Valid Cognition. Tshad ma'i lam khrid*. Mungod: Drepung Loseling Library Society.

Gyalwa Gedun Drup [the first Dalai Lama] (Rgyal ba Dge 'dun grub, 1391–1474). 2001. *Ornament of Reasoning on Valid Cognition. Tshad ma'i bstan bcos chen po rigs pa'i rgyan*. Sku 'bum: Sku 'bum byams pa gling. TBRC W739.

Jamyang Shepa (Jam dbyangs Bzhad pa, 1648–1721). 1994. *Great Exposition of Tenets. Grub mtha' chen mo*. Lanzhou: Kan su'u mi rigs dpe skrun khang. TBRC W00KG09694.

———. *Presentation of Awarenesses and Knowers. Blo rig gi nam gzhag*. TBRC W1CZ901.

Jetsun Chökyi Gyaltsen (Rje btsun Chos kyi rgyal mtshan, 1469–1544). 2003. *General Meaning of Chapter One. Phar phyin skabs dang po'i spyi don skal bzang klu dbang rol mtsho*. Bylakuppe: Sera Je Library.

———. 2003. *Presentation of Tenets. Grub mtha'i rnam gzhag.* Bylakuppe: Sera Jey Library Computer Project.

———. 2003. *Presentation of Grounds and Paths. Sa lam gyi rnam gzhag.* Bylakuppe: Sera Jey Library Computer Project.

———. 2004. *An Ocean of Play for The Naga Lords: The General Meaning of [the Twelve Links of] Dependent Arising. Rten 'brel gyi spyi don klu dbang gi rol mtsho.* Bylakuppe: Sera Jey Library Computer Project.

Khedrup Gelek Palsang (Mkhas grub Dge legs dpal bsang, 1385–1438). 2006. *Clearing Mental Darkness: An Ornament of Dharmakīrti's Seven Treatises on Valid Cognition. Tshad ma sde bdun gyi rgyan yid kyi mun sel.* New Delhi: Institute of Tibetan Classics.

———. *Illumination of the Difficult Points, an Explanation of Haribhadra's Commentary on the Clear Meaning. 'Grel pa don gsal gyi rnam bshad rtogs dka'i snang ba.* Lhasa: Ser gtsug nang bstan dpe rnying 'tshol bsdu phyogs sgrig khang. TBRC W3CN3440.

———. *Ocean of Reasonings: An Extensive Explanation of [Dharmakīrti's] Commentary on Valid Cognition. Tshad ma rnam 'grel tIka chen rigs pa'i rgya mtsho.* Lhasa: Ser gtsug nang bstan dpe rnying 'tshol bsdu phyogs sgrig khang. TBRC W1AC48.

———. 1980. *Presentation of the Grounds and Paths Called "A Scholar's Delight." Sa lam gyi rnam gzhag mkhas pa'i yid 'phrog ces bya ba bzhugs so.* Sarnath, Varanasi: Gelugpa Students' Welfare Committee. TBRC W8LS22455.

Purbu Chok Jampa Gyatso (Phur bu lcog byams ba rgya mtsho, 1825–1901). 2008. *Explanation of the Presentation of Objects and Object-Possessors as Well as Awarenesses and Knowers. Yul yul chan dang blo rigs gi rnam par bshad* pa. Bylakuppe, India: Sera Jey Library. English translation: Napper 2008.

———. 1999. *The Magic Key to the Path of Reasoning: A Presentation of Collected Topics Revealing the Meaning of the Texts on Valid Cognition. Tshad ma'i gzhung don 'byed pa'i bsdu sgrva'i rnam bzhag rigs lam 'phrul gyi lde mig.* Bylakuppe, India: Sera Jey Library.

Sakya Paṇḍita Kunga Gyaltsen (Sa pan Kun dga' Rgyal mtshan, 1182–1251). *The Treasury of Reasoning. Tshad ma rigs gter. Sa skya bka' 'bum,* 11: 7–58. Kathmandu: Sachen International. TBRC W00EGS1017151.

Tsongkhapa Lobsang Drakpa (Tsong ka pa Blo bzang grags pa, 1357–1419). 2010. *Arranging the Path of Valid Cognition. Tshad ma'i lam gyi rim pa'i bsgrigs.* Mungod: Drepung Loseling Library Society.

———. 2009. *The Essence of Eloquence: Treatise Differentiating Interpretable and Definite Meanings. Drang nges legs bshad snying po.* TBRC W8LS17300.

———. 2009. *The Golden Garland of Eloquence. Legs bshad rin po che gser gyi phreng ba.* Lhasa: Ser gtsug nang bstan dpe rnying 'tshol bsdu phyogs sgrig khang. TBRC W1KG16138.

———. 2009. *Illumination of the Intent. Dbu ma dgongs pa rab gsal.* Lhasa: Ser gtsug nang bstan dpe rnying 'tshol bsdu phyogs sgrig khang. TBRC W1KG15604.

———. 1979. *Purifying Forgetfulness of Valid Cognition. Tshad ma'i brjed byang chen mo.* Blo bzang grags pa'i dpal; Gsung 'bum / Tsong kha pa (zhol). New Delhi: Mongolian Lama Guru Deva. TBRC W635, 809–96.

———. 1998. *Songs of Spiritual Experience: Condensed Points of the Stages of the Path. Lam rim nyams mgur; byang chub lam gyi rim pa chung ba.* Dga' ldan bkra shis chos 'phel gling gi chos spyod. Volume 1, 183–92 .

English Works and Translations

Āchārya Buddharakkhita, trans. 1985. *Dhammapada: The Buddha's Path of Wisdom*. Kandy: Buddhist Publication Society.

Bodhi, Bhikkhu, ed. 2006. *A Comprehensive Manual of Abhidhamma: The Abhidhammattha Sangaha*. Translated by Nārada Mahāthera and Bhikkhu Bodhi. Kandy: Buddhist Publication Society.

Cabezón, José Ignacio. 1992. *A Dose of Emptiness: An Annotated Translation of the sTong thun chen mo of mKhas gDrup dGelegs dpal bzang*. Albany: State University of New York Press.

Dalai Lama Tenzin Gyatso. 2002. *Illuminating the Path to Enlightenment: A Commentary on Atiśa Dipamkara Shrijnana's "A Lamp for the Path to Enlightenment" and Lama Je Tsongkhapa's "Lines of Experience."* Translated by Geshe Thupten Jinpa. Lama Yeshe Wisdom Archive.

———. 2002. *Supplication to Seventeen Nālandā Scholars (Dpal nalenda pan grub bcu bdun gyi gsol 'debs)*. Translated by Venerable Lhakdor. Edited by Jeremy Russell. Dharamsala: Thekchen Choeling.

Dreyfus, Georges B. J. 1997. *Recognizing Reality: Dharmakīrti's Philosophy and Its Tibetan Interpretations*. Albany: State University of New York Press.

Dunne, John D. 2004. *Foundation of Dharmakīrti's Philosophy*. Boston: Wisdom Publications.

Hopkins, Jeffrey. 2005. *Absorption in No External World: 170 Issues in Mind-Only Buddhism*. Ithaca, NY: Snow Lion Publications.

———. 1999. *Emptiness in the Mind-Only School of Buddhism: Dynamic Responses to Dzong-ka-ba's The Essence of Eloquence: I*. Berkeley: University of California Press.

———. 2003. *Maps of the Profound: Jam-yang-Shay-ba's Great Exposition of Buddhist and Non-Buddhist Views on the Nature of Reality*. Ithaca, NY: Snow Lion Publications.

———. 2002. *Reflections on Reality: The Three Natures and Non-Natures in the Mind-Only School, Dynamic Responses to Dzong-ka-ba's The Essence of Eloquence, Volume Two*. Berkeley: University of California Press.

Jackson, Roger R. 1993. *Is Enlightenment Possible? Dharmakīrti and rGyal-tshab-rje on Knowledge, Rebirth, No-Self, and Liberation*. Ithaca, NY: Snow Lion Publications.

Jetsun Chökyi Gyaltsen. 2005. *Presentation of Tenets. Grub mtha'i rnam gzhag*. Translated by Glen Svensson. FPMT Education Department.

Jinpa, Thupten, and the Compendium Compilation Committee. 2020. *Science and Philosophy in the Indian Buddhist Classics: Volume 2, The Mind*. Boston: Wisdom Publications.

Klein, Anne Carolyn. 1991. *Knowing, Naming and Negation: A Sourcebook on Tibetan Sautrāntrika*. Ithaca, NY: Snow Lion Publications.

Napper, Elizabeth, trans. 2008. *Explanation of the Presentation of Objects and Object-Possessors as Well as Awarenesses and Knowers, by Pur-bu-chok*. FPMT Education Department.

Lati Rinbochay, with Elizabeth Napper. 1986. *Mind in Tibetan Buddhism: Oral Commentary on Ge-shay Jam-bel-sam-Pal's "Presentation of Awareness and Knowledge, Composite of All the Important Points, Opener of the Eye of New Intelligence."* Ithaca, NY: Snow Lion Publications.

Pabongkha Dechen Nyingpo. 2006. *Liberation in the Palm of Your Hand.* Translated by Michael Richards. Boston: Wisdom Publications.

Panchen Losang Chökyi Gyaltsen. 2013. *Lama Chöpa.* Translation compiled and published by FPMT Education Department.

Perdue, Daniel E. 1992. *Debate in Tibetan Buddhism.* Ithaca, NY: Snow Lion Publications.

Rogers, Katherine Manchester. 2009. *Tibetan Logic.* Ithaca, NY: Snow Lion Publications.

Samuels, Jonathan (Sherab Gyatso), trans. 2023 (forthcoming). *Tibetan Buddhist Epistemology II: The Geluk School. The Library of Tibetan Classics* 21. Somerville, MA: Wisdom Publications.

Sopa, Geshe Lhundup, with Jeffrey Hopkins. 1989. *Cutting through Appearances: Practice and Theory of Tibetan Buddhism.* Ithaca, NY: Snow Lion Publications.

Tsongkhapa. 2000–2002. *The Great Treatise on the Stages of the Path to Enlightenment: Lam Rim Chen Mo.* vols. 1–3. Translated by The Lamrim Chenmo Translation Committee. Edited by Joshua Cutler and Guy Newland. Ithaca, NY: Snow Lion Publications.

Yongzin Yeshe Gyaltsen. 2005. *A Necklace for Those of Clear Awareness: Clearly Revealing the Modes of Minds and Mental Factors.* Translated by Toh Sze Gee. *Sems sems 'byung gi sdom tshig nor bu'i phreng ba dang de'i 'grel ba blo gsal mgul rgyan.* FPMT Education Department.

Wylie, Turrell. 1959. "A Standard System of Tibetan Transliteration." *Harvard Journal of Asiatic Studies,* 22: 261–67.

INDEX

A

Abhidharma, 243, 314n223

absurd consequences, 18, 41–42, 114, 239

afflicted mind, 118, 119, 308n120

afflictions/afflictive emotions, 81, 117, 197–98

  abandonment of, 175–76, 252

  analyzing, 252–53

  arising of, 157

  cessation of, 268

  definition, 250–51

  direct antidote to, 152, 160, 199

  mental, 5, 65, 167, 253–54

  misconceptions about, 173, 174

  objects classified from the side of, 182–83

  other-power of, 165

  person/aggregates as basis of, 188, 195, 197–98

  pervasive compounding suffering of, 162, 163

  purification of, 172

  root of, 185, 267

  six root and twenty secondary, 248, 251

  strong production of, 171–72

  truth of origin and, 167

  See also destructive emotions

afflictive obscurations, 192, 202, 260, 311n167, 313n196

aggregates (contaminated, appropriating), 202, 311n161

  as basis of suffering, 160, 162–64, 171

  four superimpositions of, 164–65

  karma and, 249–50

  meditative absorption of cessation and, 119, 309n122

  self as characteristically discordant with, 186, 187–88, 189–90, 192, 194–95, 251

  as selfless, 74, 198, 269–70, 307n85

  wish to be free of, 167

  See also view of the transitory collection

analysis

  and concentration, relationship between, 28, 151, 198, 253, 260

  on path of preparation, 261, 264

  purpose of, 268–69

  See also logical reasoning

anger, 157, 251, 252, 253, 267, 269

appearing objects, 13, 33, 60

  of direct perceiver, 32

  meaning generalities and, 44

  object possessors of, 61–63

  permanent and impermanent, 34

  pervasion and, 25–26, 303n13

apprehended objects, 13, 29, 42, 45, 57, 60

  and apprehender, distinction between, 111–12, 113–14

  Chittamātra view of, 53

  direct and indirect, 63

  direct perceivers of, 142

  in distinguishing valid cognizers, two types, 31, 32–33

  object possessors of, 61–63

  obstructions to, 50–51

  pervasion and, 25–26, 303n13

  self- and other-knowers of, 147

  of sense consciousnesses, 108–10, 308n116

inferential valid cognizers, 74, 89–90, 212
cause of, 134
dependent on correct sign, 240
explicit objects of comprehension of, 17
hidden phenomena and, 21–22
implicit and explicit realization for, 22, 27–28
manifest phenomena and, 12–13
objects of engagement and, 63
by power of fact, 228
reasoning in establishing, 83
of specifically and generally character-ized phenomena, 30–33
through belief, 12, 229–30
through renown, 229
intermediate state (bardo), 310n153
interpretable teachings, 55, 191
Investigation of the Object (Dignāga), 126, 127, 131
Investigation of the Object Autocommentary (Dignāga), 130
Ishvara (aka Śhiva), 171
isolates, 98, 99. *See also* concordant isolate; meaning isolate

J
Jamyang Shepa, 174
Jetson Chökyi Gyaltsen, 53, 180, 255, 305n56, 312n175

K
Kagyü tradition, 2
Kālachakra Tantra, 8
karma, 6, 117
arising of, 157
cessation of, 268
contaminated, threefold division of, 249
as hidden phenomena, 12
immovable, 185
impelling suffering, 166
inference through belief and, 225
meritorious and non-meritorious, 185
negative, preventing, 253–54
Nigrantha view of, 174

obscurations of, 221
other-power of, 165
person/aggregates as basis of, 188, 195, 197–98
pervasive compounding suffering of, 162, 163
strong production of, 171–72
truth of origin and, 167, 168–69
karmic formation, 160
Kham, 8
Khedrup Jé Gelek Palsang, 1, 2, 5
biography of, 7–8
works of, 8, 153, 168–69, 179–80
See also *Clearing Mental Darkness*
Khedrup Sengye Gyaltsen, 7
knowers
as free from conceptuality, 97, 98–99, 103, 105
seven types, 66, 82
synonyms, 65, 67
knowers of all aspects, 121. *See also* exalted knowers
knowing, 65, 148, 149, 203, 205

L
Lamdré Yeshe Pal, 7
Lamrim Prayer (Panchen Losang Chökyi Gyaltsen), 311n165
Lamrim tradition, 164
language, implied and indirect meanings of, 25
latencies. *See* imprints
liberating paths, 5, 6, 151, 157, 199–200, 209–10. *See also* five paths
liberation
aspiration for, 265
mind seeking, 163, 184
misconceptions about, 173–74
from samsara, 158, 180, 202–3
virtues partially concordant with, 208
wish to achieve, 200, 208–9
logical reasoning, 193, 212
for afflictions, 253
in Buddhism, role of, 81–82

ABOUT THE EDITORS

GESHE TENZIN NAMDAK first worked as an environmental researcher, having graduated with a bachelor of science degree in hydrology. He took ordination from His Holiness the Dalai Lama before engaging in his formal studies in Buddhist philosophy and psychology at Sera Jey Monastic University. He completed the entire twenty-year geshe program at Sera Jey and the traditional one-year Vajrayāna study program at Gyüme Tantric College. Currently, he is the resident teacher at Jamyang Buddhist Centre, London, and teaches worldwide.

TENZIN LEGTSOK is a Buddhist monk in the eighteenth year of the geshe program at Sera Jey Monastic University, where he studies classic Indian Buddhist treatises and their Tibetan commentaries in the tradition of ancient Nālandā University. He was ordained by His Holiness the Dalai Lama in 2001. The question "What makes for the most happy and meaningful life?" compelled him to major in philosophy at Kenyon College and gradually led him to study meditation, philosophy, and psychology with teachers among the exiled Tibetan communities in India and Nepal from 1999 until the present. For the past fifteen years he has worked to make basic Buddhist teachings accessible to various audiences in India and the United States through lectures, essays, and meditation instruction.

WHAT TO READ NEXT
FROM WISDOM PUBLICATIONS

Science and Philosophy in the Indian Buddhist Classics
Volume 1: The Physical World
Conceived and introduced by the Dalai Lama
Edited by Thupten Jinpa
Translated by Ian Coghlan

"*Science and Philosophy in the Indian Buddhist Classics* offers a rare gift of wisdom from the ancient world to the modern reader. The editors have curated a rich treasure of the philosophy and maps of the mind that have their origins in the early centuries of Indian thought, were preserved in translation for centuries in Tibet, and now are brought to all of us in this translation."—Daniel Goleman, author of *Emotional Intelligence*

Science and Philosophy in the Indian Buddhist Classics
Volume 2: The Mind
Conceived and introduced by the Dalai Lama
Edited by Thupten Jinpa
Translated by John D. Dunne and Dechen Rochard

"This is a valuable reference for anyone interested in philosophy of mind, epistemology, and psychology."—Jay L. Garfield, Smith College and Harvard Divinity School

Illuminating the Intent
An Exposition of Candrakirti's Entering the Middle Way
Tsongkhapa
Translated by Thupten Jinpa

Written as a supplement to Nagarjuna's *Fundamental Verses on the Middle Way*, Candrakirti's text integrates the central insight of Nagarjuna's thought—the rejection of any metaphysical notion of intrinsic existence—with the well-known Mahayana framework of the ten levels of the bodhisattva, and it became the most studied presentation of Madhyamaka thought in Tibet.

Mind Seeing Mind
Mahamudra and the Geluk Tradition of Tibetan Buddhism
Roger Jackson

"Roger Jackson's *Mind Seeing Mind* is an outstanding achievement, vast in scope and profound in its engagement with Tibetan Buddhist contemplative and philosophical traditions. From the origins of the Mahāmudrā teaching in India, through its refinement and development among the Kagyü masters of Tibet, to its transmission to Jé Tsongkhapa and his Gelukpa successors down to the present day, Jackson guides the reader on a journey resembling the exploration of a great river from its turbulent headwaters to the spreading streams of its delta. *Mind Seeing Mind* is a model study of the historical and doctrinal literature of Buddhism in Tibet."—Matthew T. Kapstein, École Pratique des Hautes Études, Paris, and the University of Chicago

Insight into Emptiness
Khensur Jampa Tegchok
Edited and introduced by Thubten Chodron

"One of the best introductions to the philosophy of emptiness I have ever read."—José Ignacio Cabezón

About Wisdom Publications

Wisdom Publications is the leading publisher of classic and contemporary Buddhist books and practical works on mindfulness. To learn more about us or to explore our other books, please visit our website at wisdomexperience.org or contact us at the address below.

Wisdom Publications
199 Elm Street
Somerville, MA 02144 USA

We are a 501(c)(3) organization, and donations in support of our mission are tax deductible.

Wisdom Publications is affiliated with the Foundation for the Preservation of the Mahayana Tradition (FPMT).